YOGA MORALITY

For Alan
with kind regards
and best wishes,

Georg

YOGA MORALITY

Ancient Teachings
At a Time of Global Crisis

Georg Feuerstein

HOHM PRESS
Prescott, Arizona

Cover photograph by Zachary Parker
Cover design, interior design and typeset by Zachary Parker, Kadak Graphics

Library of Congress Cataloging-in-Publication Data

Feuerstein, Georg.
 Yoga morality : ancient teachings at a time of global crisis / Georg Feuerstein.
    p. cm.
 Includes bibliographical references (p. 271) and index.
 ISBN 1-890772-66-6 (pbk. : alk. paper)
 1. Yoga. 2. Conduct of life. 3. Ethics. I. Title.
 B132.Y6F484 2007
 294.5'48--dc22
                        2006029644

HOHM PRESS
P.O. Box 2501
Prescott, AZ 86302
800-381-2700
www.hohmpress.com

This book was printed in the U.S.A. on recycled, acid-free paper using soy ink.

07 08 09 10 11   5 4 3 2 1

This book is dedicated to Brenda, my wife,
for challenging, encouraging, and joining me in my environmental forays,
and for sharing my passion for Sanskrit, India's spiritual traditions,
and particularly the difficult path of inner growth and illumination,
and for doing so with a love that warms my heart and feeds my soul.

CONTENTS

ACKNOWLEDGMENTS

I sincerely wish to thank Subhash Kak, David Frawley, and Lyman and Lucia Spencer for various kindnesses accorded to me in recent years. I also would like to thank Kendra Crossen Burroughs for her perceptive input on this work.

Most importantly, my heartfelt thanks go to Lee Lozowick, Dasya Zuccarello, and Regina Sara Ryan, as well as the other good spirits of Hohm Press, who understand that spiritual practice must go hand in hand with environmental conscientiousness in order to amount to anything. Hohm Press is among the few American publishers that have switched to recycled paper, where the rest is lingering in an almost medieval mindset oblivious to our present-day environmental crisis.

Author's Preface

Since its inauguration in 1972, the Union of International Associations has identified over 30,000 global "issues" (read: problems), which between them have more than 150,000 connections. These challenges characterize what many now refer to as our present-day "global crisis"—from the pollution of earth, water, and air to the depletion of nonrenewable resources like oil and arable soil, to widespread deforestation and desertification, to rapidly melting glaciers and rising sea levels, to overpopulation and world hunger, to the displacement of large populations because of the Greenhouse Effect, collapsing ecology, or ethnic and political persecution, to the return of diseases once thought to have been eliminated and the appearance of elusive viruses, to the mass extinction of animal species on a scale comparable to the disappearance of the dinosaurs 65 million years ago, to the proliferation of nuclear arms and uncontrolled arms trade, to increasingly lethal terrorism and the return of fascism (which treats the state as God), and on and on.

Most people are as yet dangerously unaware that humanity is at this very moment facing an unprecedented challenge in its long history. Many are uninformed, but many more simply don't want to see, because either they are indifferent or they can't face reality. It is my understanding, however, that in the years to come we will all be forced to acknowledge that our species is in dire straits, because those difficulties will have become very personal. Many experts fear it is already too late to prevent the worst from happening.

Anyone thinking that environmentalists have prophesied doom and gloom for many decades now and that after all we are still here, should think again. Nor is it only staunch environmentalists who are ringing the alarm bell these days and, moreover, the number of warning voices has greatly multiplied. Until now the media have avoided reporting on the single most important news—the *magnitude* of the crisis we are facing not only environmentally but also socially and geopolitically. By feeding the reader only fragments ("sound bytes") of the total picture, they effectively trivialize the actualities and thus render them innocuous. Still, there are plenty of publications chronicling the state of affairs and, before long, even the media will finally have to tackle this unpopular topic and assume responsibility for conscientious reporting of the unsavory truths. Among other things, we may expect them to talk about existing governmental emergency programs to control the population when the panic starts.

When the American government declared war on terrorism after the tragedy on September 11, 2001, it essentially redefined world politics and the nation's understanding of human liberty. In 1979, President Jimmy Carter created the Federal Emergency Management Agency (FEMA) granting it a wide range of executive powers in case of emergencies and a multi-billion dollar secret budget—an organization that has sometimes been called the "secret U.S. government." In 2003, President George W. Bush, Jr., incorporated FEMA along with twenty-two other government offices into the newly launched Department of Homeland Security (DHS). Under the pretext of preventing future terrorist attacks, the U.S. government endowed DHS with unprecedented powers and a budget of well over 30 billion dollars a large chunk of which is unaccountable to the public. Other nations have their own versions of this kind of emergency organization, which are not designed purely for disaster relief but also clearly involve political machinations that revolve around controlling the population at the cost of personal liberty. These are just the beginnings of many more changes that will inevitably encroach more and more on our personal lives, whatever our nationality may be.

Of course, there are countless things we can and must do to prepare ourselves for the inevitable at a personal level and also at the collective level. Morris Berman, for one, thinks that the best we can do is to live authentically, bearing the big crisis in mind. As he articulates in his thought-provoking book *The Twilight of American Culture*, today's critical developments are most likely to lead to the collapse of the American empire and its dependent states.[1] Another orientation is present in books like Richard Heinberg's *Power Down* and *The Party's Over* or Donella Meadows, Dennis Meadows, and Jørgen Randers' *Beyond the Limits*, Andres R. Edwards's *The Sustainability Revolution*, and not least Charles Dobson's *The Troublemaker's Teaparty: A Manual for Effective Citizen Action*.[2] These works clearly spell out our practical options. There are also many organizations that champion various causes and practical solutions.

The present volume, however, has a slightly different purpose. I want to look at the present situation primarily from the viewpoint of a spiritually committed person, especially but not exclusively a practitioner of Yoga. To be precise, I am interested in answering—from the perspective of a Yoga scholar and practitioner—the question of how we may live consciously, responsibly, authentically, and without fear in the midst of mounting turmoil.

Although *spirit* and *spiritual* are admittedly old-fashioned and possibly quite outdated and somewhat problematic terms, I continue to avail myself of them, because I surmise that most of my readers will know roughly what I mean by them. I appreciate, however, that some people have a problem with these words, and so I would like to proffer the following clarifying comments: For me, *spirit* is short-hand for ultimate Reality, that is, Reality as it is beyond all conceptualization. The word *spiritual*, again, denotes anything that relates to that Ultimate, in particular the act or attitude of voluntary and consistent self-transcendence, which is the fulcrum of Yoga and other similar traditions.

In my view, the distinction between *spiritual* and *religious* is one of degree. *Spirituality* emphasizes the systematic and sustained practice of radical self-transcendence with the view of fully realizing ultimate Reality, which in agreement with mysticism is understood to be the very core of our human nature. *Religion* also encourages self-transcendence but is more conventional in its approach, emphasizing sound moral behavior and obedience to the will of the ultimate Reality pictured as a person (i.e., God/Goddess).

How, then, should we conceive the relationship between spirituality and mysticism? *Spirituality*, in principle, requires no doctrines for its fulfillment, whereas *mysticism* is shod through with religious notions. I hasten to add that Yoga extends over a wide spectrum of orientations, some of which should be considered to be more religious, others more mystical. For instance, Bhakti-Yoga (the devotional path) is clearly a heavily religious branch of yogic spirituality, while Karma-Yoga (the path of self-transcending action) focuses on moral behavior and involves few typically religious notions. Then again, Jnāna-Yoga (the path of wisdom) or the Buddhist Dzogchen/Mahāmudrā approach, which all engage the self-transcending process as a training in awareness, or mindfulness, are neither religious nor mystical and thus perhaps best expresses what I mean by radical spirituality. Since Bhakti-Yoga and Karma-Yoga, however, also have perfect transcendence of the human condition as their final goal, they too must be considered spiritual. An example of a mystical spirituality would be Kundalinī-Yoga (the path of mental and bodily transformation via the activation of psychospiritual energy, or *shakti*).[3] But, strictly, all such labels are only approximations and need to be used with appropriate flexibility.

In defending my use of the word *spirituality*, I am not unaware of the unfortunate fact that since the 1970s this term has been ruthlessly exploited by merchants of "religious" consumer goods. This point is well argued from a political perspective by Jeremy Carrette and Richard King in their sharp-edged book *Selling Spirituality*.[4] The authors expose the cultural destructiveness of neoliberalism with its attendant commodification and homogenization of life. I happen to agree with them that we "should be rightly suspicious of calls for a return to the religious traditions of the past."[5] At the same time, we ought not to blithely discard those traditions, even if this were possible, for they constitute an amazing resource of collective human wisdom.

In writing the present book, I have set myself two related tasks. My first objective is to introduce the yogic moral teachings in their cultural context, freely crisscrossing between Hindu, Buddhist, and Jaina Yoga—the three major *forms* of the Indic Yoga tradition. My second objective is to show the relevance of Yoga's moral teachings for contemporary humanity, particularly in light of today's global crisis. *Morality*, I know, is not a fashionable term, but, like *spirituality*, it remains useful, and therefore I have availed myself of it without hesitation and apology. Perhaps it is precisely the conspicuous absence of a moral perspective from our contemporary Western society that makes some people intolerant toward the word itself. It is a word, however, that is perfectly appropriate in the present context.

Let me begin by saying that Yoga is not to be measured by the glamour of its spectacular physical postures or fabulous states of meditation, which hold so much fascination for us moderns. Yoga, which lies at the heart of India's great cultures of Hinduism, Buddhism, and Jainism, is as indicated above a spiritual tradition. As such it is concerned with personal growth and the ultimate goal of complete self-transcendence to the point of perfect inner freedom. The core process of Yoga, which conducts the yogic practitioner from a state of inauthentic existence to authentic being, is unglamorous and proceeds through the gradual, quiet transformation of one's body-mind and everyday life. Thus the foundation of all genuine Yoga practice, like any other spiritual discipline in the world, lies in the realm of moral behavior. It is impossible to be a good yogin or yoginī without also being a morally mature individual. This book is dedicated to exploring what this means.

I have long contemplated writing in more detail about the moral dimension of Yoga, which I see missing from much of contemporary Yoga teaching and practice. I did address moral issues in quite a few of my published works on Yoga—how could I not, considering that the yogic masters fully acknowledged that spiritual growth and moral growth go hand in hand? As well-loved Swami Sivananda of Rishikesh put it:

> Ethics is the foundation of Yoga. . . . Ethics is the gateway to God-realisation.

> Without ethical perfection, no spiritual progress or realisation is possible. A Yogic student or aspirant must be strictly ethical. He must be truthful and pure in thought, word and deed. He must possess excellent conduct. He must not injure any living being in thought, word and deed. He must practise rigidly right thought, right speech and right action.[6]

Again, "Mahatma" Gandhi—perhaps the best-known modern practitioner of Karma-Yoga (the path of self-transcending activity)—wrote in his celebrated autobiography that the "conviction that morality is the basis of things" took deep root in him, while the insight that "truth is the substance of all morality" became his sole occupation.[7] And Albert Einstein, a thoroughly Western voice, noted:

> The most important human endeavor is the striving for morality in our actions. Our inner balance and even our very existence depend on it. Only morality in our actions can give beauty and dignity to life.[8]

So long as we are alive, we must act. Even choosing to remain inactive is a kind of action, a stance that—like any action—has both wanted and unwanted consequences. By not voting in an election, for instance, we are not merely inactive but indirectly contribute to the political outcome. Or, to furnish another example, by not taking a stand on ecological issues and implementing an eco-wise way of life, we inevitably contribute to the ongoing decline of our environment. Therefore, as Krishna pointed out in the *Bhagavad-Gītā* ("Lord's Song") long ago, it behooves us to understand action and its consequences.[9] It is my hope that this book will help thoughtful readers in making proper sense of the nature of their activities in light of the great enduring principles of spirituality and morality.

Who would deny that our lives have become incredibly complex? Our contemporary civilization is a formidably multifaceted enterprise, and more than ever we are in need to shape our lives consciously based on the best wisdom available. Such wisdom, I propose, can be found in the spiritual traditions of India. Even though these traditions were created millennia ago, their insights into the human condition are as valid and vital today as they were then. After all, only external circumstances have changed over the course of history, while our psychological reality has largely remained the same: As a species, we are still afflicted with fear, anger, hatred, envy, jealousy, greed, pride, competitiveness, and ethnocentrism. We still ask "ultimate" questions, if only tentatively and mostly privately and then only in crisis situations: Who am I? Whence did I come? Whither do I go? What shall I do? Even those who have decided that posing these existential questions is pointless still face their own demise with apprehension or affected indifference. We still fight wars, and they generally are more destructive than they have ever been, even holding the dread prospect of global annihilation. Our species still knows poverty, hunger, disease, exploitation of people, animals, and Earth's environment, as well as torture and tyranny—perhaps more so than ever.

According to traditional Hindu and Buddhist reckoning, humanity finds itself in the midst of a dark cycle, the so-called *kali-yuga*, which is marked by a progressive diminution of our physical and mental capacities, as well as moral and spiritual decline. Whether or not the age-old model of world epochs is correct, it certainly fits the bill.[10]

Clearly, as a species we have not found answers to these seemingly perennial problems, or rather we have ignored the answers furnished by our spiritually and morally most mature individuals. Nor have our modern technological "solutions" brought us any closer to peace, harmony, and contentment. If anything, modern technology has put large boulders in our way, and for the first time in known history, our species is confronting the growing possibility of global destruction. The medical establishment and social planners are slowly acknowledging the remarkable fact that the so-called advances made by our contemporary "post-modern" society have had a hidden cost: We are in poor mental health, with a large number of people suffering from obsessions, phobias, and generic anxiety, as well as a great deal of despair, unhappiness, and not least self-involvement.[11]

Our leadership is far from being exempted from this adverse condition, which explains the dangerously pathological manifestations in national and international politics. Addressing 3,000 neurologists at the World Congress of Neurology held in London in 2001, psychiatrist James Tool, president of the World Federation of Neurology, argued strongly in favor of regularly testing world leaders over the age of sixty for signs of mental instability. Many would want to see such testing done before a candidate actually enters the political arena.

This book, then, is an attempt to outline the moral teachings of Yoga as an integral aspect of Yoga's program of spiritual self-transformation. I have opted for a panoramic approach. When better informed Westerners discuss Yoga, they often only pay attention to Patanjali's classical eightfold path with its five moral disciplines.[12] But these disciplines constitute the ethical ground of *all* yogic teachings. Many scriptures other than Patanjali's *Yoga-Sūtra* contain valuable and even more comprehensive discussions of the moral dimension of the yogic path.

There are inspiring writings particularly in the Buddhist Yoga tradition, such as the literature on the *bodhisattva* path. And who would not be impressed by the careful cataloguing of moral practices found in Jainism, which has developed its own unique yogic teachings? In addition to the classical Hindu philosophies, as well as Buddhist and Jaina literatures, I have also used relevant materials from the Vedic era some 5000 years ago up to the time of the Gnostic tracts of the *Upanishads*.[13] Going forward in time, I have availed myself of the writings of modern Indian thinkers and sages, notably "Mahatma" Gandhi and Sri Aurobindo. Their teachings will give the reader an appreciation of the fact that there is a marvelous continuity of insights on the core issues of existence in the *philosophía perennis*. Whenever it seemed useful to do so, I have also resorted to Western understanding, particularly in the hard and soft sciences to illustrate a point, and, as mentioned at the beginning of this preface, this kind of book would make little sense if I did not also make the materials relevant to the present global crisis.

This book seeks to fill a yawning gap in the existing literature on Yoga and counterbalance the unfortunate trend witnessed today toward overpopularizing the yogic heritage. Often Yoga's modern votaries are no longer even aware of the spiritual and moral aspects of the age-old tradition they presume to practice. This state of affairs has long saddened me, because when stripped of its spiritual and moral teachings, Yoga cannot lead to inner freedom, peace, and happiness, as it was designed to do.

I have absolutely nothing against the physical exercises promoted today under the wrong rubric of Hatha-Yoga. On the contrary, I have intermittently practiced some of them in order to remedy physical challenges. I confess, though, that personally I much prefer an hour's walk in Nature to indoor exercising. The postures of Hatha-Yoga can indeed help a person restore or maintain his or her bodily wellbeing, but let us recall that their original purpose was to transmute the body as part of an extensive program of self-transcendence and self-transformation. Authentic Yoga—including genuine Hatha-Yoga—has always had its focus on the high ideals of mental health and spiritual realization.[14] The contemporary shift away from these two time-honored and interrelated goals not only distorts the yogic heritage but also shortchanges those who have adopted some of the yogic practices into their quest for physical health and fitness.

We ought never to be discouraged by our failures to live up to our own highest ideals, but learn from our stumbling, raise ourselves up, and try again. Inner growth is not linear and cannot be explained or guided by rigid formulas. Nor should we let the run-of-the-mill morality of others deter us from listening to our own conscience, so long as we are committed to self-honesty and the ideal of nonharming. We must, as the *Bhagavad-Gītā* insists, follow our own inner law even at the risk of committing a blunder. With truth and integrity as our guiding ideals, we will not fail in the long run.

It should not require much imagination to appreciate that a person can be superbly fit but mentally lethargic, emotionally insensitive, morally corrupt, and spiritually bankrupt. After all, we have the historical example of the Third Reich, which placed a premium on physical fitness and health to guarantee its military success and long-term survival. It is certainly desirable to have a fit and healthy body, but we would profit more from a stable and perceptive mind combined with a loving, caring heart. Yoga is primarily about the latter ideals, which have been pursued and realized for millennia by the great masters of the various branches of Yoga. It makes implicit sense to listen to their wisdom teachings and imbibe especially their ideas about morally sound action that stops the vicious cycle of harmful behavior and leads to greater happiness for all.

In writing this book, I have naturally had to scrutinize my own moral history and acknowledge flaws and failures. We cannot grow without properly understanding and acknowledging the many karmic tracks our intentions, verbal behavior, and physical actions leave behind. Each of us has an arm-long record of moral misjudgments and slipups extending, as the Yoga masters assure us, across countless lifetimes. "Who," Jesus of Nazareth is said to have asked, "will cast the first stone?" So, let us not look at the moral flaws of others but focus on our own shortcomings, and more importantly, concentrate on transforming our character to prevent moral failings in the future. The wonderful part about being human is that we can learn from our mistakes and catapult ourselves out of the karmic orbit created by the sum-total of our past motivations. To put it in religious terms, the only valid kind of repentance is acting differently, that is, striving to become morally sound, or virtuous. To speak of *virtue* or *virtuous* is not popular in our time and, in some circles, is even deemed ridiculous. But that is so only because we have largely lost sight of the things that really matter in life. Hypnotized by the ideology of consumerism, sold so efficiently by the corporate world and governments alike, we see only what is directly in front of us, and even then we see things only through distorting ego-tinted lenses.

I am not known for being politically correct. Hence, as with my other books, the present work does not pander to the contemporary cynics, nihilists, and religious fundamentalists. It unabashedly advocates the reclamation of our common spiritual and moral heritage, as shaped and fulfilled by the great masters of the past. Even where we beg to differ from them philosophically, we can and must learn from the example of their moral and spiritual practice. If we fail to do so, I believe, the present-day moral and spiritual bankruptcy, combined with the growing ecological and sociopolitical disaster, will prove hugely self-destructive.

I dedicate this volume to all those—whether or not they call themselves Yoga practitioners—who pursue the spiritual path with vigor, dignity, and skillful action in the world.

Georg Feuerstein
Traditional Yoga Studies
www.traditionalyogastudies.com

ENDNOTES, AUTHOR'S PREFACE

1   See Morris Berman, *The Twilight of America* (New York: W. W. Norton, 2000) and Derrick Jensen, *The Collapse of Civilization and the Rebirth of Community: Volume 1* (New York: Seven Stories Press, 2005).

2   See the Bibliography for details.

3   See Shamdasani, Sonu, ed. *The Psychology of Kundalini Yoga: Notes of the Seminar Given in 1932 by C.G. Jung* (Princeton, N.J.: Princeton University Press, 1996).

4   See Jeremy Carrette and Richard King, *Selling Spirituality: The Silent Takeover of Religion* (London: Routledge, 2005). See also Susan Bridle, "The Man With the Golden Tongue," *What Is Enlightenment? The Modern Spiritual Predicament: An Inquiry Into the Popularization of East-Meets-West Spirituality*, no. 12 (March 2001); Wade Clarke Roof, *Spiritual Marketplace* (Princeton, N.J: Princeton University Press, 1999). The preceding publications should be read along with Christopher Lasch, *The Culture of Narcissism: American Life in an Age of Diminishing Expectation* (New York: W. W. Norton, repr. 1991).

5   Carrette and King, *Selling Spirituality*, p. 181.

6   Swami Sivananda, *All About Hinduism* (Shivanandanagar, India: Divine Life Society), 1947. Online version (www.dlshq.org/download/hinduismbk.htm) dated 1999. "Ethics" here is of course not so much the theory of moral conduct, but practical morality itself.

7   M. K. Gandhi, *The Official Mahatma Gandhi eArchive & Reference Library* at www.mahatma.org.in/quotes/

8   Mark Winokur, *Einstein: A Portrait* (Corte Madera, Calif.: Pomegranate Artbooks, 1984), p. 102.

9   See Sarvepalli Radhakrishnan, *The Bhagavadgītā* (London: Routledge & Kegan Paul, 1960).

10   The *kali-yuga*, or unfortunate age, is traditionally supposed to have started with the God-man Krishna's death in 3002 B.C. at the end of the devastating Bharata war (an unlikely date for the war and Krishna) and to last for 360,000 years—a span of time that, given humanity's record thus far, will most likely exceed our species' life expectancy.

11   According to the World Health Organization, one out of four individuals in both developed and developing countries will suffer from mental health problems sometime in his or her life. Well over 100 million people are suffering from clinical depression at this very moment.

12   See Georg Feuerstein, *The Yoga-Sūtra of Patañjali: A New Translation and Commentary* (Rochester, Vt.: Inner Traditions, repr. 1989).

13   See Sarvepalli Radhakrishnan, *The Principal Upanisads* (London: Allen & Unwin, 1953).

14   See Mikel Burley, *Hatha-Yoga* (Delhi: Motilal Banarsidass, 2000).

CHAPTER 1

SPIRITUALITY AND MORALITY

When people think of Yoga, they most likely think of physical fitness and twisted postures. Those who are better informed know that Yoga is India's age-old tradition of spiritual realization aiming at inner freedom and the overcoming of suffering through the transcendence of the ego, or "I-maker." Thus Yoga is primarily spiritual practice, or spirituality.

Curiously, quite a few Western Yoga practitioners, including some very popular teachers, have sought to strip Yoga of its spiritual orientation by denying that it has anything to do with spirituality, mental discipline, or inner development. They have even argued that Yoga is devoid of moral teachings, implying that everyone can live as they please. Nothing could be farther from the truth! From earliest times, Yoga has been intimately connected with humanity's spiritual aspiration to penetrate the veil covering the ordinary mind and to see Reality as it is, beyond dogma, doctrine, presumption, and conjecture. Yoga, in other words, has always primarily been a discipline of enlightenment, of personal growth to the point of complete inner freedom and unclouded perception of Truth.

The spiritual and moral poverty of many schools of modern Yoga ought not to blind us to the real nature of Yoga, which is overwhelmingly obvious from its long history and also its present-day traditional forms. At this point, I should clearly distinguish between religion and spirituality. Often both terms are used interchangeably, but it might be useful to demarcate religion from spirituality. I understand the former to refer to a person's values, beliefs, attitudes, and practices in regard to a supreme Person called "God" or "the Divine," which typically are shared by a community of believers. Also typically, religion in this sense involves a founder and an élite of priestly specialists who are charged with upholding the religious tradition. The emphasis is on "doing the right thing"—morally sound behavior—in order to receive God's grace and have the community's approval and thus support. Also, the religious concept of God is that of a supreme authority, a Superperson (usually of the male gender) who somehow exists outside of oneself and with whom interaction is possible but only as creature versus Creator. The characteristic form of interaction with this personal God is devotion and prayer.

Spirituality, by contrast, can be understood as a more individualized striving for *direct* knowledge of, or union with, the supreme Reality, which is most often conceived as impersonal and which is the very core of one's being (one's "Self" or "Buddha Nature"). Hence the knowledge of, or union with, the supreme Reality is also frequently called "Self-realization."[1] Other terms for this event are "enlightenment," "realization," and "liberation." Since the supreme Reality is not only the Ground of all existence but also the ultimate Core of our inner being, it is not an *external* force or agency to which we can address our petitionary prayers. Strictly speaking, we cannot even unite with it, as it already is our true nature. Some spiritual traditions, however, employ the language of merging or uniting as a concession to the conventional (duality-oriented) mind. What all spiritual approaches have in common is that the person seeking to realize the supreme Reality must submit to a course of intense self-discipline, self-transformation, or self-transcendence, which goes beyond prescribed moral rules but nevertheless involves sound moral behavior.

The transformation expected of a religious practitioner, by comparison with a spiritual practitioner, is rather lenient. Spiritual practice ultimately always aims at a radical transmutation of the practitioner. The superlative ideal of spirituality is not religious conformism but utter ego-transcendence to the point of enlightenment.[2] From a spiritual perspective, religion could be called a beginning stage in the process of self-transformation. In this sense, then, Yoga is spirituality rather than religion, though some yogic schools clearly have a more religious flavor than others.

Yoga, which is a creation of the genius of Indic humanity, exists in three major forms, which arose in the context of Hinduism, Jainism, and Buddhism—the three great cultural complexes of India.[3] These forms of Yoga—Hindu, Jaina, and Buddhist—and their various branches all universally agree that human existence is shot through with suffering. The cause of this suffering is not any outside agency but the artificial psychological construct we call the "I," or ego. The ego is our ongoing misidentification with a particular body-mind, whereas in truth we forever transcend all physical, emotional, and mental realities. In Hindu Yoga, this Spirit is widely called *ātman* or *purusha*. In Jaina Yoga, it is known as "Perfect Self" (*siddha-ātman*), while the Buddhists often speak of it as "Buddha Nature" (*dharmatā*) or "Reality Body" (*dharma-kāya*).

The word *ātman* means literally "self." As a personal pronoun it can mean "oneself, himself, herself, itself." In philosophical contexts, it typically stands for the transcendental Self, or eternal Spirit. The word *purusha*, which is equally old and can be found already in the ancient *Rig-Veda*, means literally "person" and is used in this prosaic sense in conventional speech. In philosophical contexts, however, it refers to the transcendental part of the human being—the supreme Being, or Spirit.

Our spiritual Identity/Self is by definition infinite, eternal, and immutable. By contrast, the ego-personality is finite, mortal, and highly changeable. The relationship between the transcendental Self and the "lower" self, or ego, is explained differently in the various schools of Yoga. The nondualist schools of Yoga acknowledge the existence of only a singular Self, whereas the schools of qualified nondualism and dualism speak of many transcendental Spirits. The latter appears to be also the position of Patanjali's Classical Yoga, as we can infer from his *Yoga-Sūtra* (c. 200 A.D.).[4]

Some traditions, such as Kashmiri Shaivism, describe the ego in terms of "self-contraction" (*ātma-samkoca*): The infinite Self curiously contracts in on itself, creating the artificial sense of individuated existence in opposition to other individuated existences (or ego-selves).[5] Thus the ego is the main culprit behind our universal human experience of suffering—be it as an inner sense of incompleteness, inadequacy, unfulfillment, fragmentation, unease, unhappiness, anguish, or physical discomfort and pain.

But in most Yoga traditions, the ego-self is not regarded as the root-cause of suffering. The Yoga authorities point to spiritual ignorance as the source of all evil. This ignorance is said to precede the formation of the ego-self: We are born in ignorance of our true nature as Spirit. This leads us to develop an increasingly stronger sense of limited self (expressed in "I," "me," and "mine"). This psychological process is complete with the individuation of the adult human individual. From a conventional perspective, this is considered a desirable accomplishment. From a yogic perspective, it is merely a process of estrangement from our true identity, the Spirit. In his *Yoga-Sūtra* (2.3ff.), Patanjali addresses this self-alienation in his teaching on the five causes of affliction: ignorance, "I-am-ness", attachment, aversion, and the survival instinct.

In this schema, "I-am-ness" (*asmitā*) corresponds to the "I-maker" (*ahamkāra*) of other schools. It arises out of the seedbed of spiritual nescience and, in turn, gives rise to the kind of basic reactivity that characterizes ordinary life: Attachment to what we experience as pleasant and aversion to what we experience as unpleasant. Once we feel we are a *someone*—an embodied individual with a particular mind and personality—we also behave accordingly, constantly affirming our separateness from all other individuated beings. When the ego-sense has become firmly entrenched, we also seek to protect and perpetuate it endlessly, which is in fact the survival instinct.

Yoga is an all-out endeavor to deconstruct the ego-construct— our "artificial" self-sense—and uncover our true nature, the transcendental Spirit/Self or Witness.[6] As such, Yoga is intensely personal, because it seeks to dissolve our individuated inner world. Yet, at the same time, it is highly impersonal, because its avowed goal is the transcendence of all aspects of our human personality, which is a product of space-time coincidences. A third dimension of Yoga lies between the personal and the impersonal, which is the whole area of moral behavior.

It is in its practical morality that Yoga seeks to overcome the ingrained obsession with the ego-self by connecting the ego-personality with other ego-personalities through the common ground of virtue. Yoga morality is based on the insight that all beings are vitally interconnected and that for all of them to function optimally (and thus to survive as individuated beings), they must accept a common ground at the level of social interaction. If everyone were to behave totally egocentric and, out of self-interest, even behave immorally, no human society would be possible. Violence, lying, stealing, and so on undermine the very fabric of social life.

Thus Yoga—like other religio-spiritual traditions—maintains the notion that virtues like nonharming, truthfulness, nonstealing, chastity, and greedlessness are universally valid, as they promote the inevitable interconnectedness that exists between beings. These universal virtues are thought to make possible not only peaceful coexistence but also the pursuit of inner freedom, as envisioned by the liberation teachings of India. It is self-evident that in a society that is full of deceit, aggression, ideological control, and vice, it is almost impossible to succeed in spiritual life. Hence the Yoga scriptures recommend that an aspirant should find a peaceful country with friendly people.

Whether or not a Yoga practitioner lives in community with others, he or she has to uphold the five universal moral virtues mentioned by Patanjali and a good many more. The reason for this is that these virtues are powers that are effective even purely at the level of the mind. Hence they must be observed in body, speech, and mind. What this implies is that our interconnectedness with other beings occurs not merely in the shared physical environment but also—and for the yogin or yoginī possibly even primarily—in the vastness of our shared noetic space. Hostile thoughts are just as harmful as hostile physical actions or hostile speech. They harm others and ourselves, and thus they throttle life rather than cause it to flourish.

The ego-personality, which, in the language of Kashmir's Shaivism, is itself a "constriction" (*samkoca*), tends to be delimiting and confining.[7] When, through intensive spiritual practice, we become able to loosen this egoic constriction in our own case, we will enter into a mood of "expansion" (*vikāsa*) that corresponds more to our true nature, which is infinite and unlimited. This expansion, of course, is not an expansion of the ego, which would be equivalent to ego inflation. Rather, it is an expansion in the sense of an opening in consciousness where rigid walls are broken down, so that our true identity can shine forth. The Yoga tradition speaks of "knots" at the heart that must be loosened in order to reveal our innermost free core.

Inner freedom and Yoga's universal morality are thus not at all contradictory, though the conventional mind may experience them as such. We often confuse inner freedom with an attitude of "anything goes," which means that the ego-personality is at liberty to wallow in its karmic patterns of desire. But true freedom is precisely freedom from the compulsion of the ego and its conditioning. Who we are when we are truly free remains to be seen in each case. So long as there is a physical body along with a specifically endowed mind, we can expect uniqueness in form and content. That is to say, even when a Yoga adept has attained complete inner freedom, he or she continues to look a certain way and, to some extent, display the signs of animating a certain personality. Typically, though, the personality of a liberated being is rather flexible and not easily stereotyped. Some personality patterns obviously are predictable, because much of our mental makeup is DNA-driven. Thus a liberated adept may have a modal personality but still display a wide range of responses to life situations, which are not easily predictable. Even though enlightenment is mind transcending, this does not mean that the mind ceases to exist, just as the body continues to exist until it naturally disintegrates upon death. The mind transcendence of the enlightened being consists in the cessation of his or her identification with a particular body-mind.

Historically, however, the behavior of a liberated adept—or even an adept close to the ultimate realization of freedom—shows a basic grounding in the universal moral virtues. It would seem that inner freedom and goodness go together and that a liberated master who is evil simply is an impossibility. Of course, prior to full liberation or enlightenment, adepts can manifest character traits that we would normally classify as highly undesirable or even psychopathological. Therein lies the danger of entrusting one's spiritual life to a teacher who may have all kinds of extraordinary realizations and capacities, which may even seem to us as supernatural, but who has not yet transcended the ego-illusion himself or herself.[8]

Yoga connects virtue with the cosmic order itself. The universe is not arbitrary but an ordered whole, even though its order may not always be obvious to us or even fit into the expectations of conventional logic. Interestingly, the word *dharma*—which has a wide range of meanings, including "morality"—stems from the root *dhri* meaning to "hold" or "maintain." Virtue or morality is the glue that holds (*dhri*) human life together, just as the cosmic law (*rita*) holds together the macrocosmic structures and processes.

Of course, the Yoga practitioner does not aspire to virtue for its own sake. Goodness in itself is an abstract ideal that does not stir the yogin or yoginī. Rather, virtuous behavior is meant to free up energy and attention for the spiritual process of liberation. It is an essential part of the Yoga practitioner's extensive program of self-purification in which all the dross created by the false ego-identity is eliminated until the ego-identity itself can be replaced by the transcendental Self/Spirit. Moral behavior, then, has a cathartic effect that, if engaged with the requisite understanding, ends in the removal of the artifice called "ego."

On the way to inner freedom, morality is a sound facilitator. After attaining inner freedom, morality is the natural expression of an ego-free being. We must, however, not confuse the universal morality or radical spirituality with the conditional morality of the average ego-based individual. The latter is largely self-serving and not conducive to Self-realization. Yogic morality is founded in the wisdom of the great adepts, who have realized their true nature. It is geared toward self-transcendence and inner freedom. Moreover, it is a wisdom that each of us can replicate within ourselves if we care to follow the guidelines of the sages. As we grow spiritually, we become less and less dependent on external rules and discover more and more the kind of spontaneous morality that springs from real understanding, authentic wisdom.

Here we must remember that Yoga is thoroughly experiential. We can verify its fundamental tenets, which themselves are the product of intensive experimentation. No belief is required to succeed in Yoga, although at least provisional acceptance of a few of its central ideas—notably the existence of a transcendental Spirit—can facilitate our inner growth.

For the yogic adept, morality *is* spirituality, and vice versa. Hence we should not be surprised to see Yoga masters pay so much attention to the moral precepts, which are guidelines for wise living, having been distilled from extensive and intensive spiritual practice. That we find the same universal virtues in religious traditions is simply an indication of the former's intrinsic merit. The difference between a spiritually based morality and a religion-based morality is not one of essence but merely one of attitude.

As mentioned before, it seems useful to distinguish spirituality from religion. Both are concerned with the ultimate Reality (Divine, Godhead, Deity, God, Goddess, Self, Spirit). Religion, as the word suggests, seeks to "reconnect" or "re-link" (*religare*) an individual with the ultimate Reality, which is generally considered to be the Creator of all things. This reconnection is supposed to happen through belief in the articles of faith (whatever they may be) and obedience to the moral laws (e.g., the Ten Commandments) provided by the founder of each religious tradition. Thus the "path" of religion is based on submission to an external authority that dictates to the believer what is right and wrong, allowing little room for personal insight and an unmediated encounter with the Divine. The image of God is typically that of a superauthority ("Heavenly Father"), who blesses or condemns and punishes—an archetypal image that historically has instilled a fair measure of fear and guilt in religious believers (the "children" of God).[9]

In the case of spirituality, the reconnection with the ultimate Reality is of a radical kind. First of all, the Supreme is not viewed as a father or mother figure but as the ultimate spiritual essence of our being and of all existence. Some schools of Yoga speak of the "Inner Ruler," the God within. The spiritual path is not mere obedience to an external authority (be it a priesthood or sacred scripture) but consists in "remembering" our identity with the ultimate Reality. This remembering calls for a healthy dose of self-initiative and self-reliance. Most of all, however, it demands our steady practice of voluntary self-transcendence from moment to moment. On the spiritual path, we do not behave morally or practice the teachings in order to please God and win his favor but because it ripens (or purifies) our personality to the point of enlightenment (or "awakening").

Religion wants to create a "God-fearing" individual, who lives a morally sound life. Spirituality encourages us to find the Divine within ourselves and in all things, which is the essence of enlightenment. Religion aims at creating a "good" person but leaves the ego contraction intact; spirituality insists on transcending the ego itself, thereby creating a being who lives spontaneously out of the infinite wisdom of the ultimate Reality.

Manifestly, religion and spirituality occupy positions on the same spectrum of responsiveness to the ultimate Reality, and the boundary between them is quite fluid. There are religious orientations that are more spiritual, just as there are spiritual approaches (such as Bhakti-Yoga) that have a more religious flavor. As is demonstrated by the mystics of the world's religious traditions, when religion is taken seriously, it evolves into spirituality. We can see this in the example of Thomas Merton, a Trappist monk who in his later years explored Eastern teachings. Despite the shackles put on this intrepid spiritual explorer by the Christian Church, he found his way to the recognition that "Contemplation is the highest and most paradoxical form of self realization, attained by apparent self-annihilation."[10] The leap into radical or deep self-transcendence is the decisive step from mere religion to deep spirituality.

Spirituality is more or less synonymous with the discipline of radical self-transcendence—the kind of transcendence that cuts to the root (*radix*) of *the* existential problem, which is the ego. Every act of deep self-transcendence, as I will discuss in Chapter 4, symbolically recapitulates the primordial self-sacrifice of Macran-thropos (or *mahā-puruṣa* in Sanskrit). One of the facets of self-transcendence is an altruistic concern for others. Most people re-gard altruism as a desirable virtue, even though they themselves would admit to falling short of the ideal. Since the Enlightenment, however, some philosophers have protested against this consen-sus opinion. Instead, they have argued in favor of selfishness of one kind or another as a legitimate source of moral action.

One of the most outspoken modern critics of this ilk was the "objectivist" philosopher-novelist Ayn Rand, who commanded a large following during her lifetime and whose works are still widely read. Rand vigorously argued that every person is basi-cally selfish, though some mask this fact by a show of pretended altruism. She made selfishness the central virtue of her rational-ist ethical-philosophical system. In her book *The Virtue of Self-ishness*, she defines virtue as any action by which one secures and protects one's life and happiness.[11] She obviously understands "selfishness" in a way that is quite distinct from popular usage of the term, which ordinarily signifies indifference to others and the pursuit of one's personal whims. Rand's "selfish" person is no mere brute but, in the interest of his or her own welfare and hap-piness, firmly commits to cultivating benevolence, justice, and other virtues respected by any rational individual. She rejects altruism because it does not acknowledge the individual's need for self-respect and independence in supporting his or her own life. Rand's ideal person—as illustrated in the person of Howard Roark, the central hero of her novel *The Fountainhead*—neither sacrifices himself for anyone else nor expects others to sacrifice themselves for him. In her subsequent novel *Atlas Shrugged*, the main character, John Galt, is still more stripped of personality and turned into a mouthpiece of Rand's philosophy. Her car-toon-like superrational heroes are uniformly fearless, forthright, and independent.

We may agree with Rand's impression that the human being is "self made," but not quite in the sense she intended. Also, from an Indian Gnostic perspective (which accepts the validity of multiple lives), her insistence that we all are born without sin—as a *tabula rasa*—is highly questionable. We only need to ask a mother, and she will confirm that her children were all different even as newborns. None of us comes into the world as a blank slate. Rather, as the Indian sages would contend, we have inscribed in the deepest layers of our mind the secrets of our karmic destiny ("sin"), just as our body carries the DNA encryption of our parents. The rationalist dream of independence to which Rand subscribed is just this: a dream, fantasy, or hope. We are by definition interdependent beings, and when we deny this and affirm independence too forcefully, we get ourselves and others, as well as our biotic environment into trouble. Witness the present global crisis!

As with every philosophy, Rand's system contains a kernel of truth, perhaps even a good many valuable insights. The kind of altruism that received her consistent criticism and scorn is indeed imbalanced. Since we ourselves are sentient beings too, we must also take care of our own needs—our welfare, health, and happiness. Only when we are whole ourselves can we in fact serve others appropriately. Any other attitude is probably neurotic.

Rand rightly highlighted the selfishness in what most people call "friendship" and "love," though she did find these to be acceptable behaviors. She vehemently rejected, however, any program that put strangers before our own personal welfare and happiness, other than in exceptional circumstances of emergency. According to her philosophy, we are under no obligation to assist a poverty-stricken neighbor, though we may do so for our own reasons. Many of the noble actions of the Buddhist bodhisattvas would have been quite incomprehensible to her.

Rand's self-centered ethics, like that of Baruch (Benedict) Spinoza before her, is significant in that it reminds and even obliges us to look at the extremes of egocentrism and altruism respectively.[12] As the Italian economist-sociologist Vilfredo Pareto noted, most ethical theories represent attempts to make sense of altruism vs. egoism and establish some sort of compromise between them.[13] Spinoza, by the way, is remembered as a kind, compassionate individual. Born in 1634 in Holland into a family of Sephardic Jews, he earned his living as a lens-maker but by vocation was a rationalist philosopher. His book on ethics—*Ethica Ordine Geometrico Demonstrata*—approaches its subject with mathematical-geometrical precision. Though condemned, cursed, and vilified by his contemporaries for his rejection of Deism and scriptural truth, Spinoza remained calm throughout these tribulations and is said to have died without fear in his heart.

From what we know about his all-too short life, he was utterly dedicated to the pursuit of truth, and no threat could make him deviate from the philosophical path. His moral integrity, considerateness, kindness, and exemplary patience were such that his few friends and admirers, as well as subsequent rediscoverers of his work deemed him a saintly individual. Bertrand Russell, in his *History of Western Philosophy*, called Spinoza "the noblest and most lovable of the great philosophers."[14] It is unfortunate that for a whole century after his death, it was considered unacceptable to talk nicely about Spinoza and his intellectual legacy, and that even now his contribution to philosophy is so little known and appreciated.[15]

For Spinoza, the highest virtue was to know God, which for him was ultimate Being or Reality. This superlative virtue, like any other, he saw anchored in the inmost nature of the human being. Hence, he felt, it was perfectly legitimate and even necessary to preserve oneself; he saw suicide, for instance, as the act of a confused and weak-willed person. Because virtue is an integral part of who we are in our innermost nature, he taught that we should desire virtue for its own sake. As Heidi Morrison Ravven, a professor of religious studies at Hamilton College in Clinton, New York, has shown, there is good neuroscientific evidence in support of Spinoza's position that moral life is natural.[16] Notably, neuroscientific research on emotions and socialization has led researchers to conclude that all experiences have an emotional-evaluative flavor. Virtue seems hardwired into the brain and has survival value. This finding is important for the model espoused in the present volume, which is known as "virtue ethics": the proposition that ethical theory is best built on the notion of innate virtues rather than utilitarian principles or duties. I will explain this position, which is the position of all traditional systems of spiritual growth, in the next chapter.

ENDNOTES, CHAPTER 1

1   The Hindu Yoga tradition knows the term *ātma-jnāna* or "Self-knowledge," but the realization for which it stands must not be confused with a cognitive state. It is gnosis only in the loose sense that the *fruit* of this realization implies a radical shift in understanding: The ego is no longer the focal point of experiences, but post-enlightenment life is now lived with the ātman or transcendental Self as the true center. See the excellent book by Herbert Fingarette, *The Self in Transformation: Psychoanalysis, Philosophy and the Life of the Spirit* (New York: HarperCollins, 1977). This work remains one of the finest exploration of the connection between psychoanalysis, existentialism, and India's wisdom traditions. It includes a helpful discussion of the notion of karma from a psychoanalytic perspective.

2   Some people insist on distinguishing between enlightenment (as an accomplishment while being embodied) and liberation (as a realization that occurs once the body-mind has been jettisoned. But this distinction is not entirely convincing, and therefore I have not adopted it here. An enlightened being, in my view, is liberated whether he or she is embodied or disembodied. Thus the Buddha's *nirvāna* was the same prior to his body's demise as it was thereafter, even though the latter condition is indicated by the term *parinirvāna*, simply to suggest that the entity called Gautama the Buddha had ceased as an embodied being.

3   See Georg Feuerstein, *The Yoga Tradition: Its History, Literature, Philosophy and Practice* (Prescott, Ariz.: Hohm Press, 2d rev. ed. 2001). This tome serves as the principal textbook for an 800-hour distance-learning course designed by me and also is used in a number of Yoga teacher training programs in the United States and elsewhere.

4   For a discussion of the metaphysics of Patanjali's Classical Yoga, see Georg Feuerstein, *The Philosophy of Classical Yoga* (Rochester, Vt.: Inner Traditions International, repr. ed. 1996). See also my distance-learning course on this school of Yoga, which is offered by Traditional Yoga Studies.

5   One of the most user-friendly introductions to the intriguing metaphysical system of Kashmiri Shaivism and its associated practices is Swami Chetanandana, *Dynamic Stillness—Part One: The Practice of Trika Yoga* and *Dynamic Stillness—Part Two: The Fulfillment of Trika Yoga* (Portland, Or.: Rudra Press, 2001).

6   On the witnessing function, see Arthur J. Deikman, *The Observing Self: Mysticism and Psychotherapy* (Boston, Mass.: Beacon Press, 1982).

7   On the metaphysics and psychology of Kashmiri Shaivism, see Jaidev Singh, *Śiva Sūtras: The Yoga of Supreme Identity* (Delhi: Motilal Banarsidass, 1979) and *Spanda-Kārikās: The Divine Creative Pulsation* (Delhi: Motilal Banarsidass, rev. ed. 1980).

8   I have addressed this issue in connection with the phenomenon of crazy wisdom. See my book *Holy Madness: Spirituality, Crazy-Wise Teachers, and Enlightenment* (Prescott, Ariz.: Hohm Press, 2d ed. 2006).

9   On the paternalistic image of God, see Stewart Elliott Guthrie, *Faces in the Clouds: A New Theory of Religion* (New York: Oxford University Press, 1993) and Richard Dayringer and David Oler, eds., *The Image of God and the Psychology of Religion* (Binghamton, N.Y.: Haworth Pastoral Press, 2004). It is this mental icon of God that the German philosopher Friedrich Nietzsche dismissed when he defiantly announced the death of God.

10   See T. Merton, *The New Man* (New York: Farrar, Straus & Cudahy, 1961), p. 19.

11   See A. Rand, *The Virtue of Selfishness: A New Concept of Egoism* (New York: Signet Books, reissue ed. 1989).

12   See Don Garrett, ed., *The Cambridge Companion to Spinoza* (Cambridge: Cambridge University Press, 1995) and Genevieve Lloyd, *Routledge Philosophy Guidebook to Spinoza and the Ethics* (London: Routledge, 1996).

13   See Vilfredo Pareto, *Cours d'économie politique professé à l'université de Lausanne* (1896–1897). This two-volume work was reissued in 1962 as a single tome, the first of 31 volumes in Pareto's Collected Works by Librairie Droz in Geneva.

14   B. Russell, *The History of Western Philosophy* (New York: Touchstone Books, 1972), p. 569.

15   In the context of the present discussion of virtue, it may be permissible to mention that Ayn Rand's own life had a contrasting flavor. She enjoyed enormous success, even adulation, as a writer and thinker during her lifetime. Like Spinoza, she was forthright but apparently less considerate. Where we see calm reasonableness in Spinoza, we witness fiery conviction in Rand. Her personal life was stormy, because she sought to exact from her friends and close followers rational standards that, as a private individual, she herself was unable to demonstrate consistently. See the controversial Ayn Rand biography by Barbara Branden, *The Passion of Ayn Rand* (New York: Doubleday, 1986).

16   See Heidi Morrison Ravven, "Did Spinoza get ethics right? Some insights from recent neuroscience," in J. Thomas Cook and Lee Rice, eds., *Spinoza on Mind and Body* (Würzburg, Germany: Königshausen & Neumann, 2004), pp. 56–91. This is vol. 14 in the Studia Spinozana series.

CHAPTER 2

THE CONCEPT OF MORAL LAW

As stressed in Chapter 1, Yoga is a *spiritual* discipline, which aims at enlightenment, or liberation. All forms of spirituality share a strong interest in tapping into our highest human potential, which is the ability to transcend the human condition itself. That is to say, all authentic Yoga seeks to go beyond the conventional levels of human activity—the all-pervasive worry over food, shelter, companionship, procreation, material means (especially money), emotional contentment, creativity, power, and general self-expression and self-esteem. Whenever the impulse for self-transcendence is absent, we do not have genuine Yoga before us. (What does this say about contemporary Yoga?)

In its goal of radical self-transcendence, Yoga even intends to reach beyond the level of normative behavior, or learned morality. In order to live authentically, the sages insist, we must transcend the human-made categories of "good" and "evil," which vary from culture to culture, even sometimes from group to group. For instance, in one culture it might be considered completely moral to punish a thief by lopping off his hand. In another culture, such eye-for-an-eye legalism would be regarded as barbaric. Or, yet another culture might reject the electric chair as inappropriate but wholeheartedly accept beheading as a valid alternative punishment. Many more examples of such cultural variation in the moral domain could be cited. Moreover, in our own contemporary Western society, which is no longer held together by the glue of a single religious tradition or a shared lifestyle, moral relativism is abundantly evident.[1] Confronting multiple lifestyles and moral standards, Westerners tend to be quite confused about morality, to say the least.

In previous centuries, Christianity supplied a unifying morality for the Occident, but with the waning of ecclesiastical authority in the eighteenth century and a growing disinclination to participate in Christian religious life, more and more Westerners have come to face a scary void. In some ways, the scientific world-view has largely replaced the preceding religious world-view. It has done so, however, as a limiting and often destructive ideology—or what has been called "scientific materialism"—which is built on an exaggerated version of the ideal of objectivity. Science, which is primarily or, as some would argue, exclusively concerned with *how* things work, is not qualified to answer metaphysical questions, which deal with *why* things are the way they are. Contrary to popular belief, for science to remain human it must be based on sound philosophical footings and, indeed, sound moral principles. An amoral science or technology, I believe, is prone to quickly become an immoral and hence harmful pursuit.

Today we can witness the widespread negative effects of just such a stance. Secular humanism, which subscribes to amoral science as gospel truth, has done considerable damage.[2] Its reductionistic ideology, which itself has become a de facto religion, dismisses religion, myth, metaphysics, and paranormal science—all so-called supernatural and authoritarian beliefs—and in the process has chucked out much that is of intrinsic value in human life. Its quasi-religious texts are the *Humanist Manifesto I* (1933) and the *Humanist Manifesto II* (1973). Its high priest is the American philosopher Paul Kurtz, the chairman of the Council for Secular Humanism and author of over forty books. Of course, not all the tenets of secular humanism are without merit. On the contrary, many are valid and to the point, but as a socio-cultural movement and substitute religion, secular humanism has proven a failure.

Yet, when we turn for moral guidance to philosophy, which in bygone ages included metaphysics, we find that contemporary philosophers are for the most part no longer interested in metaphysical questions or practical moral issues. Even many theologians—our next obvious choice for moral advice—are also not particularly eager to tackle moral problems. They might refer us to the moral counsel of a priest, parson, or rabbi. Unless they happen to be fundamentalists who have pat answers for everything, however, these good people in turn are frequently as perplexed as we are ourselves.

The problem with fundamentalism of any kind is that the "gospel truth" it preaches springs from a narrow literal interpretation that distorts rather than illuminates. In the case of religious fundamentalism, the great insights and inspirations of the founders of religions become transmogrified into inflexible dogmas and rigid rules of behavior. This does not mean that all fundamentalist beliefs are necessarily wrong, but rather it suggests that we must scrutinize them with special vigilance.

Manifestly, all religious traditions include moral teachings that highlight certain universal values. Those values are universal in the sense that they are deemed highly desirable by any thinking person of sound mind because they allow societies to function harmoniously and effectively. I am referring to the kind of moral values that, for instance, are embodied in the Ten Commandments of the Pentateuch or in the moral disciplines of Patanjali's so-called Classical Yoga. The latter moral code, to be sure, is shared in principle by all other forms and branches of Yoga. In other words, it is fundamental to all schools of Hindu, Buddhist, and Jaina Yoga—the three basic forms of the yogic heritage of India.

To fully appreciate the role of morality within the yogic tradition, we must evoke the Indic concept of *dharma*. As mentioned previously, this Sanskrit term is derived from the verbal root *dhri* meaning "to hold, support, bear, carry" and literally means "that which supports." It is cognate with the Latin word *firmus*, meaning "firm," "fixed," "strong," "reliable," "solid." By implication, dharma is thought to firmly uphold or sustain social life and also cosmic existence as such. Depending on the context in which the term appears, it can mean "morality," "righteousness," "prescribed conduct," "virtue," "duty," "law," "custom," "norm," "ordinance," "usage," "established order," and "justice," but also "substance," "quality," "reality," and "teaching."

The word *dharma* has a long history, which begins with the archaic *Rig-Veda*, the oldest Indic scripture and the source of Brahmanism ("orthodox" Hinduism). In this ancient text already, it signifies "morality" and "custom." The *Atharva-Veda* (12.1.17), which also belongs to the earliest literary creations of the Indic civilization, extols the greatness of dharma with the following words: "The Earth is upheld by *dharma*."

The Vedic concept of *dharma* is connected with, and in some hymns of the *Rig-Veda* synonymous with, the equally essential Vedic notion of the universal order or cosmic harmony. The cosmic order (*rita*) is dharma at the level of the macrocosm, while dharma can be considered to be a microcosmic manifestation of the macrocosmic harmony.[3] To put it differently, the inner moral law corresponds to the overarching "natural" laws that govern the cosmos at large. In the language of medieval European hermeticism, "As above, so below."

It was the eighteenth-century German philosopher Immanuel Kant, a great rationalist, who wrote in the conclusion of his *Critique of Practical Reason*: "Two things fill my mind with ever new and increasing admiration and awe the more often and more intensively I ponder them: the starry heaven above me and the moral law within me."[4] Of all the thousands of words written by Kant, these were the ones to be inscribed on his gravestone.

Any sensitive person cannot fail to be touched by the grandeur and astounding orderliness of the rhythms of Sun, Moon, the other planets, and the array of stars. He or she would also be filled with awe and wonder at the beauty and orderliness of the mesocosm—the human body and its environment with seasons, ebb and tide, cycles of rain and sunshine, and not least the miracle of plant, animal, and human growth. Furthermore, anyone who has ever looked through a microscope at a crystal, a plant cell, or a drop of pond water will have been astonished by the spectacles of the microcosm, which reaches down to the subatomic level. All three realms of Nature—microcosm, mesocosm, and macrocosm—display a rhythmicity that suggests a common ground. Finally, what of the wonderful regularity of mathematics without which the more subtle patterns of Nature would forever elude us?

One way of looking at this cohesiveness is via the notion of interconnectedness (*bandhu*), or kinship between all beings and things, which is quite ancient and which was a favorite subject of meditative inquiry already at the time of the Vedic seers some five thousand years ago. This idea, which has been revived in modern times by ecology but also quantum theory, covers a range of insights. Among these archaic insights is the mystical belief expressed in the above-mentioned maxim "As above, so below": Manifestations at the material level reflect forms at the mental or subtle level of existence. Likewise, the well-known but poorly understood "law of retribution" or "moral causation" (*karma*), is an expression of the deep interconnectedness and orderliness of the cosmos.

What is important to realize in the present context is that since time immemorial the Indic sages have avowed that (a) in order to live harmoniously human beings must structure their lives according to the universal interconnectedness and natural order-liness of life and (b) they cannot transcend the human condition without first consciously synchronizing themselves with the cosmic order.

Implied in this age-old belief is the idea that self-transcendence is a natural aspect of human life. In fact, when we look closely enough, self-transcendence is an integral part of the process of growth in general: A form changes either automatically (biologically) or intentionally in the course of its life; one condition is surpassed by another. In modern times, the great Bengali yogi-philosopher Sri Aurobindo expressed this insight relative to human beings in evolutionary terms as follows:

> In the right view both of life and of Yoga all life is either consciously or subconsciously a Yoga. For we mean by this term a methodised [sic] effort towards self-perfection by the expression of the secret potentialities latent in the being and a union of the human individual with the universal and transcendent Existence we see partially expressed in man and in the Cosmos. But all life, when we look behind its appearances, is a vast Yoga of Nature attempting to realise her perfection in an ever increasing expression of her potentialities and to unite herself with her own divine reality. In man, her thinker, she for the first time upon this Earth devises self-conscious means and willed arrangements of activity by which this great purpose may be more swiftly and puissantly attained. Yoga, as Swami Vivekananda has said, may be regarded as a means of compressing one's evolution into a single life or a few years or even a few months of bodily existence. A given system of Yoga, then, can be no more than a selection or a compression, into narrower but more energetic forms of intensity, of the general methods which are already

being used loosely, largely, in a leisurely movement, with a profuser apparent waste of material and energy but with a more complete combination by the great Mother in her vast upward labour.[5]

In the case of human beings, liberation is simply the final step in a long process of both automatic and intentional acts or processes of self-transcendence. To begin with automatic biological transcendence: Our body naturally grows out of the union of sperm and ovum into a zygote, then a fetus, embryo, independently existing neonate, child, adolescent, and adult until the bodily elements dissolve again upon death. Each step in this developmental series transcends the preceding step or steps.

The mind evolves as well, and therefore can be said to also pass—like the body—through acts of transcendence: The mind of a neonate is not the same as that of a toddler, a teenager, or an adult. It changes with experience and knowledge. Moreover, as the yogins assure us, the mind continues beyond death following its own laws at the mental level. Again we have a clear instance of one state being transcended in favor of another—automatically.

We are involved in more or less *intentional* self-transcendence whenever we love, feel compassion for someone else, or make personal sacrifices. We also transcend ourselves when we learn, change our mind about something, take up a dietary or exercise regimen, break a negative habit pattern, overcome fear, courageously protest against an objectionable behavior or rule, and so forth. Not all these actions are of equal importance or value but they all are self-transcending nonetheless. Of special interest, however, is what I have called intentional self-transcendence.

Full-fledged self-transcendence sets in when we deliberately and voluntarily follow a spiritual path by which we seek to go beyond the normal sense of self, which is the conventional idea of inhabiting a single body that is distinct from all others. The state of ecstasy, which reveals the interconnectedness or no-thing-ness of everything, is an instance of radical self-transcendence. Alas, it is only temporary and therefore, from a yogic perspective, it is not ultimately satisfactory. Only with the event of liberation does self-transcendence become fully established. In other words, liberation is radical self-transcendence by which we let go of the illusory or conventional self (ego) and recover our true identity as the omnipresent Reality. Prior to this event, we experience ourselves as individuated embodied "selves" rather than as the transcendental Singularity (*ātman*) that is the transcendental Ground of our being and of all existence. The Vedic seers and their Hindu successors have assigned to this ultimate Ground the technical term *brahman*. In the Buddhist Yoga tradition, this ultimate Reality is primarily known as Buddha Nature or the Void. The masters of Jaina Yoga call it *sat*, or "Reality" The different labels and even their underlying conceptual differences should not blind us to the fact that all definitions of liberation imply complete ego-transcendence.

It is not clear when Indic humanity discovered the *ātman/brahman* Reality. Already in the 5000-year-old *Rig-Veda* (1.129), however, we find a hymn that praises the One which "breathes breathlessly by itself" and which is to be known through the Solar Yoga of the seers. Another hymn, which belongs to the *Atharva-Veda* (10.8.44), talks about the "wise, unaging, youthful Self" which, when realized, helps one overcome the fear of death. As scholars are gradually discovering, the composers of the Vedic hymns were not naïve country bumpkins, as originally thought, but seer-bards whose poetry was highly sophisticated and gave expression to extraordinarily profound spiritual intuitions. Much of the deeper meaning of the Vedic hymnodies was lost over time, making room for watered-down interpretations and ritualistic literalism. It took a Yoga master of the caliber of Sri Aurobindo (1872–1950) to retrieve some of the spiritual teachings of the *Vedas* and set a new tone in the study and exegesis of the Vedic hymns.[6] His pioneering efforts, unfortunately, are rarely taken into account by the academic establishment.

Sri Aurobindo made it clear that the Vedic seers were not merely praying for material wealth, sons, and cattle, but their hearts were set on discovering the One beyond the Many. Thus we can say that the ideal of liberation was integral already to the Vedic culture.[7] The pronounced spiritual orientation of the Vedic people notwithstanding, we should not of course expect the general population to have pursued the ideal of liberation. Then, as now, this was very likely the pursuit of only a select few—the seers and sages. Unlike today, though, the people at large in all likelihood revered and listened to those who strove for liberation and perhaps even hoped that, one day, they too might have the same spiritual dedication and capacity.

If the seers and sages probed into the mysteries of the cosmic order, the ordinary person in Vedic times at least attempted to respect the moral law revealed by the great mystics. In their social teachings, the sages emphasized moral orderliness and, in due course, integrated dharma into the well-known Hindu schema of the four "human goals"—material welfare, enjoyment of various kinds, morality, and liberation.[8]

According to this schema, all four pursuits are deemed legitimate. Thus it is good and appropriate to dedicate a portion of one's life to the pursuit of acquiring a solid material basis, since without some measure of material security, it is difficult to do justice to the duties of a householder, which include taking proper care of one's spouse and offspring. Householders also are permitted and expected to experience the joys of life—from the birth of a child to the comfort of one's home, socializing, sexual intercourse, the consumption of tasty and nutritious food, aesthetic pleasure, and delight in knowledge. Likewise, proper conduct is considered a basic right and duty of householders. In addition, they should also keep an eye on the highest human goal of liberation and appreciate that, at the appropriate time, they must renounce their householder life and dedicate themselves to the great spiritual ideal of complete self-transcendence through the means of Yoga.

It would seem that this social model was at least partly invented in order to stem the flood of renouncers, who abandoned their homes and families in order to pursue the ideal of liberation or, possibly, just to drop out and be done with social obligations. Eager to preserve harmony and balance, the sages and law-makers praised the value of a sound moral life. They argued that without proper attention to dharma, we could not make progress on the spiritual path. By assigning such importance to dharma, the sages opened a veritable can of worms, for the social duties falling under the category of dharma do not inevitably mesh well with the pursuit of spiritual liberation and the obligations specific to the life of a renouncer. The inherent tension between morality and the pursuit of liberation is a major theme of the Sanskrit literature of the so-called Epic Era. It forms the substance of the massive *Mahābhārata* and *Rāmāyana* epics.[9]

The *Bhagavad-Gītā*, which is embedded in the *Mahābhārata*, captures the spiritual and moral dilemma of a member of the ruling class—Prince Arjuna of the Pāndava dynasty. His inner conflict arose out of the stark reality of war. Standing in his chariot on the battle field and surveying the opposing army, he was overcome by great doubt: Did he have the right to slay his enemies even though they had unjustly ousted him and his brothers from their kingdom? After all, the opposing army included family members and respected teachers and elders. Filled with compassion, Prince Arjuna posed the following question to his charioteer and guru, Krishna:

O Krishna, seeing these my own people standing [before me] eager to fight, my limbs fail, my mouth is parched, my body is trembling, and my hair stands on end. (1.29)

I do not wish to kill them, O Madhusūdana [Krishna], even if they should slay me; not even for the sake of the rulership over the three worlds, how much less for the sake of the Earth? (1.35)

Even if they, with their minds corrupted by greed, cannot see that to destroy the family is evil, and treachery toward a friend is criminal—how should we, O Janārdana [Krishna], not be wise enough to turn away from this sin and see evil in the destruction of the family? (1.38-39)[10]

Arjuna agonized that by destroying the family, he also would destroy the everlasting family norms, which then would lead to a breakdown of morality and the collapse of the social order. Bemoaning the imminent death of thousands of kinsmen, he refused to give the signal to start the first battle. The remainder of the 700-stanza-long text of the Gītā consists in a dramatic dialogue between Prince Arjuna and his enlightened charioteer and guru Krishna. The latter disclosed to him, right there on the battlefield, the secrets of Yoga by which the prince could resolve his moral and spiritual dilemma.

Krishna's activist Yoga was meant to show Arjuna—and every other householder—a way out of the maze of karma while yet doing one's appointed duty. In Arjuna's case, his obligation as a warrior and defender of justice and order was to embark on what obviously would be a devastating war. No one, declared Krishna, can ever be truly inactive. We might sit in a remote, quiet mountain cave but find that our body-mind is still agitated. So, Krishna maintains that it is better to join Nature in its creative work by doing one's allotted tasks and thereby avoid the pitfall of escapism. Krishna's answer, to be sure, was controversial in his day and also in subsequent eras. He urged the prince to do his duty as a warrior, arguing that Arjuna would merely harvest sin by not proceeding with a lawful combat in which the principle of dharma itself was at stake.

To his credit, Arjuna did not accept his teacher's wisdom without much questioning. How could harmful action ever lead to good, he asked? In this, he voiced the opinion of the entire tradition of renunciation in India, which has never accepted war and harming in general as a solution to anything. But the more prominent tradition catering to householders—the ordinary man and woman with family ties and a sense of group identity or national pride—has largely followed Krishna's ideal of self-transcending activity, or Karma-Yoga. In modern times, social reformers like "Mahatma" Gandhi, Vinoba Bhave, Ram Mohan Roy, and Narayana Guru best exemplified this activist orientation. Gandhi's "passive resistance" to the British hegemony in India is well known. Although Gandhi aspired to uphold the principle of nonharming, his political stance nevertheless led to bloodshed, not least his own death at the hands of a fanatical Hindu nationalist. Nor did Gandhi subscribe to nonharming at any cost. As he often remarked, the mouse does not practice nonviolence by allowing itself to be gobbled up a cat. Martin Luther King, who had taken his inspiration from Gandhi, similarly observed that self-defense is an excusable form of violence.

At the core of Karma-Yoga lies a concern with right action. As the realized master Krishna put it long ago, articulating what was on his disciple's mind:

What is action? What is inaction? About this even the bards are bewildered. I shall declare to you that action which, when understood, will set you free from ill. (4.16)

Indeed, one ought to understand action, one ought to understand wrong action, and one ought to understand inaction. Impenetrable is the way of action. (4.17)

Since, according to Krishna, it is impossible to abstain from all action while one is alive, it behooves one to avoid wrong action and instead cultivate the kind of action that does not produce negative traits within oneself. Krishna's middle path of Karma-Yoga is based on the formula that no undesirable destiny, or karma, is created when one pursues the right action in a spirit of self-transcendence:

He whose every enterprise is free from desire and motive, whose action is baked in the fire of knowledge—him the wise call "learned." (4.19)

Having relinquished [all] attachment to the fruit of actions, ever content and independent, though engaged in action—he does not act at all. (4.20)

For him who is free from attachment and liberated, whose consciousness abides in knowledge while performing [all deeds as an inner] sacrifice, action is entirely dissolved. (4.23)

Ultimately, so Krishna taught, one would do well to make the Divine itself the focus of one's attention. This kind of self-surrender implies nonattachment to the results of one's rightful actions. One need not even be overly concerned with the rightfulness of one's actions, because by keeping the mind firmly set on the Divine, one's actions will inevitably be lawful, conducted out of compassion and love. This is the grand ideal of Bhakti-Yoga, which is Krishna's suggested approach for those whose heart is awakened.

Others, who wish to remain active in the world but do not feel particular devotion to the Divine Person, may resort to Karma-Yoga. Yet others, who feel strongly moved to renounce the world, may avail themselves of Saṃnyāsa-Yoga, or the path of renunciation. Krishna was clear, however, that this last option of abandoning one's involvement with the world is inferior to the other two.

To understand Krishna's activism, we must familiarize ourselves with two associated concepts—*sva-bhāva* and *sva-dharma*, one's inner being or nature and one's own norm or inner law. *Sva-bhāva*, which literally means "own being/becoming," stands for a person's fundamental character or personality: the kind of individual we are when no one is looking, that is, when we do not put on an act. It relates to the basic quality of our mind and psyche. Thus a person may have an artistic or intellectual temperament or be more of the "action type." He or she may have a philosophical bent of mind or live for the moment, hold strong convictions or be wishy-washy, or be revengeful or forgiving, and so forth.

Prince Arjuna, who had been born into the warrior estate, served the Indic tradition to illustrate the kind of personality that has a strong active component and has a well-developed sense of rightness and justice. By dint of his upbringing, Arjuna had also acquired a taste for and superb mastery of the military arts. He enjoyed pitting his wit, strength, and skills against a worthy opponent in playful combat. Yet he was not a belligerent individual, though also did not fear confrontation, injury, or death. Thus he was ideally suited for the life of a soldier and protector of the social order.

Prince Arjuna's inner nature—as a courageous warrior—was obvious to his contemporaries and has been equally obvious to any traditional reader of the *Bhagavad-Gītā* since then. Arjuna himself, however, experienced a serious conflict about his inner law. When facing the enemy on the morning of the first of eighteen battles, he felt utterly confused about his duties as a military leader.

According to the Indic tradition, one's inner law arises from one's basic constitution. If the enemy lines had not included so many of Prince Arjuna's relatives and beloved teachers, he would have had no doubt about his obligations. He would have fought fearlessly and tirelessly but without hatred for the enemy. But the self-doubt he was experiencing at the outset of the Bharata war sapped his will to fight and even his will to live.

Krishna, the enlightened charioteer and king of the Yādavas, recognized Arjuna's dejection as a momentary lapse in self-understanding. He reminded his disciple of his inner nature and inner law and urged him to fight for the preservation of dharma and in the spirit of Yoga.

The importance of dharma to the philosophy of the epic age is illustrated by the story of Yudhishthira's dog, as told in the *Mahābhārata*. Many years after the war, Prince Yudhishthira, one of Arjuna's brothers, came to die. Because the prince had steadfastly sought to preserve the principle of dharma in all his actions—even when they proved ruinous to himself and his family—he had earned a place in the heavenly realm. God Indra, leader of the divine hosts, invited Yudhishthira to alight the celestial chariot so that he could transport him to Heaven. When Yudhishthira wanted to bring his faithful dog along, Indra was outraged, but the prince refused to ascend to Heaven without the dog. At that moment, the dog revealed his true form as Yama, God of Death, who praised Yudhishthira's unfailing adherence to what is right. Just as the dog had loyally stood by the prince, Yama explained, so everyone must always be loyal to the supreme principle of dharma.

Just prior to the Epic Era, the nature of morality was explored in the spiritual cultures of Jainism and Buddhism. In Jainism—today a minority "religion" of India—dharma is considered central to the spiritual path.[11] According to this tradition, the stock of karma cannot be exhausted without moral discipline—notably nonharming. So long as karmic "stuff" clings to the Spirit, it cannot realize its inherent freedom. Proper moral conduct prevents the accumulation of karma, and existing karmic matter obscuring the Spirit is removed through intense austerities, or Yoga. Thus, much of the yogic path of Jainism is concerned with moral practices, which are grouped under the heading of "proper conduct." Even at the threat of death, the Jaina practitioner must not waver in his or her commitment to uphold the moral virtues.

According to Haribhadra Sūrī (c. 750 A.D.), proper conduct— along with veneration of one's teacher, the deities, and other beings of authority (notably one's parents and elders), penance, and an inclination to attain liberation—belongs to the "preparatory service." The practice of meditation is intended for more advanced practitioners, who has gained deep insight into the illusory nature of the ego and is intent on reaching enlightenment in this lifetime.

Buddhism, which came into existence in the mid-sixth century B.C., also places a premium on virtuous conduct.[12] In fact, the term *dharma* in its various meanings is so common in Buddhist scriptures that some writers have suggested that when we understand it properly, we also understand Buddhism. The word *dharma* came to stand for the Buddha's teaching itself, which indicates the importance given to virtuous conduct. Dharma is said to prevent the creation of new negative karma that would keep the individual entrapped in the wheel of life—birth, karmic activity, and death followed by rebirth. After Gautama Buddha's time, his teaching was further developed into what is called Mahāyāna Buddhism, which focuses on the virtuous path of the bodhisattva, the being dedicated to the spiritual liberation of all. The great moral virtues were turned into actual yogic practices. Motivated by compassion and guided by wisdom, the bodhisattva makes an all-out effort to realize enlightenment in order to promote the spiritual welfare of all others more effectively. He or she seeks to perfect the six virtues of generosity, patience, moral conduct, vigor, meditation, and transcendental wisdom. The absence of nonharming from this list should not alarm as, as nonharming is implied in the practice of moral conduct.

In the second century A.D., Sage Patanjali, the compiler of the well-known *Yoga-Sūtra*, taught that at the highest level of ecstasy—just prior to full spiritual liberation—the yogin is showered with virtue.[13] I will discuss Patanjali's perspective on moral disciplines in detail in subsequent chapters.

What I have tried to show thus far, if only sketchily, is the superlative importance of dharma in the great spiritual traditions of India. I would like to conclude this chapter with a brief consideration of the type of ethics we are dealing with in the yogic tradition. The dual meaning of *dharma* as "morality" and "virtue" contains an important clue on how we ought to look upon Hindu ethics and, by extension, also the yogic ethics of Buddhism and Jainism. As proposed by Bimal Krishna Matilal in his book *Ethics and Epics*, the treatment of dharma in the *Mahābhārata* and *Rāmāyana* epics suggest an ethics that fits the Western philosophical label of "virtue ethics."[14] This was subsequently taken up by Nicholas F. Gier, a professor emeritus of philosophy at the University of Idaho at Moscow, in his seminal essay on "Hindu Virtue Ethics."[15]

First of all, to provide a little bit of a philosophical background for the lay reader, ethics is the *study* of morality. In other words, ethics is theory and morality is practice, though in daily discourse the adjectives "ethical" and "moral" are widely used interchangeably. The major types of ethics are: metaethics, normative ethics, and applied ethics. Metaethics, which is heavily philosophical, explores questions like "What is ethical behavior?" and "Where does ethical behavior originate?" Normative ethics is concerned with finding practical principles by which we can conduct our lives in terms of right (what we *ought* to do) and wrong (what we *ought not* to do). Applied ethics addresses contemporary moral problems that are especially knotty, notably abortion, capital punishment, and animal rights.

Virtue ethics straddles both metaethics and normative ethics. It is an approach that stands in stark contrast to other leading orientations in ethical thought, which focus on action itself, such as utilitarianism and deontology ("duty-ism"). An instance of the former orientation is the maxim formulated by the nineteenth-century British philosopher John Stuart Mill "the maximum good for the maximum number of people." An instance of the latter is Immanuel Kant's formulation of absolute moral laws embodied in his famous categorical imperative. Needless to say, virtue ethics also is in opposition to ethical egoism á la Ayn Rand and Friedrich Nietzsche and to ethical nihilism, which rejects all authority, tradition, and standards.

What is unique about virtue ethics is its focus on the individual, arguing that moral action flows naturally from a moral character. For the good or bad, we typically act in keeping with who we *are*. In the West, virtue ethics has had a long ancestry, which commenced with Socrates, Plato, and Aristotle, as well as the Stoics and Epicureans (with their hedonistic slant). In fact, this type of ethics seems to have been the dominant orientation in antiquity. Thus, not surprisingly, we find virtue ethics to be at the core of the wisdom teachings also of India and the Far East. In Chinese Taoism, its position is summed up as follows in Lao Tzu's *Tao Te Ching*:

> The sage has no will [lit. "heart"] of his own. The hundred families' wills are his will.

> "The virtuous (*teh*) I meet with virtue; the nonvirtues I also meet with virtue; such is the virtue of virtue. The faithful I meet with faith; the faithless I also meet with faith; such is the virtue of faith."

The sage dwells in the world mindful, very mindful about his business with the world. He universalizes his will, and the hundred families fix their eyes and ears on him. The sage regards them as his children. (vs. 49).[16]

Here Lao Tzu states that the sage has given up all self-will and lives for the larger good. He is inherently virtuous, and therefore all his actions and relations are always virtuous. Because he is virtuous, he always cares about the welfare of others and ever seeks to avoid harming anyone by being utterly mindful of the consequences of his actions. For this reason, he commands the respectful attention of the people whom he treats with the same care as he would his own children.

In the *Mahābhārata* epic, Prince Yudhishthira—an embodiment of the eternal dharma—inquired of Brihaspati who was the truest friend of a human being. Mother? Father? Teacher? Friends? No, replied the old sage, guru of all deities:

One is born alone, O king, and one dies alone; one crosses alone the difficulties one meets with, and one alone encounters whatever misery falls to one's lot. One has really no companion in these acts. Father, mother, brother, son, preceptor, relatives, and friends leave the dead body as if it were a piece of wood or a clod of earth. Having grieved momentarily, they all turn away from it and proceed with their own concerns. Only *dharma* follows the body that is thus abandoned by them all. Hence, it is plain, that *dharma* is the only friend and that it alone should be sought by all.[17]

Virtuous behavior, according to the Indic traditions, leaves a karmic imprint on the mind which travels from lifetime to lifetime. Brihaspati informed Yudhishthira that while dharma leads to the heavenly worlds, nonvirtue/vice leads a person straight to the hell realms. This teaching must be understood in the context of the much older Upanishadic teaching that one becomes what one contemplates. Our behavior, which is an expression of our mental state or character, further shapes our character. In this sense, character is truly destiny. Without any wisdom teachings, we would indeed only recycle ourselves and never truly grow beyond our karmic state of mind. Even the cultivation of dharma, as Brihaspati's words make clear, only leads to heaven. But, according to the teachings of Yoga, heaven falls short of ultimate freedom, or liberation. Hence Patanjali states in his *Yoga-Sūtra* (4.7) that the karma of a yogin is neither black nor white.

In other words, to attain ultimate freedom we must jettison *all* karma, all factors that maintain us in conditioned existence. I will say more about this in subsequent chapters. In any case, even though dharma, or virtue, does not lead directly to liberation, it prepares the ground for the jump into unconditional transcendence. Nonvirtue, by contrast, distinctly leads away from freedom into ever greater bondage, or implication in the conditional realms of existence. We can understand heaven as an experience of great joy, and hell as an experience of intense suffering. Either condition is created solely by our own volitions, or motivations, or as Lao-Tzu put it, our "heart." The choice and responsibility are ours alone.

ENDNOTES, CHAPTER 2

1   On moral relativism, see Paul K. Moser and Thomas L. Carson, eds., *Moral Relativism: A Reader* (New York: Oxford University Press, 2001).

2   See Paul Kurtz, *In Defense of Secular Humanism* (Amherst, N.Y.: Prometheus Books, 1983) and Josef Pieper, *"Divine Madness": Plato's Case Against Secular Humanism* (San Francisco: Ignatius Press, 1995).

3   See Madhu Kanna, ed., Rta: *The Cosmic Order* (New Delhi: D.K. Printworld, 2004).

4   This is my paraphrase. See Immanuel Kant, *Critique of Practical Reason.* Trans. by Werner S. Pluhar (Indianapolis: Hackett Publishing, 2002).

5   Sri Aurobindo, *Synthesis of Yoga* (Pondicherry, India: Aurobindo Ashram, 1972), p. 2.

6   See Sri Aurobindo, *On the Veda* (Pondicherry, India: Sri Aurobindo Ashram, 1964).

7   A growing number of Indian and also Western scholars today are coming to the conclusion that the Indus-Sarasvati civilization, which was the home of the Vedic culture, could possibly claim to having been the cradle of human civilization, as opposed to Sumer. I have argued in favor of this hypothesis in the book *In Search of the Cradle of Civilization*, coauthored with Subhash Kak and David Frawley. Since the publication of this work in 1995, however, I have come across evidence that suggests an even earlier date for the beginnings of human civilization . . . outside of India. The large city of Mehrgarh, dated 6500 B.C., is "recent" by comparison with the age calculated for the Egyptian Sphinx by some investigators. See, e.g., John Anthony West's *The Serpent in the Sky*; Robert Bauval and Adrian Gilbert, *The Orion Mystery*; Graham Hancock and Robert Bauval, *The Message of the Sphinx*. While this hypothesis is highly controversial, I am now more inclined to accept it because of other supportive evidence. See also the iconoclastic and disquieting work *Forbidden Archaeology* by Michael A. Cremo and Richard L. Thompson, who cite numerous artifacts that, if we can find no other explanations for them than the revolutionary ones proposed by them, would turn our understanding of prehistory completely upside down. Cremo and Thompson's contention that there have been civilizations prior to our own (whatever age or provenance we may assign to it) is a well-accepted idea in esoteric circles.

8   See Alain Daniélou, *Virtue, Success, Pleasure, and Liberation: The Four Aims of Life in the Tradition of Ancient India* (Rochester, Vt.: Inner Traditions International, 1993).

9   For an abridgment of the voluminous *Mahābhārata* epic, see William Buck (Berkeley: University of California Press, 1973). The same scholar has also published an abridgment of the *Rāmāyana* (Berkeley: University of California Press, 1976). On the dialectic between liberation and morality in the Hindu civilization, see Nicholas Sutton, *Religious Doctrines in the Mahabharata* (Delhi: Motilal Banarsidass, 2000). See also J. A. B. van Buitenen, *"Dharma and Moksa," Philosophy East and West: A Journal of Oriental and Comparative Thought*, vol. 7, no. 1 (1957), pp. 33–40 and vol. 7, no. 2 (1957), p. 37.

10   The translation is mine. For a mostly reliable English rendering with an exceptional commentary, see Sarvepalli Radhakrishnan, *The Bhagavadgītā* (New York: Harper Torchbooks, 1973).

11   On the Jaina path, see Robin Williams, *Jaina Yoga: A Survey of the Mediaeval Śrāvakācāras* (Delhi: Motilal Banarsidass, repr. 1991).

12   See Jamgön Kongtrul Lodrö Tayé, *Buddhist Ethics*. Trans. and ed. by The International Translation Committee (Ithaca, N.Y.: Snow Lion, 1998).

13   This state is technically known as *dharma-megha-samādhi*, and the idea behind it was probably influenced by Mahayana Buddhism, which is familiar with the notion of *dharma-megha* or "cloud of virtue."

14   B. K. Matilal, *Ethics and Epics: Philosophy, Culture and Religion* (Oxford: Oxford University Press, 2002). This is volume 2 of The Collected Essays of Bimal Krishna Matilal, edited by Jonardon Ganeri.

15   See Nicholas F. Gier, "Hindu Virtue Ethics," www.class.uidaho.edu/ngier/hinduve.htm.

16   This is my paraphrase. For a sensitive translation, which avoids surplus verbiage, see Stephen Addiss and Stanley Lombardo, *Tao Te Ching* (Indianapolis: Hackett Publishing, 1993).

17   Retold after *Mahābhārata*, Book 13, Chapter 111 according to the translation by K. M. Ganguly, *The Mahabharata of Krishna-Dwaipayana Vyasa* (New Delhi: Munshiram Manoharlal, repr. 2003).

CHAPTER 3

INTERCONNECTEDNESS
AND THE WEB OF LIFE

The word *yoga* means literally "union" or "discipline." Hence it is appropriate to define Yoga as "unitive discipline" or the "discipline of integration," leaving it open what precisely is meant by this. We ought to be flexible in our understanding of "union" and "discipline," because Yoga is understood differently by the various schools, though of course there is considerable overlap between the diverse explanations of the yogic path and understanding of life.

Several writers have opted to interpret Yoga as spiritual integration, notably the Theosophists I. K. Taimni and Rohit Mehta.[1] Translating the term *yoga* as "integration" offers perhaps fewer problems than the more common rendering of "union." The latter, strictly speaking, applies only to theistic schools that favor a personal God with whom the Yoga practitioner seeks to unite in some fashion. This interpretation does not, however, cover the many nondualistic approaches, which are based on the metaphysical assumption that Reality is singular. Thus Reality is neither only inside nor outside of us and hence cannot become the object of any kind of union, or unitive mystical experience. The fashionable term "integration" avoids this difficulty but at the same leaves us wondering just what is intended by it.

If we use it to designate a process of psychomental balancing, of synchronizing all the aspects of our mind or psyche, we would definitely capture one of the many connotations of the term *yoga*. For we can compare the yogic process to aligning all the "lenses" of our personality, so that the arrangement produces a highly focused laser beam: our single-minded intent to transcend the ego and thereby awaken to our true nature—the ultimate Reality. In light of this, it is perhaps best to speak of Yoga as the intentional discipline of spiritual realization, or liberation.

According to the nondualistic traditions, which seek to express the truth as seen from the "perspective" of enlightenment, the duality we experience at the level of the unenlightened mind is purely illusory along with the experiencing mind itself. In reality, we are eternally free and unconditioned. As the Vedānta scriptures put it: We are the singular Self, which also is the underlying foundation of the cosmos.[2]

Unfortunately, so long as we are unenlightened, we are under the powerful spell of dualistic experience. This means that the aforementioned equation is at best only intellectually true for us. Nonduality is not our immediate realization, or we would indeed be enlightened. Thus, at the unenlightened level, we must and do operate with dualistic concepts and imagery. We experience ourselves as a limited self, or entity, with a name, personal history, body, mind, emotions, and impulses, etc. We experience the world as outside or apart from us. Even the Self is only a concept that seems separate from our being and whose realization we aspire to by means of Yoga. We "unite" with spiritual practices or "disciplines" by means of which we hope to find our true Identity, which is the Self of all beings and things. We "integrate" our various powers and capacities to focus on the difficult work of self-transcendence, which entails the gradual "dismemberment" of our mistaken identity as a particular entity in space and time.

As we transform ourselves—step by step withdrawing our numerous projections (or mistaken identities)—we undergo what can be called a process of thorough self-transformation. This process, which is "character shaping," is successful to the degree that we can actually rid ourselves of the ego/self that we are seeking to transform. We use the idealized Self—the timeless transcendental Identity beyond all forms—as our guiding light, which has been interpreted as a process of "integration," "union" (with the "higher" Reality) or even "disjunction" (from the false self-sense). We become more and more who we truly are when all contingencies are removed.

From the nondualistic perspective, duality is what happens when the nondual Reality is not obvious to us. Duality, however, is never the actual state of things but a hallucination, dream, or misrepresentation. When we see this with absolute clarity, duality evaporates. This moment is often called "awakening" (*bodha*), implying that we previously were asleep, or dreaming. The awakened one is *buddha*. The unawakened dreamer of duality is merely "stupefied" or "confused." Upon awakening, the awakened one realizes that nothing ever happened: the experience of duality was like a momentary daydream, a brief instant of inattention within the waking state; even this is saying too much. Whenever language, which inevitably operates on the basis of the dualistic mind, is involved we are ultimately trapped in inconsistencies and contradictions.

At a gathering at Vulture Peak, the Buddha silently held up a flower; only his lay disciple Mahākashyapa smiled with recognition. This favorite Zen story illustrates mind-to-mind transmission of the essence of the teaching, but it also suggests the immediacy of enlightenment: We are inherently liberated and need only recognize this truth in order to lift us out of our apparent condition of ignorance and suffering. As anyone would agree, this is easier said than done. While enlightenment is instant, the path of purification, which reveals our true nature to us, is gradual and for most practitioners painstaking. It includes paying attention to the moral disciplines. As the Tibetan lama Gyatrul Rinpoche remarked:

> . . . we must make efforts to realize our Buddha nature, even though we all possess it. Just as you would not know that butter is the essence of milk unless you churned the milk—and not just a few churns will do; you really must churn with effort—in the same way, you must practice with effort and diligence to understand your own true nature. Nevertheless, you must remember that practice only reveals what is already present. If you churn water hoping to get b utter, it will not happen, will it? We undergo the hardships of the spiritual path because our essence is already Buddha. It is already perfectly realized. If it were not, practice would be pointless. The process is like refining ore that you know has gold in it. You work long and hard to extract the gold from the rock, but if you knew the rock had no gold in it, why would you try to extract it?[3]

As mentioned in the preceding chapter, if we want to understand yogic morality, we must take into account what Yoga has to say about the nature of the cosmos at large. In particular, we must familiarize ourselves with the archaic notion of interconnectedness or what in more recent times has been called the "Web of Life." The basis for this concept is the experience that everything seems to be related, that the reality presenting itself to our senses and mind is apparently a seamless whole. This should not really surprise us since, according to ancient and also modern cosmology, the world evolved out of a single "substance." For the modern cosmologist, it was the inexplicable Big Bang that triggered the vast and incomprehensible process of evolution. Out of an incredibly dense zero-dimensional energy point (or what the Indians would call *bindu*), the universe unfolded in recognizable stages leading to the creation of first insentient and then sentient forms imbued with life and consciousness.

The thinkers of yore likewise postulated a zero-dimensional homogeneous whole that gave birth to space and time—the *brahman*. They, like their modern counterparts, could not give a reason for this awe-inspiring process by which the One converted itself into Many. But they, too, understood that "in the beginning," space and time did not exist. Unlike modern cosmologists, however, the early sages who pondered our wondrous universe believed that the process of evolution began with the mind and then continued through diverse stages of physical unfolding.

Contrary to contemporary scientific cosmology, which is essentially materialistic, the Vedic seers did not regard the mind as an accidental end product of evolution, an "epiphenomenon" of the human brain. For them, the "subtle" or psychomental layers of the cosmos came first, whereas the material universe must be considered as the densest cosmogonic condensate. We have here a total reversal of the materialistic perspective. The human body and the physical cosmos as a whole, according to the Indian sages, are an "epiphenomenon" of the mind, that is, explications of more subtle levels of reality. This Vedic view implies that the physical cosmos is shot through with mind or psyche—a notion that few of today's scientists would endorse. Yet, we cannot fail to note that some formulations of quantum theory come curiously close to the ancient cosmological views, which perhaps says something about their durability.

In any event, if we regard matter as condensed energy, as both the ancient and modern cosmologists are telling us, then we can easily see how material (bodily) forms all have a common "energetic" background. For the traditionalist, this fundamental "energy" is psychospiritual rather than mechanical, electrical, or even nuclear. It is the matrix for subsequent evolutionary developments at the subtle (mental) level and at last also on the physical level.

Because everything shares in this common, transcendental Ground, which the ancients called *brahman*, all forms can be said to be interconnected at that primary level. Of course, at that transcendental level, forms as we know them do not exist. They are mere potentials (*shakti*). But there also is what we could call a "family resemblance" between forms at the mental (or psychoenergetic) level, which we might designate as "archetypes" or habit grooves. Finally, at the physical level, we see connectedness in terms of shared biotic environments, which is the focus of ecology. The Vedic name for this ramifying interrelatedness is *bandhu*. This term can also mean "relative" or "blood relationship" suggesting close kinship between members of a group.

From the Vedic and yogic point of view, every living being and inanimate thing arose out of the ultimate spiritual Matrix and continues to inhere in it. Hence brahman is said to be the transcendental Ground of all existence, while all beings and things are manifestations of that same formless One. We all are related to each other via that One, which is not only our origin but also the continuing foundation of our individual and collective existence in the world of space-time. In addition, we have a kinship relationship by virtue of belonging to the animate (biotic) realm of Nature, the animal kingdom, the genus of mammals, the human species, a specific ethnic group, culture, or family group.

Since time immemorial, kinship has played a huge role in all traditional societies, which value the extended family, the clan, and the tribe. Only in our modern age do many people of the so-called First World place individualism above kinship relationships. The extended family barely exists anymore, and even the nuclear family is being threatened with extinction in some Western nations. Today there are more broken homes than whole ones.

The egotistical individualism rampant in the Occident looks like an evolutionary dead-end. It certainly would have left our ancestors baffled and possibly horrified, as it does in fact confound and trouble the hearts of the sensitive people and visionaries of today's tribal societies. The latter's warning voices are on record, though being largely ignored to the detriment of all.

Be that as it may, the same attitude of shortsighted egotism applied to organizations and governments has increasingly led to the depletion of Nature's resources and perilous pollution. The danger of systemic environmental collapse is looming large. But Western societies, self-centered and pampered as they are, refuse to take a long-term view of these critical problems and thus imperil not only their own way of life but the future of all life forms on Earth. Non-Western, traditional societies are often too beleaguered by their First-World cousins' rapacious politics and economics to adopt a more wholesome course. More and more ecologists and other environment-conscious scientists are taking a pessimistic view of the decades ahead, because their warnings to governments and the public have by and large gone unheeded. Clearly, we must urgently recover the age-old value of kinship with all life.

Thus Yoga, which affirms the Vedic concept of *bandhu*, has a great deal to teach us. Even though it does not specifically state so, its moral teachings derive from the feeling of kinship with all living beings and, we might add, with the environment as a whole. If the ancient sages did not specifically mention the environment, it is only because they viewed the entire world as ensouled or animated. To them, our present-day sharp distinction between the biotic environment and inanimate objects would not have made much sense.

Grounding morality in the value of kinship makes implicit sense. Under normal circumstances, we tend to treat relatives with greater respect than we do strangers. We do not wish to intentionally harm family members (see Arjuna's dilemma discussed in the preceding chapter); if anything, we feel inclined to benefit them. The closer someone is to us, the more positive our feelings become. From a yogic perspective, however, we ought to see all beings as belonging to our human family (*kula*). The yogin or yoginī knows no strangers. Hence, traditionally, they regard everyone as either "brothers" or "sisters." Yoga seeks to instill reverence for all of life. When everyone is family and when the world itself is not a hostile place, we cannot possibly want to indulge in negative intentions, emotions, and actions. Our caring for others, by contrast, is likely to be expressed in countless acts of human kindness.

One essential question demands an answer: If the goal of Yoga is to lead us beyond the human condition, why would it be so important to acknowledge kinship as a principal foundation of morality? Translated into Buddhist terminology, how does the call for compassion tally with the insight and realization of the ultimate emptiness (no-thing-ness) of all things? Many Buddhist scholars have addressed this crucial point in their teachings. If, as they teach, all beings and things lack an essential self, or inherent nature, then why should one feel compassion for them? According to Vajrayana, the Diamond Vehicle of Tibetan Buddhism, the spiritual aspirant must tread the path of the bodhisattva for whom compassion is the central guiding light to liberation. The bodhisattva is not merely interested in his own enlightenment but is completely dedicated to the great ideal of ending the suffering of all other beings by leading them to Buddhahood, or liberation. It is tempting to consider compassion almost more important than wisdom, or insight into the emptiness of all things. I will discuss this in more detail in Chapter 11, but here are some essential points in anticipation.

Both compassion and wisdom are interdependent. Without insight into emptiness, compassion runs the risk of becoming mere sentimentalism. Conversely, wisdom without compassion is like dry firewood that cannot be lit because of the lack of fire.

Most Mahayana and Vajrayana Buddhist teachers, though, are agreed that we must train in compassion first and then graduate to the path of insight into the nature of existence. They even warn of teaching emptiness (*shūnyatā*) to someone who is intellectually and emotionally unprepared for such a teaching.

Compassion emphasizes the interconnectedness and interdependence of all beings and things, whereas wisdom sees into their true nature, which is empty of essentiality. More specifically, emptiness refers to the mistaken notion that we are a "someone," a solid, stable, unchanging entity that, as it were, stands outside the stream of time. The "I," according to Buddhism, is a construct, and the path to liberation consists in deconstructing this illusory self. At the same time, the Buddhist practitioner must, like a good mother, cultivate a positive regard for all other illusory selves in the world and help them discover the truth about their condition. For, only when we lift the veil of misconception, or illusion, can we terminate our suffering.

At one level, the Web of Life is a web of intrigue; at another level, it is a web of suffering; at yet another level, it is a web of karmic necessity. All three metaphors are contained in the concept of *bandhu*, or kinship.

First, the reality we share is a reality of common conceptualizations. Some writers, therefore, have called it our consensus reality. Now, if the way we saw and related to reality would be pure, that is, without intervening interpretations, projections, or superimpositions, there would be no problem. But the fact is that we do *not* experience reality as it really is. Rather, as modern psychology has demonstrated, our perceptions go through the filter of interpretation. They are suffused with all kinds of presumptions, including the major presumption that there are concrete beings and things. It is the great contribution of Gautama the Buddha to have pointed out very clearly that the common understanding of a "person," a "thing," or the "world" at large is in fact based on a misinterpretation of the ever-changing, fluid process we call "existence." We are habituated to thinking of ourselves as stable, concrete entities experiencing numerous other stable and equally concrete entities or objects. This simplistic way of perceiving everything amounts to a generally accepted intrigue. While this oversimplification of the complexities of existence undoubtedly is of practical usefulness, in spiritual terms it is an unmitigated disaster, as it prevents us from realizing our inherent freedom.

Second, our conceptual oversimplification of existence not only binds us to the illusion of living in a universe of countless concrete and separate beings and things, which seem to have no common ground, it also causes us much suffering.[4] That we are subject to suffering is a basic insight of Hindu, Buddhist, and Jaina Yoga. As the Buddha put it, "Birth is suffering; life is suffering; death is suffering." When we review our life and the lives of other humans and nonhumans in an unprejudiced manner, we cannot but agree with this profound insight. Even though we occasionally experience joy and happiness, those moments do not alter the insight that suffering prevails. Suffering does not need to come in the form of illness, pain, or deprivation; every frustration, disappointment, loss, or instant of boredom, envy, anger, and other negative emotions boil down to suffering. Facing our own eventual and unpredictable demise, which fills most people with fear or apprehension, is a form of suffering. Judging from the literature on death and dying, for many people in our time the experience of dying is very traumatic and attendant with great discomfort and pain.

From the Buddhist perspective, suffering continues in the post-mortem state in which the consciousness stripped of a physical body but not yet liberated confronts the products of its own anxieties, delusions, and misconceptions as we might encounter them in a bad dream. In due course, that consciousness becomes reconnected with a physical body and once more undergoes the manifold experiences of embodiment.

Third, when we contemplate the continuity between one embodied existence and another, we see what I have called the "web of karmic necessity" in full operation.[5] Ever since the mid-twentieth century, *karma* has become a household word in the West. It has long defined much of the philosophical or religious thinking of India. The concept itself is thought to have originated some 3,000 years ago with the Gnostic literature of the *Upanishads*. These Sanskrit scriptures followed the archaic hymnodies of the *Vedas* and their ritual developments in the scriptures of the *Brāhmanas* and *Āranyakas*. The *Upanishads* are traditionally regarded as forming the concluding portion of the Vedic revelation upon which much of Hinduism is based.

When we look more closely at this sacred corpus, we find that there is a far greater continuity between the *Upanishads* and the *Vedas* than generally assumed.[6] In many ways, the *Upanishads* simply explicate what is found implicit in the earliest Sanskrit literature. While it is probably true that the *Vedas* do not contain a full-fledged teaching on karma and reincarnation, the Vedic ideas proved fertile ground for further development. The first clear-cut statements about karma and the associated teaching of rebirth can be found in the oldest *Upanishads*. Thus the *Brihad-Āranyaka-Upanishad* (4.4.2), often held to be the oldest text of this genre, states:

> Just as a caterpillar when it has come to the tip of a blade of grass draws itself together before moving toward [another blade], so does this self, after having shed the body and dispelled ignorance draw itself together before moving toward [another body].

> And as a goldsmith takes a piece of gold to turn it into a new and more beautiful shape, so does this self, after

having shed this body and dispelled ignorance, fashion for itself [in the subtle realm] a new and more beautiful shape like that of the ancestors, spirit entities, the [lower] deities, Prajāpati, Brahma, or of other beings.

There is a kinship between one life and another. Life, death, and rebirth are not connected arbitrarily. There is no total disruption between one embodiment and the next. The continuity between them is ensured by the law of karma as it expresses itself in the consciousness of the individual. Physical death, all spiritual traditions assure us, does not mean complete extinction, or annihilation. Consciousness is said to survive in some fashion, though the details of this post-mortem survival differ somewhat from system to system. What all systems have in common is the notion that the conditions of a person's post-mortem state and eventual rebirth are governed, to put it colloquially, by his or her karma.

Most Yoga masters would argue that understanding and accepting karma as valid is a precondition for the spiritual path. I will not rehearse here all the arguments made in the traditional literature in favor of the validity of karma. I have learned that in spiritual matters, as with politics, people hold deeply entrenched positions. I would merely encourage those who are skeptical but sufficiently open-minded to explore this subject more deeply.[7]

My present purpose is to discuss karma as an integral aspect of cosmic interconnectedness. Karma is the glue that holds together the process of existence, which otherwise would consist only in unrelated events that pop up and vanish at random. Karma is often called the law of cause and effect at the moral level. It is meant to explain why things happen the way they do in our present life and also how our actions and volitions in this life determine the quality of our post-mortem state and future life or lives. Thus the notion of karma serves as a very comprehensive explanation, which is intended to provide a partial answer to the timeless question about the meaning of life and death. For a fuller answer, we would also have to take into account the teachings about liberation and the path to liberation.

On the one hand, karma along with the idea of rebirth helps us understand our current condition. On the other hand, it gives us a strong reason for aligning our mental and physical behavior with the highest moral and spiritual values. Even if we do not subscribe to the ideal of liberation, or wish to devote our energies to realizing it, we still would do well to take karma into account in all our actions. According to the Indic teaching about karma, our actions and volitions leave a karmic imprint upon our consciousness that, in synchrony with other similar imprints, defines our post-mortem state and subsequent rebirth. Simply put, morally positive actions and volitions engender positive outcomes here and hereafter, while morally negative actions and volitions give rise to negative outcomes. "Morally positive" are those behaviors that in Albert Schweitzer's terms amount to reverence for life, including one's own life.[8] That is to say, morally positive behaviors—whether expressed at the physical level or merely entertained as intentions at the mental level—uphold the great universal moral principles spoken of earlier. "Morally negative" behaviors are manifestly those that disregard or even undermine those principles.

Rather than supporting an irresponsible fatalism, as some writers have maintained, the karma teaching actually calls us to act, feel, and think with utmost care and responsibility. It puts the individual firmly in charge of his or her destiny. At the same time, it affirms that we are not islands unto ourselves but are interlinked with everyone and everything else. Ecology and eco-philosophy are modern efforts reminding us of the interconnectedness and interdependence of all forms of life—an understanding that was lost with the eighteenth-century "Enlightenment" leading to the flawed assumption that humans are superior to all other life forms and are entitled to ransacking Nature for their selfish ends.[9]

Today we are facing the fallout of this intellectual hubris and its creations, notably our rampant technology and out-of-control (largely Western) consumerism. It is my belief that unless the human race finds its way back to modesty and moderation, it will soon become as extinct as the dinosaurs. Only this time, the cause of extinction will be of our own making. I confess, at this late hour, I do not hold out much hope for sanity to be restored in time to avoid a global catastrophe. But conceivably our human destiny is not determined entirely by the ignorant masses, uncaring leaders, and exploitative organizations. We also may reckon with the positive, life-enhancing work and "good karma" of those who quietly go about fulfilling their bodhisattva vow to eliminate all suffering in the world and to uplift sentient beings.[10]

There is an important point in this statement: Our good karma not only benefits us individually but, if it is significant enough, also has positive repercussions in the world around us. Our good thoughts and deeds are the agents by which we can improve the lot of all sentient beings. The bodhisattva always endeavors to create a surplus of good karma, so that, increment by increment, others too may come to enjoy the same clarity, serenity, and ease. It is easy enough to see how someone's positive actions can contribute to the general welfare of others. But our positive thoughts also have their effects. As the "Mantra Project" at Duke University and many other similar studies have demonstrated, heart patients who are being prayed for have fifty to one hundred percent fewer undesirable side effects than those patients who do not receive prayers.[11]

If we do not yet enjoy enough free attention and energy to care deeply for the betterment of all sentient beings and the world as a whole, then we can at least dedicate ourselves to minimizing our negative thoughts, emotions, and actions. In due course, we will find that our life is improving and that thinking, emoting, and acting positively is becoming easier. Remembering our kinship with everyone and everything, we ought to maximize not merely our own pleasure but the welfare of all. As we ease the burden of others, they have a better chance of gaining the kind of insights that will eventually free them from the ego-illusion and thus from all suffering.

The cultivation of virtue or karmic merit with which the bodhisattva is so concerned creates the necessary conditions for himself and others to pierce the veil of spiritual ignorance. It does not, as stated in the preceding chapter, lead directly to liberation; rather by implication a virtuous character is an ego-transcending character. In Hindu terms, it suggests a person in whom *sattva*— the factor of lucidity or transparency—is preeminent. This lucidity, in turn, makes for more profound insights into the nature of reality, which then leads to virtuous (liberating) actions and yet deeper insights, as well as all those other qualities that intensify self-transcendence. While a virtuous life does not lead directly to transcendental realization, it is a necessary condition for it.

ENDNOTES, CHAPTER 3

1 See I. K. Taimni, *The Science of Yoga* (Adyar, India: Theosophical Publishing House, 1961) and Rohit Mehta, *Yoga: The Art of Integration* (Adyar, India: Theosophical Publishing House, 1990).

2 The word *vedānta* means literally "end (*anta*) of knowledge (*veda*)," that is, the conclusion of the Vedic gnosis. It is a collective term for all those philosophical traditions that evolved out of the Vedic revelation. These are largely nondualistic but *Vedānta* also knows of dualistic schools. In its nondualistic branch, *Vedānta* has *Jñāna-Yoga* (the Yoga of wisdom) at its practical core. For an experience-based philosophical treatment of nonduality, see Franklin Merrell-Wolff's *The Philosophy of Consciousness Without an Object* (New York: Three Rivers Press, 1983). This author, a mathematician-philosopher, was overwhelmed by a nondual realization, which he subsequently rejected in favor of understanding.

3 Gyatrul Rinpoche, *Generating the Deity*. Trans. by Sangye Khandro (Ithaca, N.Y.: Snow Lion Publications, 2d ed. 1996), p. 20.

4 On the Buddhist notion of suffering (*duhkha*), see M. V. Ram Kumar Ratnam, *Dukkha: Suffering in Early Buddhism* (New Delhi: Discovery, 2003).

5 See Yuvraj Krishan, *The Doctrine of Karma: Its Origin and Development in Brahmanical, Buddhist and Jaina Traditions* (Delhi: Motilal Banarsidass, 1997); Aparna Chakraborty, *Karma: Freedom and Responsibility* (New Delhi: Kaveri Books, 1998); Jagat Pal, Karma, *Dharma and Moksha: Conceptual Essays on Indian Ethics* (Delhi: Abhijeet Publ., 2004); Herman W. Tull, *The Vedic Origins of Karma: Cosmos as Man in Ancient Indian Myth and Ritual* (Albany, N.Y.: SUNY Press, 1989); Christopher Key Chapple, *Karma and Creativity* (Albany, N.Y.: SUNY Press, 1986); Rajendra Prasad, *Karma Causation and Retributive Morality* (New Delhi: Munshiram Manoharlal, 1989). For a broad overview on reincarnation, see Hans Tendam, *Exploring Reincarnation: The Classic Guide to the Evidence for Past-Life Experiences* (London: Rider, 2004).

6 On Upanishadic teachings, see David Frawley, *From The River of Heaven: Hindu and Vedic Knowledge for the Modern Age* (Lotus Press, 1990). See also Basantakumar Chatterjee, *The Teachings of the Upanishads* (Calcutta: University of Calcutta Press, 1952).

7 See the references provided in footnote 5 in Chapter 15.

8 See Albert Schweitzer, *The Teaching of Reverence for Life* (New York: Henry Holt, 1965); *Reverence for Life: Sermons 1900–1919* (New York: Irvington Publishers, 1993).

9 On ecophilosophy, see Henryk Skolimowski, *Dancing Shiva in the Ecological Age* (New Delhi: Clarion Books, 1991).

10 There are numerous books on the Mahayana path of the bodhisattva. See, e.g., Chökyi Dragpa, *Uniting Wisdom and Compassion: Illuminating the Thirty-Seven Practices of a Bodhisattva* (Somerville, Mass.: Wisdom Publications, 2004) and Dalai Lama, *The Compassionate Life* (Somerville, Mass.: Wisdom Publications, repr. ed. 2003).

11 See, e.g., Larry Dossey, *Healing Words: The Power of Prayer and the Practice of Medicine* (New York HarperCollins, 1993).

CHAPTER 4

THE IDEAL OF SACRIFICE

Sacrifice is not a prominent notion in our time. We have difficulty in comprehending so-called primitive societies or extinct civilizations in which sacrificial rituals played a central role, as they did in ancient India and its remaining pockets of traditionalism. We are at a complete loss when trying to understand, for instance, the large-scale human sacrifices that preoccupied the Mesoamerican civilizations, notably the Mayas, Toltecs, and Aztecs.[1] A glimpse into this extreme ritual will, I believe, help us better understand the allegorical or inner sacrifice demanded in Yoga.

To focus on the Mayas for a moment, they believed that the cosmic order could be restored or maintained by spilling the blood especially of nobles and braves, who had been vanquished in battle. The potency of the sacrificial ritual was directly linked to the degree of difficulty involved in conquering the enemy. The Mayas were not particularly interested in slaves and ordinary warriors, or women and children, who were thought to have only limited value as sacrificial victims. At times of social or economic stress, however, these unfortunates were sacrificed as well to restore the balance of cosmic forces.

Those selected for human sacrifice were painted blue (the color of deoxygenated blood), tortured to the point of shedding precious blood, and then killed by ripping the heart out of the sliced-open chest. The heart was held up to the Sun and then burnt to ashes to nourish the deities. The sacrifice emulated the archetypal sacrifice of Quetzalcoatl, the ubiquitous feathered god, by which he created the universe—an idea that, as we will see, had its counterpart in the human sacrifice (*purusha-medha*) of ancient India. From the Maya perspective, human sacrifice was not so much an instance of death as of spiritual rebirth and life (in the hereafter). By conquering fear and pain, the ritual victim was given the opportunity to enter heaven and avoid the lords of the underworld and the gloomy fate awaiting their prey.

To be sure, this gruesome practice of ritual cardiectomy offends our modern sensibilities. Yet, it would seem, that for the victims themselves this was at least intended to be an ennobling way to die, which would lead them directly to the heavenly fields. In later times, the Aztecs slaughtered conquered enemies indiscriminately and brutally by the thousands, which merely inspired terror in the surrounding kingdoms. It is hard to imagine that any captive of the Aztecs went willingly to his or her grave or was able to do so with dignity.

Behind the callous custom of tearing the heart out of the chest of a living prisoner lies the ritual equation of blood with power and life. As in many cultures, the Mayas believed that one had to spill the blood of the living in order to enhance the life of the deities, guardians of the cosmic order. The superlative role of blood can be seen in the widespread Maya custom of bloodletting, which was meant to ensure the fertility of the Earth. The more powerful one's position was in the social order, the more bloodletting was expected. The rulers of Maya towns were appropriately called "blood lords." This custom is the reverse of the situation found in secular societies like our own in which the powerful and wealthy squeeze the lifeblood of the disempowered and poor.

Today when we say someone "has made a sacrifice," we indulge in a rather prosaic linguistic survival from earlier periods; all we mean to suggest by this phrase is that someone "has taken the extra step" or "has gone out of his or her way" to achieve a positive result. No actual ritual offering is involved in this kind of metaphoric sacrifice.

In Christian circles, however, the archaic idea of sacrifice is still being kept alive in the central doctrine that Jesus the Christ surrendered his life for the sake of all the faithful. He, the "lamb," made a sacrifice of himself, so that the sins of his followers would be forgiven. This literal, physical self-sacrifice reinterpreted along symbolic lines is as close as we moderns come to the archaic practice of actual sacrifice, apart from the psychopathic aberrations of mass murderers. The idea, however, looms large in the Yoga tradition both in terms of actual ritual offerings of purified substances and the symbolic offering of oneself in the process of self-transcendence.

As any Sanskrit dictionary tells us, the Sanskrit word *yoga* stems from the verbal root *yuj* ("to yoke, unite, discipline"), which is closely related to the verbal root *yaj* ("to worship by means of sacrifice") forming the important term *yajna*, or "sacrifice." Thus Yoga can be succinctly defined as the discipline of self-sacrifice/self-surrender, which in more contemporary terms would be self-transcendence; that is, the transcendence of the illusion of being a limited body-mind-personality.

A cognate word is *yāga*, which has the same connotations as *yajna*. It is often used in the sense of *antar-yāga*, or "inner sacrifice," which is the mental act of complete renunciation of all one's attachment to external things and social relationships. But most importantly, the yogin is expected to renounce the ego, or self, which is the constructed identity by which we either cling to or let go of the body, mind, and world. This kind of letting-go is one of the core attitudes to be cultivated on the path of Yoga and was first spelled out in the *Upanishads*, dating back to 1000 B.C. and earlier. To explain the full meaning of Yoga as inner sacrifice and self-sacrifice is the purpose of the present chapter.

Yajna is among the oldest terms of the Sanskrit vocabulary and is found numerous times in the 5000-year-old *Rig-Veda* and very many more times in the succeeding ritual literature (notably the *Brāhmanas* and *Āranyakas*), which elaborates on the sacrificial ceremonies and their accompanying myths in the Vedic era.[2] The idea of sacrifice is pivotal not only to early Brahmanism but also to later Hinduism and has significant cosmological, social, and individual implications, which I will discuss on the following pages.

Cosmologically, the significance of sacrifice is expressed in the following hymn of the *Rig-Veda* (10.90), which extols Primordial Man, the Macranthropos, the ultimate Person (*purusha* = *purushottama*), or spiritual Reality:

Primordial Man had a thousand heads, a thousand eyes, a thousand feet. Enveloping the Earth from all sides, He [yet] exceeded it by ten fingers' width. (Verse 1)

This Primordial Man is indeed all that has been and will be—the Ruler of immortality who grows bigger by food [i.e., sacrificial offerings]. (Verse 2)

His greatness is mighty. Primordial Man is greater than this [universe]. All beings are one quarter of Him; three quarters are immortal in Heaven. (Verse 3)

Primordial Man ascended with three quarters while one quarter of Him was here [in this world]. Then he strode out everywhere over what eats [i.e., sentient beings] and what does not eat [i.e., insentient existence]. (Verse 4)

From Him the Shining One was born; [and yet,] from the Shining One, Primordial Man [in His immanent form came to be]. As soon as He was born, he spread eastward and westward over the Earth. (Verse 5)

The deities performed the [original] sacrifice with that Primordial Man as offering. Spring was its ghee, summer the fire-wood, autumn the [sacrificial] offering. (Verse 6)

That first-born Primordial Man, [was laid out] on grass [and] sprinkled [with holy water]—by means of That [Supreme Being] the deities, the accomplished ones, and the seers sacrificed. (Verse 7)

From that all-offering sacrifice was extracted ghee-and-yogurt [i.e., the seminal essence] by which He created beasts, birds, creatures of the forest, and domesticated animals. (Verse 8)

From that all-offering sacrifice were produced the hymns and chants. From that [sacrifice] were produced the poetic metres. From that [sacrifice] sprang forth the sacrificial formulas. (Verse 9)

From that [original sacrifice] sprang forth horses and [other creatures with] two jaws. From it were produced cattle. From it came [also] goats and sheep. (Verse 10)

When they divided Primordial Man, how many portions did they make? What do they call His mouth, his arms, his thighs and feet? (Verse 11)

The priest (*brahmin*) was His mouth. The warrior was fashioned from the arms. His thighs became the worker. From the feet the servant was produced. (Verse 12)

The Moon was born from His mind, and from His eyes the Sun was produced. [The deities] Indra and Agni [hailed from His] mouth. From [His] breath Vāyu was produced. (Verse 13).

From [Primordial Man's] navel came the mid-region. From the head the sky was created. The Earth [was created] from the feet and the [four] directions from the ears. Thus the worlds were fashioned. (Verse 14)

The deities [used] seven border markers [i.e., the seven poetic metres?] and prepared thrice seven layers of fuel [i.e., the aspects of the human body-mind?] when they bound Primordial Man as the beast [i.e., the sacrificial victim] for that sacrifice. (Verse 15)

By means of [this original] sacrifice the deities worshiped sacrifice. These were the first norms (*dharma*). The mighty ones went to Heaven where the accomplished ones, the earlier deities, are. (Verse 16)

Although this hymn dedicated to the Macranthropos is among the last materials to be included in the *Rig-Veda*, its great importance can be gauged from the fact that it is repeated or explained in various ancient Sanskrit scriptures.[3] Much later, in the *Bhagavad-Gītā* (9.16), we find Lord Krishna—representing Primordial Man—exclaiming "I am sacrifice." In his fine commentary on the *Gītā*, Sarvepalli Radhakrishnan elucidates this solemn declaration as follows:

The Vedic sacrifice is interpreted as an offering of our whole nature, an entire selfgiving to the Universal Self.

What we receive from Him, we give back to Him. The gift and the surrender are both His."[4]

Krishna, in his transcendental nature, is the very Macranthropos from whose immensity the universe was born by an act of unprecedented self-sacrifice. As an incarnation (*avatāra*) of that Macranthropos, the God-man Krishna wanted everyone to follow his divine example. The sacrifice of Primordial Man, who produced the cosmos out of himself, must now be symbolically recapitulated by anyone wishing to recover his or her own spiritual wholeness. This *imitatio Dei*, or simulation of the Divine, demanded by tradition consists in a life of active self-transcendence. As can be readily appreciated, this symbolic self-sacrifice involves a reversal of the cosmic self-sacrifice of Primordial Man. In order to create the universe, Primordial Man had to split himself up into a transcendental part ("three quarters") and an immanent part ("one quarter"). As human beings, by contrast, we are already inherently self-divided and in order to achieve wholeness, we must consciously transcend the "one quarter" of manifestation, which is our body-mind. This principle of reversal is fundamental to all Yoga and, in fact, to all spirituality.

In the days of the *Vedas* and subsequently, sacrificial rituals were an important aspect of the "Solar Yoga" of the priests and seers. Only in the Upanishadic epoch did the sages begin to internalize rituals, that is, use their own body-mind as the sacrificial altar and their own love and devotion as offerings into the fire of rigorous self-discipline, even self-offering. Just as the ultimate Being originally heated itself up to create the universe, so also the seer-sages had to undergo an intense process of inner maturation through asceticism (*tapas*), which the Vedic and Hindu scriptures often compare to the transformative act of cooking.[5]

Before I continue with my consideration of this symbolic self-sacrifice, however, I need to address the question of what the Vedic priests considered a viable sacrificial offering. In later times, the God-man Krishna generously said that he, as the Divine Person, would accept any offering, however humble, as long as it was made with a pure heart. The Vedic priests, by contrast, felt that they needed to offer their best and most prized possessions. For them, this was livestock, especially cattle and, on special occasions, horses. To this day, the traditionalists of the Mimamsa school continue to make sacrificial offerings of this kind, even though over the centuries they have met with much opposition from those who understand nonharming in a more comprehensive way.

Visitors to India are taken aback when they witness the daily bloody sacrifices of goats at the Kālī temple in Calcutta. It is at this temple that Sātī's right toes are said to have fallen to earth after Vishnu had dismembered her corpse into fifty-one pieces. Sātī ("Furrow"), Shiva's spouse, had killed herself by self-immolation because her father had publicly humiliated her. Shiva dragged her charred corpse from the funeral pyre and, utterly disconsolate at her death, carried her remains on his shoulders while dancing wildly. Because his frenzied dance threatened to destroy the whole world, Vishnu used his magical discus to slice up the corpse in order to end Shiva's grief and rampage, which it did. Wherever the pieces fell, the earth was instantly sanctified and charged with power. Thus there are fifty-one power spots spread throughout India on which temples have been built—the *shakti-pīthas*, or Goddess shrines, that even today are favorite pilgrimage centers.

Even though most contemporary Westerners consume liberal amounts of meat, few find the idea of slaughtering animals for sacrificial purposes appealing or acceptable. I suspect, though, that this has more to do with facing the brutal reality of slaughtering an animal than any bias against sacrificial rituals in general. People nowadays are so accustomed to hygienically packaged meat, which often does not even look like meat anymore, that an animal's bleeding throat offends their sensibilities. Whenever I have asked my meat-eating friends and students whether they would eat meat if they had to kill their own hen, pig, or cow, they invariably answered in the negative. Some of them qualified their statement by saying that if there was no other source of protein available, they would reluctantly kill animals for food. Curiously, some felt that they would not be so troubled about killing fish, and several of them had in fact done so.[6]

Now, the ancients certainly did not feel squeamish, being much more in touch with the stark realities of life and death than modern people tend to be. At the same time, however, they would not have been motivated to kill creatures for mere pleasure, as we can witness among today's hunters equipped with the latest weapons. The Vedic priests impartially slaughtered sacrificial victims because they felt this was necessary for an efficacious ritual, just as they impartially slaughtered livestock for their daily food. They followed a strict moral code, which limited harming to necessary situations—meat for food or ritual purposes. Around the time of Vardhamāna Mahāvīra and Gautama Buddha, the ideal of vegetarianism became prominent throughout Indic society, and this new viewpoint put enormous pressure on those priests who desired to remain true to the Vedic tradition of animal sacrifices.[7] The ideal of the inner sacrifice won out in most schools of thought. The old fire sacrifices were gradually replaced by ceremonial offerings (*pūjā*) in which food and flowers take the place of living creatures. The animal sacrifices to the "black" Goddess Kālī are today an exception to the rule.

Sātī's self-sacrifice is symbolic of the Yoga practitioner's inner sacrifice, or self-offering. But from a historical perspective, it may also be regarded as an allusion to an ancient practice that most modern people would find horrifying: that of human sacrifices. I mentioned this custom in regard to the Mayas and Aztecs, but it would appear that human sacrifice was an institution of many, if not most, ancient societies—from China to Greece and Rome and the Meso-American and South American civilizations.[8] In Vedic India it was known as *purusha-medha*.[9] Most contemporary Hindus would vehemently reject any suggestion that human sacrifices were performed in the early Vedic era, and modern scholars are divided in their opinions. Many would argue that all suggestive references in the early Sanskrit literature are to be understood symbolically. If so, we may still see in them echoes of rituals that were once enacted literally, distasteful though this is to our modern sensibilities. Why should human sacrifices have been absent from ancient India, when they were definitely practiced widely throughout the ancient world? The *Vedas*—the great poetic compositions of seers and sages—reflect cultural developments extending not merely over several centuries but millennia. It is conceivable and even highly likely that in its earliest phases, the Indic civilization included in its ritual repertoire also human sacrifices. Nor must we consider such a practice as incompatible with the high civilizational accomplishments we can witness in the architectural and literary relics of the Indus-Sarasvati Civilization. At least we may conclude this from a comparison, for instance, with Sumer and first-dynasty pharaonic Egypt where the human sacrifices were known.

To understand the archaic ritual of human sacrifice, we must suspend our present-day judgment for a moment and try to comprehend it from within the logic of the worldview of ancient civilizations. Human life was deemed more precious than any other form of life and hence was thought to make the greatest sacrificial offering to the deities, or invisible powers. In many ancient societies, kings were regularly sacrificed in order to restore an imbalance in the social order for which the rulers were held responsible. But often the sacrificial victims were recruited from the underprivileged—prisoners of war, outcasts, vagrants, and other marginal types. In ancient India, designated victims were sometimes given privileged treatment for the year preceding their ritual execution. This custom parallels the treatment granted to the victim in the horse sacrifice, where the elected horse is allowed to roam freely in rich pastures for a whole year before it is ritually slaughtered.

In each case, the sacrifice was intended to ensure the continued weal of the community or to restore it if for some reason it had been undermined. The ancients lived in a magical universe in which the natural interconnectedness of things was felt very acutely and interpreted in terms of a personal and collective obligation. Today we are slowly rediscovering the interdependence of all life— largely because of the ecological crisis resulting from centuries of disrespect toward the Earth environment. We certainly ought not return to the literal sacrificialism of bygone days, but we surely are called now to make a "human sacrifice" in the form of personal consistent spiritual practice—steady self-transcendence through responsible action, kindness, compassion, and caring for all sentient beings.

A form of literal self-sacrifice is present in the custom of *satī*, also known as *suttee*, in which a widow voluntary commits her body to the flames of her dead husband's funeral pyre. In doing so, she seeks to emulate Shiva's divine spouse Sātī. This strange practice is first mentioned in the *Mahābhārata* epic, which describes how Mādrī threw herself on her husband King Pāndu's funeral pyre. As Joerg Fisch has shown in his book *Burning Women*, this custom was widespread in the cultures of the ancient world.[10] Among others, it was practiced by the ancient Egyptians, Greeks, Goths, and Scythians. In India, it was outlawed in 1928 by the officials of the British Raj. Occasionally, however, one still hears of a particularly traditionalist Indian woman ascending the funeral pyre before she can be stopped. Today even tradition-minded Hindus, with a few rare exceptions, disapprove of *satī*.

From the vantage-point of the twenty-first century, human sacrifice—including acts of self-immolation as in *sātī*—is rightly considered intolerable. Animal sacrifices likewise are an anachronism that, in my opinion, should be abolished along with the brutalities of the meat industry. Even more anathema are the hundred or so instances of human sacrifice in honor of Kālī that are reportedly still occurring in India every year. They should be absolutely prevented like any other murder, including the slaughter of innocent men, women, and children in the many wars fought throughout the world in the name of "liberation," "justice," "democracy," or "progress."

As I argued in Chapter 3, if everything is related to everything else, then we must expect certain "family" obligations. These can be summarized in the principle of sacrifice. Thus, the Vedic/Hindu culture knows of five major sacrificial obligations that ought to be discharged daily:

1. The *homa* sacrifice, which entails making offerings into the fire by which the obligation toward the collectivity of deities and in particular one's chosen deity is discharged.

2. The *bhūta* or "ghost" sacrifice, which "feeds" lower spirits and the animal kingdom.

3. The *pitri* or "ancestor" sacrifice, which consists in making oblations to ancestors who dwell in subtle realms of existence.

4. The *brahma* or "brahmic" sacrifice, which entails the study of the sacred or spiritual texts, which are sacred to the priestly or brahmin estate.

5. The *manushya* or "human" sacrifice, which consists in

treating guests with the same respect and welcome that one would accord a deity (or, in Judeo-Christian language, an angel).

The above five sacrifices are intended to align the sacrificer with the rest of the living cosmos. This attitude, which acknowledges the "kinship" (*bandhu*) between all beings, is strikingly different from our modern self-centered way of life.

Moreover, for the most part, modern Westerners do not pay any attention to invisible beings like deities, discarnate masters, ancestors, and lower spirits. Under the spell of rationalism, which has flourished ever since the Enlightenment movement, most Westerners have difficulties with the invisible—despite the invisibility of mathematical laws, grammatical structures, rules of logic, subatomic particles, electricity, magnetism, gravity, or feelings like love, compassion, and trust, or abstract concepts like justice, goodness, truth, freedom, democracy, and nation. For them, seeing is believing. Jungian psychotherapist June Singer examined this cultural trait from a psychological viewpoint in her book *Seeing Through the Invisible World*.[11]

For the ancient peoples, the invisible was a living reality to which they were sensitive, whose forces they respected and at least partly feared, but to which they were never indifferent. Their cosmos was a hierarchy of nested levels of existence of which the human eye could perceive only a small fraction—the material world. The mental eye, especially if trained, was believed to be able to peer into the immaterial realms populated by spirits, ghosts, angels, demons, and so forth. With the dawning of the Age of Reason, such beings were dismissed as pure fantasy.

Halloween is our secularized nod to the invisible (ghostly) world. We wear scary or hideous outfits to startle the unwary but mostly only to contribute to the general mood of celebration and hilarity. If we are religiously inclined, we might pray to, or remember, our favorite patron saint, Jesus Christ, or the equally invisible Virgin Mary. A growing number of Christians, however, have difficulty accepting the Church dogma of the invisible figure of the Devil other than in a symbolic sense.

Death is the threshold to invisibility—from the material realm of the body to the immaterial ("subtle") realm of the mind or spirit. Understandably, if we are unconscious or declared materialists, death makes us feel ill at ease. As materialists, we do not like to think about the dead, and the archaic idea that the deceased continue to dwell in our midst as invisible spirits causes us to shudder or react with mockery. As a sign of our respect, we might place flowers on a loved one's grave on the anniversary of his or her death, but we certainly do not consider this a daily obligation. In fact, as materialists we prefer to ignore death (both our own and others'), and when we are forced by circumstances to admit its existence, we tend to prettify it. We even pay hard-earned cash to have our loved ones "made up" before burying or cremating them, in order to keep the sobering physical reality of death at a safe distance.[12] Unless we are directly affected by someone's demise, we try to "forget the whole thing" as quickly as possible. By contrast, in some parts of Latin America, an extra plate is set at meal time for a recently deceased family member.

And yet, there is a widespread fascination with death in the form of tragic accidents and large-scale disasters, as reported in the news media. A fair number of people are intrigued by ghosts and poltergeists, which are the lurid topics of TV talk shows, scandal sheets, and movie hits like *Ghostbusters, Ghost Ship,* and *Pirates of the Caribbean.* Parapsychological research into so-called spirit phenomena, particularly troublesome *poltergeists,* also never fail to at least temporarily arouse public interest in the invisible world. But as soon as the entertainment has worn off, people tend to retreat into the one-dimensional worldview of materialism. Where the spirit world is still a part of the public consciousness, as is the case in Ireland and the Scandinavian countries, commercialism is heavily benefiting from, and likely also modifying and eroding, inherited folklore. Fairies and trolls are manufactured by the thousands to decorate gardens, homes, and window displays. We may find them "cute" or "hideous," but they seldom prompt us to ponder the vast invisible realm in which we are embedded.

Regarding the daily *brahma* sacrifice of the pious Hindus, we must note that it has no equivalent in our modern era. Comparatively few people—even when they have made a deeper commitment to their religion—take the time to delve into the religious scriptures (e.g., Bible study) of their tradition. Scriptural study is a time-honored custom in many traditional bookish societies, notably Hinduism, Buddhism, Judaism, and Christianity. Today, in the last-mentioned religious tradition, serious scriptural study has been replaced with what is popularly known as "Bible thumping"— a fundamentalist endeavor demonstrated in the ability to quote the Bible by chapter and verse without refined understanding.

In traditional India, great care was taken to transmit the sacred or "revealed" knowledge of the *Vedas* with utmost fidelity. Today, fewer and fewer Hindu children have the capacity or inclination to memorize the Vedic scriptures and study them in depth. Vedic recitation along with conducting Vedic sacrificial rituals is a dying art, and the deeper meaning of the *Vedas* was in fact lost centuries ago. Efforts to revive this disappearing art are bound to face formidable challenges, as secular values overtake sacred values in the increasingly well-to-do middle class, which is more interested in emulating Western lifestyles.

Since ancient times, the Hindus have considered "hearing" (*shravana*) the teachings, an important first step in spiritual training. It must be followed by proper reflection (*manana*) on what has been received either by way of oral transmission or by pious study of the written teachings. When the mind has attained certainty about the validity and relevance of the spiritual teachings, then it can soak up their inner or hidden significance via meditation (*nididhyāsana*). These three steps, first taught in the early *Upanishads*, are still followed by practitioners of Vedanta—the philosophical system that has Jnāna-Yoga, the integral discipline of liberating wisdom, at its core.

Like the Hindus, the Buddhists also were eager to preserve the precious teachings of the Buddha and subsequent masters. Especially the monastics—similar to their European Christian counterparts—invested much time and effort in faithfully memorizing the teachings and preserving them also in written form.[13] In c. 484 B.C., three months after the Buddha shed his body, the first gathering of monks was convened just outside the town of Rajagriha to recollect and fix the teachings that the enlightened one had bequeathed to his followers and the rest of the world. Then, in c. 383 B.C., a second council was convened to address ten specific points relating to monastic conduct.

The one thousand elders participating in the very important third council, which was convened in c. 250 B.C. at Pataliputra and patronized by the Buddhist Emperor Ashoka, concerned themselves primarily with the important matter of heresy. At that time, a number of schools determined to be heretical were excluded from the Buddhist community, and the Buddhist community split into two great camps. On one side were the strict monastics who continued on as what came to be known as Hinayana ("Small Vehicle"), and on the other side was the much larger contingent of both monastic and lay practitioners who subsequently gave birth to Mahayana ("Great Vehicle"). This was also the time when, under the newly converted emperor's influence, Buddhism became a missionary tradition.

The fourth council, convened by Emperor Kanishka in c. 100 A.D. and not recognized by the Theravada school, marked the emergence of Mahayana with its Sanskrit-based scriptures as a distinct branch of Buddhism. The followers of this "new" tradition contributed over 2,000 scriptures to the Buddhist canon. While oral transmission continued to be emphasized, copying the sacred scriptures also became a noble activity that was greatly encouraged. By virtue of the personal sacrifice of many literate monastics, we of today have the enormous privilege of being able to study Buddhism through its preserved written literature. Manifestly, self-sacrifice can assume many different forms.

Coming to the fifth and last Hindu sacrifice—the above-mentioned *manushya-yajna*—I want to very briefly note that this is generally interpreted as standing for the traditional custom of hospitality and defer a detailed discussion of this virtue to Chapter 13. It makes sense to consider hospitality in conjunction with the multifaceted virtue of generosity.

Clearly, we moderns fall far short of the five traditional Hindu sacrifices, which echo similar practices found in other spiritually based cultures. This goes hand in hand with our failure to recognize that the world we live in includes an immense hidden/invisible dimension that is yet vital to our personal and collective wholeness and haleness. Behaving like pre-Copernican flatlanders, we only see the most external aspects of life and therefore cannot function fully and with full responsibility in the world. In Indian terms, if we lack correct view, we cannot know morally sound conduct and consequently will only increase our suffering and miss out on wisdom and happiness. More than that, we will also not be able to truly alleviate the suffering of our fellow beings but likely contribute to their distress. In Buddhist language, instead of bringing ourselves and others closer to *nirvāna*, we merely reinforce the bonds of *samsāra* for them and us.

The average Westerner today has little or no interest in sacred rituals. The daily routine chores along with watching or reading the news, TV entertainment, regular physical fitness sessions, scheduled visits to the hairdresser, and the weekend spectator game have become substitute rituals. Even many of those who have won through to a spiritual way of life find rituals tedious and outmoded. In my view, they fail to see the advantage of involving the body in the spiritual process. Be that as it may, the discipline of self-transcendence does not inevitably involve ritual. But it demands that we *in fact* commit to consistent acts of self-sacrifice. Metaphorically, we must be willing to ascend our own funeral pyre or, to put it differently in traditional terms, sever our own head with the sword of wisdom as did the goddess Chinnamastā.[14]

ENDNOTES, CHAPTER 4

1   On the Mayas, which in many ways are representative of the Toltec and Aztec cultures, see David Friedel et al., *Maya Cosmos: Three Thousand Years on the Shaman's Path* (New York: William Morrow, 1993); Linda Schele and David Friedel, *A Forest of Kings: The Untold Story of Ancient Maya* (New York: William Morrow, 1990); Linda Schele et al., *The Code of Kings: The Language of Seven Sacred Maya Temples and Tombs* (New York: Touchstone, 1999); Linda Schele and Mary Ellen Miller, *The Blood of Kings: Dynasty and Ritual in Maya Art* (Fort Worth, Texas: Kimbell Art Museum, 1986).

2   See Uma Marina Vesci, *Heat and Sacrifice in the Vedas* (Delhi: Motilal Banarasidass, 2d rev. ed. 1992); H. Aguilar, *Sacrifice in the Rg Veda* (Bombay: Bharatiya Vidya Prakashan, 1976); K. R. Potdar, *Sacrifice in the Rgveda: Its Nature, Influence, Origin and Growth* (Bombay: Bharatiya Vidya Bhavan, 1953); G. U. Thite, *Sacrifice in the Brāhmana-Texts* (Poona, India: Poona University Press, 1975), and Herman Wayne Tull, *The Vedic Origins of Karma: Cosmos As Man in Ancient Indian Myth and Ritual* (Albany, N.Y.: SUNY Press, 1989).

3   See, e.g., the *Sāma-Veda* (6.4) and the *Atharva-Veda* (19.6), as well as the *Taittirīya-Āranyaka* (3.12–13) and the *Vājasaneyi-Samhitā* (31.1–6). Explanations of some of its concepts can be found in the *Shatapatha-Brāhmana*, the *Taittirīya-Brāhmana*, and the *Shvetāshvatara-Upanishad*. The teachings of the Hymn of the Primordial Man, moreover, are discussed in the *Bhāgavata-Purāna* (2.5.35 and 2.6.1–29) and the *Mahābhārata* (12.351–352).

4   S. Radhakrishnan, *The Bhagavadgītā* (New York: Harper Torchbooks, 1973), p. 245.

5   See Charles Malamoud, *Cooking the World: Ritual and Thought in Ancient India*. Trans. from the French by David White (Oxford: Oxford University Press, 1996).

6   On the sentience of fish, see Chapter 6.

7   Christopher Key Chapple, *Nonviolence to Animals, Earth, and Self in Asian Traditions* (Albany, N.Y.: SUNY Press, 1993). See also Daniel A. Dombrowski, *The Philosophy of Vegetarianism* (Amherst: University of Massachusetts Press, 1984).

8   See Patrick Tierney, *The Highest Altar: The Story of Human Sacrifice* (New York: Viking/Penguin, 1989).

9   See John Campbell, *Human Sacrifices in India* (Mittal Publications, 1986) and Felix Padel, *The Sacrifice of Human Beings: British Rule and the Konds of Orissa* (Oxford: Oxford University Press, 1996).

10   See J. Fisch, *Burning Women: A Global History of Widow-Sacrifice from Ancient Times to the Present* (Oxford: Berg Publishers, 2005).

11   See J. Singer, *Seeing Through the Invisible World: Jung, Gnosis and Chaos* (San Francisco: HarperCollins, 1990).

12   See Jessica Mitford, *The American Way of Death Revisited* (New York: Vintage Books, 2000). See also Ernest Becker, *The Denial of Death* (New York: Free

Press Paperbacks, 1997).

13   For a concise history of the development of Buddhism, see Sangharakshita, *A Survey of Buddhism: Its Doctrines and Methods Through the Ages* (Birmhingham, England: Windhorse Publications, 9th rev. ed., 2001).

14   See Elisabeth A. Benard, *Chinnamastā: The Aweful Buddhist & Hindu Tantric Goddess* (Columbia, Mo.: South Asia Books, 1994).

CHAPTER 5

UNIVERSAL MORALITY
AND PERSONAL VIRTUES

A ll ancient cosmologies describe a cosmos that unfolds in layers and persists at various levels owing to an inbuilt regularity
or order called *rita* by the Vedic sages.[1] Modern cosmologies entertain a somewhat similar notion about the universe, though most
scientists do not subscribe to the kind of nested orderliness—harmony at varyingly subtle levels down to the material level—as did
the ancient visionaries and thinkers. Instead they speak of mere
mathematical regularities against the backdrop of competing theories of how stars explode into being and billions of years later die
or how dark matter spreads throughout the known vast expanses
of interstellar space but is doing so by the sheer random dance of
energy quanta—the sort of notion that prompted Albert Einstein
to exclaim that "God does not play dice with the universe."[2]

As we have seen in the preceding chapter, traditional societies
have consistently believed that this cosmic order depended at
least in part on the collaboration of human beings: By means of
mirroring the universal harmony at the level of daily life, humans
can and must contribute to the maintenance of rhythms observed
in Nature and the world at large. In bygone eras, this was done in
two ways; first, by regular sacrificial rituals that were thought to
replicate the archetypal sacrifice of Cosmic Man (*macranthropos*)
and second, by acts of self-sacrifice. Every sacrifice entails an

element of self-sacrifice, because it is based on a conscious effort to overcome the ordinary tendency of the mind toward distraction and hence microcosmic disorder and disequilibrium.

But there also have been societies—like the Indic civilization—which developed the idea and practice of symbolic self-sacrifice, or "inner sacrifice." The Vedic seers still used the means of external sacrifices to focus the mind and raise it to ecstatic heights where they could divine the cosmic law and even pierce the cosmic envelop to discover the ultimate Singularity. Centuries later, the Upanishadic sages discovered and exalted the "inner sacrifice" as a primary tool for realizing the transcendental Reality. Their spiritual probings led to the creation of Yoga as we know it.

Yoga is inner sacrifice or self-sacrifice *par excellence*. No longer did the Upanishadic yogins require external rituals to concentrate the wandering mind, though many continued to avail themselves of this useful medium. They learned to appreciate that the mind itself was sufficient to work the miracle of deep self-transformation. The central objective of all such self-sacrificing practices like Yoga is to transcend the human condition and therefore also to transcend the cosmos itself. Such radical transcendence, however, does not imply a literal obliteration of the human being or the world. On the contrary, it has long been thought that by transcending the human condition, we come fully into our own (as the ultimate Reality) and, having done so, we can thereby contribute to the cosmic order or harmony—one of the great paradoxes of spiritual life. Only the ego is reckoned as a source of disturbance in the cosmos. Dissolving the ego illusion, by contrast, has a salutary effect on the world as a whole. It is comparable to removing an irritant from the body, whereupon its health or balance is restored.

The adepts of the medieval Tantric tradition invented a powerful symbol that captures the very spirit of self-transcendence and its salutary effects: the myth of the goddess Chinnamastā

("She who is decapitated").[3] This deity, who is one of the most visually striking (some would say macabre) goddesses of the Hindu pantheon, is typically depicted in a standing posture, holding in her right hand a bloody sword and in her left her own severed head, with blood gushing from her neck in three streams. The left and right streams respectively enter the mouths of two devotees on either side of her, while the middle stream flows directly into the mouth of her cut-off head.

According to this Tantric myth, the goddess—in her function as Mother of the universe—decapitated herself in order to feed her hungry devotees with her own blood. In other words, she committed the ultimate self-sacrifice of offering her body and life substance—blood—to benefit others. The fact that the middle fountain of blood spouting from her neck should enter her own mouth is a sign that the goddess has not committed conventional suicide. Her self-sacrifice does not negate life but enhance it. The central stream of blood issuing from her decapitated body corresponds to the flow of psychospiritual energy along the "gracious" central channel of the body. This symbolism and its underlying process are fundamental to Tantric Yoga. When the psychospiritual energy rises in the central channel from the base of the spine to the crown of the head, it not only revitalizes every cell but also helps the Tantric practitioner to transcend and transmute the body into a "divine" vehicle.

The image of Chinnamastā suggests that she possesses infinite vitality, and those who imitate her self-sacrifice through the practices of Yoga will likewise gain access to immeasurable energy—the energy of Spirit itself. Often Chinnamastā is depicted as standing on a copulating couple. The man in prone position is Kāmadeva, the god of love and passion, and the woman sitting or lying on top of him is Rātī, goddess of pleasure. This beautiful Tantric image, as I understand it, contains a twofold message. First, Chinnamastā's self-sacrificing act transcends sexuality and mere pleasure. Second, the Tantric work of self-transformation is grounded in psychosexual energy, or what Sigmund Freud called *libido*. Rather than repressing the sexual instinct, the adepts of Tantra utilize it to increase the body's vitality, which then provides the necessary energy for transcending the body (and sexuality) as a whole.

Another aspect of Chinnamastā's complex symbolism relates to the severed head, which stands for the transcendence of the ego and its identification with the physical body. Only when we have overcome our inbuilt sense that we *are* the body, or at least are inextricably linked to it, are we able to discover our true nature as nonlocal Awareness. It is not enough to have merely a conceptual grasp of this process, which is a good beginning; but actual transcendence of body identification involves the kind of psychoenergetic restructuring that Tantra and other forms of Yoga make possible. Contrary to how a casual observer might interpret Chinnamastā's gruesome image, her symbolism suggests the triumph of life over death.

Obviously, Chinnamastā's iconographic image was never intended for the squeamish. It is, however, deeply meaningful for anyone intent on practicing conscious self-transcendence. Every spiritual and moral act implies that we go beyond the habit patterns of the conventional self, the ego, and bear in mind our connection with all forms of life and even our inanimate environment. In all our activities, we must be both sacrificer and sacrificed. Only then will we—to use archaic language—help preserve the cosmic order by "feeding" the rest of creation with our energy and good will.

Naturally, the transcendence of one individual's ego illusion does not make for total cosmic harmony; that would require the dissolution of all ego personalities—a highly unlikely eventuality, though some adepts have contemplated just this possibility. One such Yoga master was the twentieth-century yogin-philosopher

Sri Aurobindo, who wrote extensively about the descent of the Supermind and the transmutation of humanity as a whole.[4] Another contemporary adept, Gopinath Kaviraj, believed that a single, sufficiently advanced realizer could uplift all of humanity in one moment.[5] He himself was undertaking a difficult practice to accomplish this. Since we are still here struggling to achieve even a modicum of happiness, we know that his mission was not blessed with success even locally, not to mention the cosmos at large. According to some Indic schools of thought, the universe exists only for the sake of sentient beings, and thus the liberation of all beings would deprive the universe of its intrinsic purpose. In this theory, then, we would even have to expect the obliteration of the cosmos itself.

Such ambitious spiritual goals notwithstanding, we may affirm in keeping with the yogic tradition that humanity holds an important place in the scheme of things. Hence it is not surprising that we should find the concomitant idea that human life is more desirable than any other form of existence. Human life affords us a rich field of experience of both pleasure and pain, which are deemed powerful stimuli for moral and spiritual growth.

The premium placed on human life in the spiritual traditions has nothing to do with the erroneous notion of the eighteenth-century Enlightenment movement that, by virtue of our reasoning capacity, the human species represents the very crown of creation. This particular hubris sprang from an overestimation of our rational faculties and the place of reason within evolution itself. While a clear, rational mind is a desirable and beautiful thing, it neither characterizes the life of most individuals nor is it sufficient in itself to guide us safely through the maze of life. Reason must be tempered by that aspect of the mind which we associate with feeling, sensitivity, and empathy. Without the "warmth" of feeling, the rational mind is little more than a calculating machine. We can see the failure of a predominantly rational approach all around us: Over the last 200 years, we have created a formidable technology but also an essentially dysfunctional civilization that now finds itself on the brink of self-destruction. Our individual and collective lives are governed not by illumined reason but by spiritual blindness and counterproductive ego-based drives and motives. A purely rational approach to life tends to deny and suppress the "irrational" side of our being, including the valuable capacities for intuition, empathy, kindness, love, and compassion.

By contrast, the spiritual traditions of the world, which always look at the larger picture, assign to reason its proper place and see it as a polar complement to the nonrational or feeling aspects of the mind. Thus they are interested in a mind that is both lucid and compassionate and that respects the algorithms of reason and the grammar of the heart. In Yoga, a distinction is made between *buddhi* (the higher mind) and *manas* (sense-bound rationality). Only the former faculty is capable of the kind of deep insight that leads us beyond mere functional existence to inspired living and ultimately to the transcendence of the human condition as such.

The spiritual traditions consider and celebrate the extraordinary personal growth of a select few individuals whose lives illustrate humanity's higher but largely untapped potential. In other words, what is great about human life from a spiritual perspective is our innate capacity to transcend it! From a modern evolutionary perspective, we could say that evolution fulfills itself in the rare individual who has come to realize and also actualize in daily life that he or she is not a human island unto himself or herself at all, but an unlimited ocean of pure Being-Awareness (*sat-cit*).

When a society has forgotten the true spiritual potential of human individuals and merely skids along the surface of existence, it increasingly is dedicated to unviable forms of thought and behavior until it becomes dysfunctional ("neurotic") and self-destructive. We learn the rules of the evolutionary game mostly by trial and error, and our growth as a species and as individuals is attendant by a great deal of suffering. Ignorant of the rules, we behave like a newly blind person in an unfamiliar environment: We bump into sharp corners and stumble over the smallest obstacles in our path.

As our ignorance is gradually removed and wisdom—the fruit of much experiential learning and reflection—dawns in our mind, our eyes open. Thus we become able to accelerate our inner maturation by intentionally cooperating with the cosmos. Such cooperation does not only consist in calculated optimal living but also in understanding, appreciating, and abiding by the cosmic laws, which present themselves at the human level as moral principles.

Ever since the Stoics, Western philosophers have pondered the question of morals—what precisely they are (or are meant to be) and where they originate. They have created a veritable jungle of ideas about and approaches to morality.[6] It would go far beyond the intended scope of this book to review all the diverse theories here, but I would like to provide brief definitions of the three most important current viewpoints on ethics: moral realism, moral relativism, and moral nihilism.

Moral realism, the most prevalent viewpoint, is the theory that there are normative "objective" truths about what a moral person ought or ought not to do. This is the position of all traditional cultures and those governed by strong religious beliefs. Of the c. 1.6 billion people inhabiting the Western hemisphere, several hundred million are more or less active adherents of Christianity, some 40 million are said to practice Judaism or Islam, while a few million follow an Eastern religion. Incidentally, I seriously question the figure given in the *Encyclopedia Britannica* of c. 800 million Christians in Europe and Northern America combined. Certainly many people in the West officially call themselves Christians but in practice are unchurched or even self-declared atheists. Be that as it may, those religious followers can be expected to subscribe to a form of moral realism in which the moral duties are clearly specified and expected to be followed.

Moral relativism, which is gaining in popularity, insists that there are no universal truths that apply across the board, but that moral standards are always relative to a group of people or even an individual. What some hold to be good, others decry as bad. For instance, the widespread practice of human sacrifice in the ancient world is today condemned by most people as bad or evil. It would seem that moral relativism marks especially the so-called New Age movement, which is strong in some parts of the United States. While there is some truth in moral relativism, it fails to acknowledge that there are certain key values that remain inviolate so long as we are dealing with a healthy individual or society. Abraham Maslow, the "father" of humanistic psychology, spoke of "meta-values" or "being values," such as goodness, justice, truth, beauty, wholeness, self-transcendence, and self-actualization.[7] (By the way, he saw love as an important "deficiency need," which must be met for normal emotional growth.)

An interesting, if sad, example is the famous British philosopher-scientist-statesman Francis Bacon, who already in the sixteenth century strongly advocated moral relativism. His philosophical stance was, it would appear, shaped by his questionable character, for in his personal life this intellectual genius showed a singular lack of moral fiber. Not only was he constantly in debt even when he earned a lavish income, he also was dismissed in disgrace as Lord Chancellor under King James I. A tribunal had found him guilty on twenty-three charges of corruption in his political and judicial offices. Possibly even more dishonorable was Bacon's enthusiastic prosecution of his former friend and benefactor Robert Devereux, the Second Earl of Essex, when the latter was tried for treason. Widely criticized for his unscrupulousness during the trial, Bacon sought to exonerate himself in several public statements. He clearly lacked moral integrity, and his life illustrates the failure of moral relativism, which is built on a strict separation of values from facts.

Moral nihilism proposes that there are absolutely no standards that are meaningful and that therefore we can do what we want, but must be prepared for the consequences in terms of public disapproval or legal intervention. We must distinguish this stance from the ideology of the so-called moral nihilist movement of late-nineteenth-century Russia, which favored moral iconoclasm (a deliberate smashing of existing moral conventions) but in order to build a new moral order based on whether something is useful or not. In contradistinction, the true nihilist believes in nothing and lacks a concept of duty or obligation, yet wants everything for himself. Moral nihilism is patently unsuitable as a prescription for harmonious living.

Within moral realism, which I favor, various approaches can be distinguished. To simplify, these can be grouped into three major ethical orientations: *duty based*, *goal based*, and *virtue based*. The duty-based (or so-called deontological[8]) orientation is exemplified by Immanuel Kant's famous categorical imperative: "Act in such a manner that the standards of your will can always serve as the foundation of law-making in general." A popular adage puts it simpler: "Do unto others as you would have them do unto you."

Goal-based or utilitarian ethics, by contrast, is not so much concerned with duty as the outcome of our actions. The classic theory is the utilitarianism of the eighteenth-century British philosopher Jeremy Bentham, who believed that the value of an action is entirely determined by whether or not it is conducive to the welfare (= happiness) of the majority of people. A generation later, Bentham's work inspired his countryman John Stuart Mill, whose political and economic views were rather influential. In his important work entitled *Utilitarianism* (published in 1863),

Mill wrote:

> The creed which accepts as the foundation of morals,
> Utility, or the Greatest Happiness Principle, holds that
> actions are right in proportion as they tend to promote
> happiness, wrong as they tend to produce the reverse of
> happiness. By happiness is intended pleasure, and the
> absence of pain; by unhappiness, pain, and the privation
> of pleasure.[9]

Mill went on to defend his position against the popular accusa-
tion that he was advocating a demeaning Epicureanism by rightly
reminding his critics, as did the Epicureans long before him, that
pleasure is not limited to sensory enjoyments but includes sublime intellectual, artistic, and even moral joys. In his own words:

> It is better to be a human being dissatisfied than a pig sat-
> isfied; better to be Socrates dissatisfied than a fool satis-
> fied. And if the fool, or the pig, are of a different opinion, it
> is because they only know their own side of the question.
> The other party to the comparison knows both sides.[10]

On the downside, utilitarianism condones the notion that
the end justifies the means, which view is unthinkable within the
framework of a duty-based ethics but which has become wildly
popular among politicians, business tycoons, and military folk.
Even Krishna's admonition to Prince Arjuna to fight a just war
was argued on the basis of a warrior's sacred obligation to uphold
the very possibility of a virtuous life.

While both duty-based and goal-based ethics deemphasize
the acting individual, virtue-based ethics acknowledges that all
actions flow from an agent who imbues all actions with the basic
qualities of his or her inner being. Virtue ethics was clearly the

predominant approach in the pre-modern era and to some degree still informs traditional cultures, notably of the East. In our own epoch, however, virtue is treated as an old-fashioned concept and most ethicists stay clear of virtue-based ethical theories. People's current obsession is with rights and goals, but these do not make full sense apart from the moral quality of the individual. We act in accordance with our nature, which is either drawn to virtue or vice or some in-between condition.

To make any sense of moral action, we must bear the agent in mind. As Alasdair MacIntyre proposed in his book *After Virtue*, virtue-based ethics was championed by most philosophers from the time of the Greeks through the Middle Ages up to the eighteenth century.[11] It went distinctly out of favor with the Enlightenment movement, whose protagonists considered the human being intrinsically selfish and motivated by minimizing pain and maximizing pleasure. This seems a paltry view of human nature, and I propose we would be wise to recover the lost perspective of virtue ethics.

This ethical orientation acknowledges the primacy of the moral agent who is free to choose good over evil, right over wrong, justice over injustice. Virtue is more than duty, or a sense of obligation. Nor is it a rational standard by which we seek to realize our own happiness or the welfare of all. Virtue is first and foremost a state of being. The *Dashâ-Vaikâlika-Sûtra* (1.1-4) of the Shvetâmbara branch of Jainism, which was possibly composed in the fifth century B.C., opens with the following verse:

Dharma is the greatest blessing: Nonharming, restraint, and asceticism. Even the deities honor a mind always set on *dharma*.

As briefly discussed in an earlier chapter, virtue is a manifestation of the psychocosmic quality of *sattva*—a Sanskrit term that literally means "being-ness" and that conveys a condition of refinement, lucidity, purity, and transparency. The sattvic person is naturally virtuous. Therefore, so the classical viewpoint maintains, we must purify ourselves and increase the *sattva* content of our whole being to *become* virtuous and thus become able to *act* virtuously. This orientation does not necessarily rule out a consideration of duty or utility, but it emphasizes the nature or character of the individual agent. In his *Nichomachean Ethics*, Aristotle introduced virtues as "dispositions" to act in certain ways. True to the Greek philosophical heritage, he, moreover, characterized virtues as tending toward the mean (*menos*)—the golden middle between excess and deficiency. Thus the virtue of courage lies between rashness and cowardice; that of generosity between wastefulness and stinginess; that of friendliness between sycophancy and frostiness, and so forth.

I appreciate that in order to even want to undergo a prolonged process of self-purification, or what one might call "sattvification"[12] of our entire being, we must paradoxically already embody certain virtues. To put it differently, if we lack the virtue of desiring a virtuous life, we will never embark on the conscious cultivation of virtues through a process of self-transcendence and self-transformation. Therefore it is important that we encourage virtuous acts in our children, even if they at first do so simply to obey us. We must, however, also give them the opportunity for self-inspection and reflection on their behavior to come to understand the larger picture and the desirability of leading a meaningful, self-transcending, virtuous life. The best we can do for them, though, is to be good role models in the exercise of virtues.

Life, especially nowadays, presents us with plenty of situations that at least potentially address diverse virtues. Then the question arises of how to respond to them virtuously. This was precisely the dilemma in which Prince Arjuna found himself some 3000 years ago on the morning of the first of eighteen fierce battles, which came to be known as the Bharata war. On the one hand, the moment called for him to fight as a trained warrior for justice, peace, and the preservation of the highest moral ideals. On the other hand, his study of Yoga, had put him in touch with the virtue of nonharming, which he deeply felt when contemplating the situation. The enlightened master Krishna, ruler of the Yādava kingdom, showed him a way out of his perplexity. To understand what Krishna was telling him, Arjuna first had to inwardly transform himself, which was made possible by Krishna's theophanic self-revelation and his patient instruction of Arjuna in the subtle points of a spiritually based ethics and metaphysics.

An example closer to home is that of the German Protestant theologian Dietrich Bonhoeffer.[13] In 1936, he was forbidden to teach theology at the University of Berlin. Seeing the plight of his countrymen under the Nazis, he struggled with the kind of Christian values he treasured—love, charity, forgiveness, etc.—and the felt sense that something needed to be done about Hitler and his regime. Finally in 1939, after much agonizing reflection, he jettisoned his pacifism and joined a secret group of high-ranking military officers who plotted to assassinate Hitler. Bonhoeffer felt he was justified in helping to remove the cause of so much evil and suffering. Fearing that his family would be arrested and punished, he courageously declined the opportunity to escape from prison and was hanged for conspiracy in 1945, only three weeks before the allied forces liberated Berlin. His action understandably led to lively debates in Christian quarters.

A significant question presents itself: If there is a choice of virtues in any given situation, which should we animate? The Indic tradition espouses, loudly and clearly, nonharming (*ahimsā*) as the master virtue. It is considered as the anchor-point of all other virtues. Only in specific crisis situations, such as when the ideal of virtuous living itself is endangered, as was the case in Arjuna's days, may the great virtue of nonharming be appropriately modified by those who, because of their psychological nature and role in life, feel moved and called to take action. What was right for Arjuna, however, would not necessarily have been right for a sage who was not a military man but had attained to a high level of renunciation.

This qualification is in keeping with the spirit of virtue ethics. We must act according to our inner nature or always run the risk of engaging inauthentic action. This position is not the same as moral relativism, for nonharming is still considered the supreme guiding ideal, but an allowance is made for those who have not yet reached higher levels of inner development and who, by dint of their inner nature and commitments in life are called, like Arjuna, to act in ways that fall short of this highest ideal. Krishna would undoubtedly have counseled an advanced spiritual practitioner differently. In the *Bhagavad-Gītā* (6.3), we find in fact one stanza which recommends self-transcending action for the aspiring yogin and quiescence (*shama*) for the master who has ascended the heights of Yoga. We may assume that only in a state of quiescence in which no particular social obligations pertain can nonharming be practiced in its fullest sense.

The teaching of ego-transcending action (or Karma-Yoga) was specifically addressed to Arjuna, a member of the warrior estate. If Krishna would have given the same teaching to a member of the working class, it would not have had the same focus on harming in the form of military action. While the principles of Karma-Yoga were intended to apply universally, Krishna took Arjuna's particular character and situation into account. Pacifism, however, is traditional India's preferred moral stance.

Hinduism, Buddhism, and Jainism acknowledge at least the following five key virtues: nonharming, truthfulness, nonstealing, nongrasping (greedlessness), and chastity. In his *Yoga-Sūtra* (2.31), Patanjali speaks of these as constituting the "great vow" (*mahā-vrata*), which shows their intrinsic importance to the yogic path. He, furthermore, states that they are valid in all spheres of life, regardless of a person's birth status, location, time, or circumstance. Clearly, these virtues belong to the code of ethics of any serious ascetic. According to Jainism, they also make up the "subsidiary vow" (*anu-vrata*) that is relevant to a lay practitioner. I will discuss these individually, as well as other related virtues in Chapters 11–14, drawing from the yogic-moral teachings of Hinduism, Buddhism, and Jainism.

The five major virtues mentioned above constitute what amount to basic principles without which human conduct would collapse into anarchy. Interestingly, in an attempt to construct a "scientific ethics," the contemporary philosopher David Resnik worked out a comparable set of moral rules based on the following principles:[14] (1) the nonmalificence principle ("Do not act in ways that cause needless injury or harm to others"); (2) the beneficence principle ("Act in ways that promote the welfare of other people"); (3) the principle of autonomy ("Rational individuals should be permitted to be self-determining"); (4) the formal principle of justice ("Treat equals equally and unequals unequally"); (5) the material principles of justice ("Punish on the basis of desert. Distribute goods on the basis of need, merit, social contribution, effort, or equality").

These fundamental principles of ethics and their possible derivatives, Resnik noted, yield specific moral rules, notably: (1) Nonmalificence (Yoga's nonharming): "Do not harm yourself or other people"; (2) beneficence: "Help yourself and other people"; (3) autonomy: "Allow rational individuals to make free and informed choices"; (4) justice: "Treat people fairly: treat equals equally, unequals unequally"; (5) utility: "Maximize the ratio of benefits to harms for all people"; (6) fidelity: "Keep your promises and agreements"; (7) honesty: "Do not lie, defraud, deceive or mislead"; (8) privacy: "Respect personal privacy and confidentiality."

Obviously, Resnik's moral rules reflect the spirit of our complex modern society and overlap only somewhat with the moral disciplines of Yoga, which seem at once simpler and broader. Conspicuous by its absence from Resnik's model is chastity. Conversely, traditional Yoga practitioners, whose life revolves around the ideal of self-transcendence, give little weight to privacy, while the virtue of justice would seem to fall under nonharming, truthfulness, and nonstealing. What Resnik calls fidelity would in Yoga be considered an aspect of truthfulness.

It is important to understand that for the yogin and yoginī, the moral disciplines are not merely abstract principles or even deduced rules. They are virtues that spring from one's character or state of being. Here is an example from our own time: While still a young child, Queen Elizabeth II had an almost mystical sense of being connected to and somehow responsible for the Commonwealth. In bodhisattva-like fashion, at the age of twenty-one, she solemnly pledged on radio while visiting South Africa to serve her subjects for the rest of her life—a vow she repeated at her accession to the throne five years later in 1952. Despite personal tragedies in her life and increasingly challenging socio-cultural times, she has valiantly kept her pledge for nearly six decades. Her sense of duty cannot be said to have been instilled in her merely by outside influences, although her father King George V to whom she was very close groomed her to succeed him. She happily embraced the burden and challenge of being a head of state, feeling early on that this was her *sva-bhāva*, or inner nature—her destiny as a servant of people. Whatever we may think of monarchism, Queen Elizabeth II's dedication to "her" people is beyond question. While the British monarchy has no executive powers, she has appointed and worked closely with eleven prime ministers—from Winston Churchill to Tony Blair. Many citizens of Great Britain have a warm feeling for the head of the royal house of Windsor, and the monarchy remains an integral aspect of Great Britain's cultural-political life.

Prince Arjuna, over three millennia earlier, temporarily forgot who he was and became confused about his *sva-dharma*, or inner law, as a ruler and protector of the people and of the principle of lawfulness in the land. Another ruler—Lord Krishna, the enlightened king of the Yādavas—had to remind Arjuna of his destined role in life and his duty to fight for the good of all on the battlefield of Kurukshetra, as chronicled in the *Mahābhārata*. Admittedly, Krishna used many cunning arguments to convince Prince Arjuna to fight in the imminent battle. But his real teaching focused on helping Arjuna to understand himself and to see the situation in the proper spiritual perspective. The moral response he hoped to elicit from the prince was not mindless obedience to some external standards but a heartfelt, lucid, and ego-transcending response based on real understanding. In the final analysis, Krishna did not want Arjuna to merely do his duty but to take action springing from his innate wisdom and a sense of appropriateness and destiny. As Krishna put it in the *Bhagavad-Gītā* (18.63):

> Thus I have disclosed to you wisdom more secret than [any other] secret. Reflect on it unreservedly and then do as you will!

Krishna left it up to Arjuna to decide the next step. Of course, in his full enlightenment, Krishna already knew how the prince would act. In fact, the epic makes it clear that the Yādava king foresaw the fateful outcome of the eighteen-day-long war.

Once before Krishna had asked Arjuna to make a momentous choice—when he gave him the opportunity to choose between his (Krishna's) good counsel or his Yādava army. Instinctively and wisely, Arjuna chose Krishna, whereas his evil-minded cousin Duryodhana greedily made his bid for Krishna's considerable army. Thus it came to be that Krishna served Arjuna as a noncombatant charioteer on the battle field, while his warriors were aligned with the enemy. Arjuna's subsequent choice to actually give the signal to do battle in fact required Krishna's counsel without which the prince would have perished in the bloody war along with everyone else.

It is important to realize that Krishna did not teach Arjuna to hate the enemy but merely to fulfill his innate law, or *sva-dharma*, after due self-inspection. At the conclusion of the *Bhagavad-Gītā* (18.73), which records the dialogue between Krishna and Arjuna, the prince finally said:

> My delusion is destroyed. Through your grace, O Acyuta [Krishna], I have attained recollection. With my uncertainty gone, I am resolved. I shall act according to your word!

This may sound like Lord Krishna succeeded in talking the Pāndava prince into a war he did not really wish to fight. But Arjuna's choice came after deep deliberation, which involved much debating and questioning of his teacher Krishna, as well as a brief experience of what could be called "cosmic consciousness"—an ecstatic vision of the Macranthropos. As Arjuna stated, he achieved "recollection" (*smriti*), which in the present context could be interpreted to mean both recollecting himself and recollecting Reality, the Truth of existence, as revealed in Krishna's theophany.[15] Thus Arjuna searched into the very core of his being, which he found to be embedded in the eternal Being, Krishna's hidden, transcendental aspect. This realization shattered all presumptions and cleared away all his doubts. He understood that Krishna's instruction, or counsel, was in fact based in Truth. Having seen the Truth for himself, he was able to accept Krishna's word not as an external authority but as a truthful statement of his own inner being.

Arjuna had to undergo a significant self-transformation before he could recognize the merit of his teacher's commendation to proceed with the war. He had to first find himself and tune into higher wisdom in order to see his situation untarnished by confusion; only then could he act in a virtuous manner. Here we have a clear instance of virtue ethics.

Even though the yogic virtues and the moral rules governing society at large intersect in many ways, Yoga morality must be distinguished from conventional morality, whether it be secular or religious. They are distinct both in terms of intent and earnestness of application. The initiate of Yoga is unconcerned with following a particular external code. He is not interested in being socially acceptable and also is indifferent to censure or praise. Rather, the yogin's or yoginī's loyalty is to personal spiritual growth, which, as I have argued, integrally involves the careful cultivation of fundamental moral virtues. Whereas conventional morality tends to be rather elastic and sluggish, yogic morality is founded on acute mindfulness or attentiveness, great sensitivity, as well as copious responsibility. Also, while conventional morality unfolds in front of the ever-watchful eye of authority—be it God, the law, or fellow citizens—the practitioner of Yoga recognizes only his or her own conscience as moral watchdog.

Naturally, the yogic approach to moral behavior entails a rare psychological and moral maturity. Psychologist and educator Lawrence Kohlberg outlined six stages of moral development through which the individual must progress consecutively in order to achieve full moral maturity.[16]

At the first level, a person's moral life is regulated by obedience to authority (parents, teachers, etc.), mostly out of fear of punishment for failing to obey. At the second level, the individual has learned to appreciate that it is beneficial to him or her to adhere to moral norms. The third level revolves around acting in such a way that a person will win the approval of others by being perceived as a "good boy" or "good girl." At the fourth level, moral behavior is governed by a concern for law and order and the fulfillment of one's obligations, which are perceived as duties. The fifth level of moral development involves an appreciation of the principle of social mutuality and a genuine concern for the welfare of others. At the sixth level, the individual becomes fully capable of universalizing moral principles and of listening to his or her highly developed individual conscience.

The first two levels are grouped together under the heading of "pre-conventional" and the next two levels are deemed "conventional," while the last two are labeled "post-conventional. Kohlberg correctly believed that the majority of people operate only at the conventional levels. Some can claim to manifest fifth-level values and attitudes, while the sixth level is reserved for the rare few.

Kohlberg had at one time considered several nominees for this advanced stage but never found enough subjects to study and define the properties of this stage more closely. He ended up labeling it a "theoretical" stage. It would appear, however, that the great Yoga adepts—such as the bodhisattvas of Buddhism—squarely occupy the sixth stage of moral evolution. They have overcome the ego-illusion and thus are free, able, and completely willing to care for the welfare of other beings. They exemplify Homo ethicus at the pinnacle of his development.

ENDNOTES, CHAPTER 5

1   On the concept of rita, see Jeanine Miller, *Vision of Cosmic Order in the Vedas* (London: Arkana, 1988).
2   Quoted by Helen Dukas and Banesh Hoffman, ed., *Albert Einstein: The Human Side* (New York: New American Library, 1954), p. 73.
3   See Elisabeth A. Benard, *Chinnamastā: The Aweful Buddhist & Hindu Tantric Goddess* (Columbia, Mo.: South Asia Books, 1994). On Hindu Tantra in general, see Georg Feuerstein, *Tantra: The Path of Ecstasy* (Boston, Mass.: Shambhala Publications, 1998).
4   See Anil Kumar Sarkar, *Sri Aurobindo's Vision of the Supermind: Its Indian and Non-Indian Interpreters* (Columbia, Mo.: South Asia Books, 1989).
5   See Kalidas Bhattacharya, *Gopinath Kaviraj's Thoughts: Towards a Systematic Study* (Calcutta: University of Calcutta Press, 1982).
6   See Lawrence M. Hinman et al., *Ethics: A Pluralistic Approach to Moral Theory* (Florence, Ky.: Wadsworth Publishing, 3d ed. 2002).
7   See Abraham Maslow, *Toward a Psychology of Being* (New York: Wiley, 3d ed. 1998).
8   The term *deontological* does not relate to *ontological* (from *ontos* "being" and *logos* "word") but is associated with the Greek word *deon*, meaning "duty, obligation," the equivalent of the Sanskrit concept of *kārya*.
9   J. S. Mill, *Utilitarianism* (1863), Chapter 2: "What Utilitarianism Is," featured online at http://etext.library.adelaide.edu.au/m/mill/john_stuart/m645u/util02.html.
10   Ibid.
11   See Alasdair MacIntyre, *After Virtue: A Study in Moral Theory* (London: Gerald Duckworth, 2d ed. 1984).
12   I have coined this neologism based on the Sanskrit term *sattva*, meaning literally "beingness" and standing for the psychocosmic principle of lucidity and reality, similar to the Neoplatonic *logos*.
13   See Dietrich Bonhoeffer, *Letter and Papers from Prison* (New York: Touchstone Books, 1997).
14   See David Resnik, "Philosophical Foundations of Scientific Ethics" based on a workshop given on July 17, 1993, at Eastern Michigan University's Corporate Education Center and published at www.physics.emich.edu/mthomsen/resn1.htm.
15   See Chapter 11 of the *Bhagavad-Gītā*, which must surely be one of the most remarkable descriptions of mystical vision in the world.
16   See, e.g., Lawrence Kohlberg, *The Psychology of Moral Development: The Nature and Validity of Moral Stages* (New York: HarperCollins College, 1984). See also Ronald Duska & Mariellen Whelen, *Moral Development: A Guide to Piaget and Kohlberg* (New York: Paulist Press, 1975) and Brenda Munsey, ed. *Moral Development Moral Education and Kohlberg* (Birmingham, Ala.: Religious Education Press, 1980). Kohlberg has written a number of books, and there is a considerable literature on his model of moral development.

CHAPTER 6

NONHARMING

Nonviolence entered world politics as a concept with "Mahatma" Gandhi and was subsequently boosted by folk heroes like Martin Luther King, the Haitian preacher Jean-Bertrand Aristide, or the Salvadoran archbishop Oscar Romero. Although nonviolence has become a popular concept, I nevertheless prefer to speak here of nonharming, which has a wider connotation.

Nonharming, or *ahimsā* in Sanskrit, is the bedrock of all spiritually based morality.[1] The three major cultural traditions of India—Hinduism, Buddhism, and Jainism—all promote the supreme moral value of nonharming. In the *Yoga-Sûtra* (2.30) of Patanjali, representing Hindu Yoga, nonharming is listed among the five observances or disciplines (*yama*), which are said to be universally applicable. Patanjali's position has its precise parallels in Buddhism and Jainism. Of these three great traditions, Jainism offers the most comprehensive treatment of nonharming.

Historical Jainism was founded in the sixth century B.C. by Vardhamāna Mahāvīra, an older contemporary of Gautama the Buddha, but tradition knows of twenty-three earlier teachers, who are known as "ford-makers" (*tīrthankara*).[2] Like Hinduism and Buddhism, Jainism offers a spiritual path leading to liberation and originally was a strictly monastic community. Later, it also acquired lay followers. Jainism is marked by vigorous asceticism and has produced a long line of great world-renouncing adepts.

The degree of asceticism favored in Jainism can be seen in the early dispute over whether Jaina monastics should wear clothes or go about naked. Around 300 B.C., the community split into those wearing clothes (i.e., the Shvetāmbaras) and those wearing only space (i.e., the Digambaras). The lifestyle of Jaina monks and nuns has exerted a strong influence on the laity, and so we find that even ordinary householders are keenly practicing the ideal of nonharming, which is known as the "supreme virtue."

According to Hemacandra's *Yoga-Shāstra* (2.31), spiritual practice is worthless if it is not based on the abandonment of all harmful activity. The *Dashā-Vaikālika-Sūtra* (1.1-4) of the Shvetāmbara branch, which was possibly composed in the fifth century B.C., opens with the following verses:

Virtue (*dharma*) is the greatest blessing: Nonharming, restraint, and asceticism. Even the deities honor a mind always set on virtue.

As a bee satisfies itself by drinking the nectar of tree blossoms, without damaging the blossoms, so also do here on Earth the liberated ascetics, who, seeking food among the blossoms as it were, delight in devoted offerings.

Like bees from flowers we subsist, without burdening anyone, on whatever has been prepared.

Thus even in such a vital aspect of life as nutrition, the Jaina monastics walk lightly on this planet, wishing to avoid harming or even inconveniencing others. Nonharming is the "great vow." As the *Dashā-Vaikālika-Sūtra* (1.11) puts it:

Sir, the first great vow is abstention from harming living beings. Sir, I will abstain from harming any living beings, be they small or large, mobile or immobile. I myself will not harm any living being. I will not harm any living being through another. I will not condone the harming of any living being. For as long as I live, I will not cause, instigate, or condone [harming others] through the threefold means of body, speech, and mind.

The Jaina moral code fobids monastics to dig in the soil, to mold lumps of clay, or to deliberately dry out lakes or even puddles. Everything must be left as undisturbed as possible, for life is to be found everywhere. They are not even to make or put out a fire because fire too has its own life forms that must be neither molested nor destroyed.

When walking, the Jaina monastics must gaze at the ground to avoid stepping on living beings, including vegetation. They must gently remove any insect that happens to have landed on their body, being careful not to place it where it would cause inconvenience to other life forms. Some monastics—the Sthānakavāsins—wear a strip of cloth called *muhpatti* over their mouth to avoid accidentally swallowing insects, etc. For the same reason, the Jaina monastics abstain from fanning themselves and swimming or even wading in water.

Similar to Hinduism and Buddhism, Jainism maintains that all harmful acts cause karma, which then binds the person to the finite world characterized by suffering. According to the *Tattvārtha-Sūtra* (7.13) by Umāsvāmin, harming or *himsā* is cutting off another's life out of carelessness. Harming can be intentional or accidental in the performance of one's allotted work. Needless to say, the Jainas abhor hunting, vivisection, capital punishment, animal sacrifice, personal revenge, and war. The rules for the laity are far less strict than those for the monastics, as lay people are permitted, within reason, to defend their own life.

The key to nonharming is said to be constant vigilance or attentiveness. As the above scripture explains (7.4), this is to be cultivated by means of the following five practices:

(1) guarding one's speech
(2) guarding one's thoughts
(3) care in walking
(4) care in lifting and laying down things
(5) careful inspection of one's food and drink

The *Tattvārtha-Sūtra* (7.11) also recommends the following four practices:

(1) benevolence toward all beings
(2) delight in all beings
(3) compassion for all beings
(4) forbearance toward all those who are misguided in their behavior

We become inattentive and negligent through negative mental states, notably anger, greed, delusion, pride, or passion. These cloud reason and cause carelessness, which may lead to the injuring or even killing of other beings. Clearly, the Jaina moral code demands acute mindfulness. This is even more impressive when one knows that the vow of nonharming belongs only to the second of eleven stages of spiritual development in the life of a lay practitioner and fourteen stages in the case of a monastic. A balanced moral life serves to free attention for the meditative process and the cultivation of those higher virtues that lead to liberation.

Only when we are whole-heartedly and also energetically established in the virtue of nonharming does life "flow" for us or, as Patanjali tells us in his *Yoga-Sūtra* (2.35), does enmity cease in our proximity. A classical example would be that of a yogin or yoginī in whose presence a tiger becomes a pussycat or a mad elephant is instantly appeased. Yogic lore is full of such stories, and we need not dismiss them generically as mere fiction or phantasy. In yogic terms, a person for whom nonharming has become second nature emanates an aura of peacefulness that is infectious.

How, we may ask, is it then possible for Gandhi, the twentieth-century apostle of nonharming *par excellence*, to become the victim of a fanatical Hindu assassin? From a traditional perspective there are at least three possible answers to this legitimate question. The first is that the claim of inner peacefulness creating calmness in other beings is wrong. The second answer is that Gandhi did not have sufficient peacefulness to protect himself against such a violent onslaught. The third possible response is that karma is karma and that it was his time to die. This final answer leaves no opening for a discussion, but I would like to consider the first two possible answers a little bit.

Having sat in front of several great Yoga masters, I know from first-hand experience that they radiate a palpable peace that certainly makes deep meditation very much easier. I also have no reason to suspect contemporary Yoga masters are lying when, in order to encourage their disciples, they occasionally share incidents from their life that illustrate the contagious nature of nonharming. And if contemporary adepts have such true stories to tell, there is no reason to dismiss wholesale traditional accounts either.

Despite the adulation Gandhi received and still receives from millions of his countrymen, he never claimed to walk among the spiritual giants of his motherland. In fact, on a number of occasions he freely admitted that his spiritual practice was a great challenge for him, in particular his vow of sexual abstinence. This confession hardly adds up to a peaceful mind, which one would expect of a high-caliber spiritual illuminatus. Several of his closest admirers and associates have written about his sadness. For instance, remembering the period just six weeks before Gandhi's death, his secretary wrote: "I found Gandhi to be the saddest man that one could picture when I rejoined him in the middle of December, 1947."[3] He also observed: "I watched day after day the wan, sad look on that pinched face, bespeaking an inner anguish that was frightening to behold."[4] In her preface to *Last Glimpses of Bapu*, Manubehn Gandhi, Gandhi's grandniece, remarked about "the agony and unrest in Bapu's mind."[5]

The Hindu honorific "Mahatma" ("Great Soul") enveloped Gandhi with an ambiance of sanctity that makes any attempt at an objective appraisal of the man and his work almost sacrilegous.[6] But however much we may admire Gandhi for upholding so resolutely the virtue of nonviolence in political action, it is impossible to overlook his bouts of depression, periodic self-doubt and self-incrimination, occasional despair, and persistent inner turmoil over his struggle with the ascetical lifestyle he had chosen. Thus Gandhi often described himself as being "surrounded by darkness" and every so often questioned his life's work, feeling that so little had changed in Indian society and politics. In one of his diary entries, we even find Gandhi blaming the enduring violence in India on a "grave defect" within himself.[7] In the last two years of his life, Gandhi undertook two long fasts to bring about changes within himself and his social environment. While he was fasting, Gandhi's mood was upbeat but as soon as the fasts ended, his mental turmoil resumed by his own admission.

Whatever we may want to make of the contagious nature of inner peacefulness, any sane person can easily appreciate that doing harm to others is less desirable than treating them kindly. Yet, we may ask whether the yogic ideal of nonharming is realistic. After all, as the American poetess Maya Angelou couched it and as the sensationalist media remind us daily, Nature supposedly has no mercy at all. Do earthquakes, volcanoes, hurricanes, tornadoes, tsunamis, drought, hunger, and disease not amply exhibit Nature's "bloody tooth"? Stars burst into existence and collapse obliterating surrounding stellar objects; galaxies collide and die extinguishing untold numbers of living creatures. How can we think of the universe as a benign place? Things are at war with each other? At the level of the material cosmos, mayhem offers a constant counterpoint to a dynamic equilibrium. As Heraclitus is said to have noted, "It is necessary to understand that war is common, strife is customary, and all things happen because of strife and necessity."

Now, if the microcosm is supposed to be a reflection of the macrocosm, how does this go with the apparent ferociousness of Nature? Are we wolves among men, after all? These questions are fair enough, and to answer them in a meaningful way, we must look at the highest rather than the lowest aspect of the universe. From a yogic viewpoint, the universe is not composed of the visible (material) spectrum only; there also are vast unmapped subtle regions, and, above all, there are the realms of the higher mind, or what the Greeks called the *logos*. We must look to those rarefied dimensions of the cosmos to appreciate that conflict defines only a small aspect of existence. In its uppermost reaches, the universe is ever more simple and ever more balanced, or tranquil. The Indian sages would say that the upper echelons are composed of the exalted "substance" of *sattva*, the psychocosmic factor of luminosity and transparency—that fine veil or filter that subtly separates the mind or mental environment from Reality itself.

True enough, the cosmos is in a process of constant self-transformation. Forms appear and disappear (or become transformed into other forms). In Patanjali's Classical Yoga, the Sanskrit term *parināma* suggests the incessant activity of change, or transformation, of the cosmos. According to Patanjali, only the Spirit, transcendental Being-Awareness, is not subject to change. The Buddha arrived at a similar conclusion when he spoke of the "three marks" of conditioned existence: finitude, impurity, and suffering.

That the world should be riddled with limitations is readily obvious to us. That it also should have an "impure" quality is a thought that is likely to be foreign to the Western mind. But we can understand this traditional label better when we consider how our experiences are shot with imperfections, flaws, or faults. Our own personality has any number of blemishes, and the mind through which we perceive the world is riddled with all sorts of prejudices, so that our perception and understanding of things are often distorted. Above all, our emotional life is largely colored by anger, fear, envy, jealousy, and other negative emotions. All these can be viewed as impurities.

Finally, many people look askance at the Indic notion that "everything is suffering." After all, we do enjoy experiences of pleasure and delight and maybe even moments of utter ecstasy. In order to understand what is meant, we need to remember one aphorism in Patanjali's *Yoga-Sutra* (2.15), which states: "Everything is suffering for the discerner." The word "discerner" (*vivekin*) is instrumental here, because we must be endowed with a degree of mental sensitivity, or discernment, to appreciate that even the most sublime and blissful experience includes an element of suffering, simply because any experience is bound to end. Just as we were overwhelmed with bliss or joy, the same bliss or joy will drop away again and leave us in a state of longing for more or possibly in a condition of emotional destitution (the mystics' famous "dark night of the soul").

In deploying discernment, we activate the higher mind, or faculty of wisdom, which in Sanskrit is called *buddhi*. This word is constructed from the verbal root *budh*, meaning "to awaken, be awake." It is the same root from which is also derived the past participle *buddha*, meaning "awakened." This organ of wisdom, corresponding to the Neoplatonic *logos*, is a suprapersonal faculty, which, ontologically speaking, resides at the apex of cosmic existence. According to Hindu Yoga, only the transcendental Reality, which is acosmic, can claim a higher place. The higher mind is in a way a portal—the only portal—to that transcendental Reality. We can compare it with a translucent veil that separates us from Reality. When we identify—and thus "activate"—the higher mind through the application of discernment, we transcend the lower rungs of the cosmos and, figuratively speaking, move as close to Reality as is possible without actually becoming one with it or, in nondualistic terms, being it.

The higher mind is inherently nonviolent. It tends as much toward peace as toward illumination. Alas, it is only one aspect of our total mental apparatus, one dimension of the multi-layered cosmos. At the lower level of mental existence, a different situation prevails. As the Latin saying has it: *Homo homini lupus*, "Man is a wolf among men." Sigmund Freud, who quoted this adage in *Civilization and Its Discontents*, remarked gloomily: "Who has the courage to dispute it in the face of all the evidence?"[8] An array of psychologists, sociologists, and philosophers have reiterated the same view, arguing that aggression is innate to human beings. But if aggression is an aspect of our intrinsic nature, so are kindness and gentleness, as well as the ability to go beyond our murderous instincts. Only an utter pessimist would deny that it is possible for us to live in peace and harmony with our fellow beings and Nature at large. We do not *need* to murder a hundred million people by warfare and torture, as we have done in the twentieth century alone. We are free to follow a different course of action. We can cultivate nonharming and pacifism as a viable lifestyle.

Nor is this a mere utopian ideal. Here and there in bygone eras, and even in our own time, men and women have succeeded in living together cooperatively, without war and strife. Some monastic communities have achieved this great ideal at least during part of their history. Village communities in sheltered environs, which are too remote and uninteresting for curious tourists, are still achieving it today. Cooperative living is preferred not for any metaphysical reasons, but simply because everyone's survival depends on it.

At a particular level in a person's spiritual development, however, nonviolence becomes something more than an economic or social exigency. It becomes an expression of the inner feeling of unity with everything—reverence for life. This is Lawrence Kohlberg's fifth level of moral development, as introduced in Chapter 5. As previously emphasized, nonaggressiveness has been hailed as a cardinal virtue in all major religious traditions of the world. It has for millennia been central to Yoga. In Patanjali's two thousand year old *Yoga Sūtra*, nonharming is introduced as one of the five practices constituting the "great vow" of the moral disciplines (*yama*).

What does the virtue of nonharming mean to the contemporary Western Yoga student? Is *ahimsā* merely a romantic ideal? Or is it, as Patanjali insists, universally and unconditionally valid? Is nonharming still plausible in our far more complex world? In our century, it was Gandhi, a master of Karma Yoga (the path of self-transcending action), who held up high this ancient ideal. He also demonstrated its political effectiveness through the policy of passive resistance. Gandhi inspired the modern philosophy and practice of nonviolent social action through demonstrations, petitions, strikes, pickets, sit ins, teach ins, go-slows, hunger strikes, and so on. Nonviolent campaigns of social reform have been surprisingly successful, bearing witness. as they do, to the transformative and even socially healing power of nonharming.

Our answer to the question posed above must be: *Ahimsā* is as relevant today as it was at the time of Patanjali and of Gautama the Buddha, another stalwart spokesman for nonviolence. What we need to examine is *how* we can translate the ideal of nonharming into daily practice for ourselves, our local community, and our global society.

Members of some Jaina sects in India wear a mask to filter the air, lest they should unwittingly inhale and take the life of small creatures. This is a religious custom that few of us would find practical to follow. Nevertheless, upon closer inspection this extreme discipline suggests a useful lesson: Our life is built on the sacrificial death of others. With every breath, we are involuntarily murdering creatures—a massacre that not even a mask can prevent. For, we constantly annihilate billions of invisible microbes, so that we may live. We ourselves are a link in the great food chain of life, destined to die and be food for microbic creatures.

We need not stop breathing or feeding ourselves, or constantly "turn the other cheek," but we must appreciate how we owe our life to other beings and how they owe their lives to us. When we truly see this vast interconnectedness, it becomes easy for us to cultivate an attitude of reverence for life, which is essentially an attitude of nonharming and of ego transcending love. Yoga means to sensitize us to the fact that we are not alone in the universe but are interdependent cells of a vast cosmic body. Spiritual life is largely a matter of taking responsibility for the things we have understood about ourselves and the world we live in. This includes assuming responsibility for our destructive aggression, as it reveals itself to us in ever subtler forms.

As Patanjali states, nonharming must be practiced under *all* conditions, which means in thought, word, and deed. Our self inspection can begin with our active life. For instance, we may ask ourselves whether our livelihood involves harming others in ways that are not morally justifiable. As a writer I have become progressively aware of the fact that I am co responsible for the destruction of forests, which are the habitat of countless species, not least human tribal groups. Some time ago, I started taking remedial actions, such as using recycled and acid free paper that will last longer, reusing envelopes and other paper rather than discarding them, and so on. I compose my writings and make all corrections on the computer, avoiding to print out manuscripts unless I absolutely have to. I shred whatever scrap paper I accumulate and then use the slivers to pad envelopes and packages. I know that I can and should do more.

In general, recycling should be a universally adopted practice. Especially in the so-called developed countries, we have been consuming Earth's resources as if there were no tomorrow. I will talk about consumerism in connection with the moral observance of greedlessness. But greed also leads to acts of violence. It could even be said to be inherently violent and harmful. Ransacking natural resources is not an exercise in kindness. The use of fossil fuels, a nonrenewable resource on which our overconsuming Western civilization has staked its fortune, serves to illustrate how greed can cause widespread harm not only to our fellow human beings but to our planet's biotic environment as a whole. According to British Petroleum, the world's proved oil reserves are estimated at around 1,188 million barrels. The worldwide *daily* consumption of oil stands around c. 80 million barrels, with the United States alone consuming a lion share of over 20 million barrels per day.

As has dawned on the world's governments, oil is becoming an increasingly precious commodity and from 2020 on its supply will increasingly lag behind demand, while the extraction of oil will become more and more expensive. It has been estimated that even a ten-percent shortage would have a devastating effect on an oil-dependent economy like that of the United States and, in the absence of alternative sources of energy, even provoke a full-fledged civilizational collapse. Oil is needed not only to power automobiles and farm equipment but also to produce plastics (including computers), building supplies, medicines, pesticides, fertilizers, and on and on. The U.S. government is well aware of this looming crisis, not least because its top officials have sizeable personal investments in the oil industry.

As Nafeez Ahmed, among many others, has shown in his book *Behind the War on Terror*, the United States did not invade

Iraq in 2003 in order to depose an evil dictator, spread democracy, or fight terrorism, but quite simply to secure its economic and political interests in the Middle East. Above all and contrary to the U.S. government's repeated public reassurances, it fought primarily over oil. Since the invasion, over 26,000 civilian men, women, and children have been killed, and the killing is continuing.

Ahmed, the executive director of the Institute for Policy Research & Development in Great Britain, relied on official sources to reach his devastating conclusions. Rightly, he and other critics of the Anglo-American attack on Iraq have argued that "the Bush and Blair governments must be held accountable and prosecuted under international law for war crimes and crimes against humanity in Iraq."[9] Being informed about the wider ramifications of our lifestyle is an integral part of being morally responsible.

Another important area of self inspection in terms of the virtue of nonharming concerns our social relationships—our family life, friendships, and business relationships. How are we destructively aggressive in them? Where could we begin to practice *ahimsā* more seriously? How do we typically express our unlove and lack of compassion or empathy? One way of going about this is to ask our relatives and friends to give us their undoubtedly painful feedback. We may find that we tend to come across as overly aggressive, cold, or unapproachable. We may be told that we don't let others express themselves, or that we are poor listeners. There are numerous ways in which we can practice unlove, just as there are countless ways in which we can be nonviolent, kind, and compassionate.

It is important to acknowledge that we can cause harm not only by our physical actions but also by our speech. Words spoken in anger or out of inconsiderateness may hurt others as much as or even more deeply than a slap in the face. Harmful words are especially damaging when addressed to children. Great damage can be done when we call a child "stupid," "worthless," or "loser."

They can absolutely shatter his or her self-esteem. But hurtful and humiliating comments like this also can do harm to an adult when uttered in anger by an authority figure. The proverb "Sticks and stones may break my bones, but words will never hurt me" may be useful as a mantra of self-exhortation, but it is in principle wrong. Abusive language definitely leaves scars. It definitely hurts the recipient and indirectly also does damage to the abuser.

A further area of psychological harming is competitiveness when it exits the realm of childhood play and becomes callous. Today competitiveness is a popular concept in education, business, and sports. Even entire countries compete with each other—economically and politically. For now, the United States is in the lead and, I propose, illustrates on a large-scale the unhealthy side of competition. Whenever we try to outstrip each other, we merely strip ourselves and others of dignity.

When we think of competitiveness in sports, we think of the Olympic Games. Originally, the Olympics held in ancient Greece, consisted in a footrace. After the thirteenth Olympiad, other events were gradually added. They were celebrations honoring the gods. Participants had to take an oath that they would for ten months train properly and then compete fairly. Fines were imposed on those who broke the oath, and the money raised from such penalties was used to create new statues of Zeus for the temple at Olympia. Since their nineteenth-century revival, the Olympic Games have become a fierce international competition in which national pride plays as much a role as personal victory. This four-yearly event, which attracts thousands of athletes, has been riddled with boycotts and scandals of bribery, as well as cheating, especially in the form of forbidden performance enhancing drugs. The Olympics have become an example of unhealthy, even lethal competitiveness.

Be that as it may, the competitive spirit has clearly no place in Yoga. Yet, around the world every year several major

Yoga competitions are held to determine who is the most able contortionist of the day. The egregious error in this sort of event is that it equates Yoga with posture practice and posture practice with flexibility and flexibility with showmanship. Yoga competitions, in my view, violate the very principles on which authentic Yoga is based. They are celebrations of the ego.

Even yogic meditation has been subjected to such parody. In 2003, a competition was held in the Golden Dome at the Maharishi University of Management in Fairfield, Iowa, to test the flying skills of practitioners of Transcendental Meditation. Seated in the lotus posture, with legs interlaced and soles facing up, twenty-five men demonstrated their jumping skill. Supposedly by entering into a "blissful" state of meditation, the body becomes able to leap like a frog. The winner managed to leap 30 inches into the air—a respectable, if bizarre, physical feat, which, however, has absolutely nothing to do with the spiritual purpose of Yoga. Even if he could have leaped to the top of a skyscraper, the feat would remain quite nonspiritual though, I daresay, would give skeptics of the paranormal something to think about. While this kind of competition may seem more ridiculous than harmful, it does give the public the wrong impression about Yoga.

An aspect of lifestyle in which serious harm is done consistently and on a large scale is our Western diet.[10] Unless we are strict vegetarians (Vegans), we consume meat, fish, eggs, and dairy products. Quite apart from any health or religious considerations, we must be concerned about the fact that our dietary habits are locked into a vast industry that is not known for its moral scruples. The meals we eat tend to come from factory farmed animals that are widely treated with unbelievable cruelty ("because animals don't feel pain as we do"). Cows are kept artificially pregnant to yield milk, while their calves are deprived of motherly affection. They are forced to eat a monotonous milk replacing diet to ensure that their flesh will be as white as the market demands, and are routinely fed unmarketable parts of their own kind—the cause of Mad Cow Disease. Let us recall here that every year over 30 million heads of cattle—individual beings—are slaughtered for American consumers and the world market.

Literally *billions* of chickens, another favorite food item, are slaughtered every year in the United States alone. They spent their short lives typically cooped up in torturously small cages of less than half a square foot. They are generally debeaked (without anaesthesia) to avoid that these highly stressed birds hurt one another. Broiler chickens, moreover, are fed hormones to speed up their growth process, causing them often to die of congestive heart failure. The Humane Slaughter Act does not apply to poultry, and consequently the slaughter methods are utterly cruel. The birds are dropped en masse into electrified water to stun them (an inefficient procedure) after which they have their throats cut by a mechanical blade. Some birds, who have remained conscious during the electric shock treatment, struggle on the conveyor belt and the blade may miss them altogether. All of them, even those who are still conscious, are next dropped into a tank of boiling hot water; every year, millions of birds are literally scalded to death in this fashion. The ones who have managed to escape all these cruel processes by fluttering to the factory floor are either killed or wounded by equipment or simply starve to death.

Pigs, another favorite item on the menu, are taildocked and kept in miniscule pens in the dark and are forced to eat out of sheer boredom. They can do nothing but wait to be slaughtered in an often brutal way. In the United States, 100 million bovine creatures experience this gruesome fate every year.

Our food habits maintain an industry of some seventy billion dollars a year in the United States alone—an industry that every day blatantly violates the ideal of nonharming. It significantly contributes, moreover, to the massive degradation of the environment. Forests and wetlands are converted into pasture land, worsening the serious problem of soil erosion and the pollution of rivers. It has been calculated that the 1.3 billion heads of cattle on Earth produce some 100 million tons of methane annually as part of their natural digestive process. This is c. 20 percent of the global production of this particular pollutant, which has been identified as the second most important factor in global warming after carbon dioxide.

With factory farming, the dairy industry has its own share of animal cruelty, and the cost of milk, cheese, and eggs goes well beyond those products' retail price. The popular concern about adequate protein intake in one's daily diet is misplaced. Protein has twenty-two amino acids, and the eight amino acids that the body cannot produce by itself are readily available through a balanced vegetarian diet. In fact, excessive protein intake has been associated with various types of cancer. I have enjoyed a vegetarian diet for years, though have thus far not made the transition to Veganism, because I find soy products hard to digest and also because there is some evidence that the regular consumption of soy can cause cancer.[11] I do, however, buy "organic" and "free-range" dairy products.

It is interesting how many people do not count fish as sentient beings. Experiments have demonstrated, however, that fish can learn from experience. Researchers at the universities of Edinburgh, Leeds, and St. Andrews in Great Britain have shown that the learning ability of fish is comparable to that of land animals. They share information amongst themselves about food, resting places, and mating. In other words, they are not the mindless creatures they are often made out to be. Other investigations have clearly established that fish have pain receptors and hence can experience pain. The notion that they lack a brain to experience pain, entertained even by some researchers, is ill founded. Thus Lynne U. Sneddon, a fellow of the Natural Environment Research Council at the University of Liverpool, observed that trout exposed to toxic substances react with stress behavior similar to other vertebrates.[12] This new finding makes sport fishing, into "the cruelest, the coldest and the stupidest of pretended sports," as Lord Byron remarked about angling with acute perceptiveness, despite his lack of moral judgment in some areas of his own life.

To put it mildly, we do not do well by our animal fellow beings. We not only eat them in massive quantities but also subject them to all sorts of cruelty and suffering in pharmaceutical research for medicines and cosmetics. Likewise, our hunger for entertainment leads to animal abuse in a variety of ways—from sport hunting to rodeos and races. Even their captive existence in seemingly innocuous zoos and circuses entails cruelty. First of all, they are deprived of enjoying their natural habitats and secondly, they are often condemned to live in very confined spaces and made to suffer cruelty and neglect. Whatever educational or entertainment value those animals might be thought to have, zoos and circuses plainly do violence to them. The movie *Born Free* tried to convey this to the public back in 1966, as did *Free Willy* in 1993. Yet, the public continues to support zoos and circuses.

Much could also be said about how our conspicuous consumption directly or indirectly disadvantages Third World nations, where every year millions of people are starving to death from hunger. In 2003, the United Nations announced that, despite international efforts, world hunger is on the rise. In Africa and Asia, some 850 million people are chronically hungry. Some people argue that the plight of nations so far away is surely their own problem. Apart from being rather heartless, such an attitude ignores the ruthless political maneuvers by governments of the developed nations in those parts of the world.

To interpolate a little bit of relevant history here, in the days of colonialism, the Portuguese, British, Dutch, French, Italians, and Germans subjected the African nations to sustained economic exploitation. They robbed that continent of gold, ivory, and spices, and, worse, enslaved its people. The foreign administrators even dared to argue that colonialism was good for the colonized countries, as it developed their economic infrastructure—an argument that is still very much alive in U.S. political circles.

With America declaring its independence in 1776, Britain lost its westernmost colonies. It was well prepared, however, for this event, because it had started its paramount rule over India nineteen years earlier, which was to last for 190 years. Upon the discovery of vast oil reserves in the Middle East, Britain wasted no time to make its political presence felt in the Gulf States, yet it was the United States that snatched the controls early on.

The United States, a young nation by comparison with the nations of Europe, made its first imperialist move in 1893 when it annexed Hawaii. Five years later, it wrested control of the Philippines from Spain. In the early twentieth century, the United States expanded its economic and political influence into South America, the Middle East, and the Far East. Since 1945, successive U.S. administrations have been involved in numerous foreign "interventions," the most recent being Afghanistan and Iraq in 2001 and 2003 respectively. Neocolonialism is alive and kicking and continues to spread mayhem and suffering.

All our actions have moral repercussions. For instance, doing our duty as an upright citizen involves paying taxes every year. But what are we to do when, as in the case of the United States, our taxes help support a vast military industry that revolves around violence and that in effect leads to countless deaths and untold pain around the world? It would be foolish to withhold taxes, but voting citizens can push for a long overdue tax reform and, more importantly, protest against the ways in which tax money is spent.

Finally, the ideal of nonharming is not confined to physical or verbal expression. Our very thoughts are powerful. They determine the subtle ways in which we relate to life, especially how we interact with others. If we are emotionally down, we tend to drag our environment down. If we feel buoyant, our happiness uplifts those around us. Even if we do not mean to harm another person, our coldness or indifference is a form of harming. Whenever we are not present as love, we inevitably reduce our own life force and the life force in others. Hence we must become fully responsible for how we are present in the world, even when we are on our own, because our field is interconnected with the fields of everyone and everything else. *Ahiṃsā*, as a manifestation of self transcending love, is a building block of spiritual practice. Genuine Yoga is impossible without it.

Nonharming is certainly not an old fashioned value. We ought to consider and talk about it more. As Gene Sharp suggests in his study *The Politics of Nonviolent Action*, one of the reasons why many treatments of political histories all but ignore nonviolent means of political action is that the further dissemination of such means would not be in the interest of politicians and military leaders.[13] Naturally, more than considering and talking about nonharming, we are strongly encouraged to practice it.

Nonviolence makes for peace of mind and, as Gandhi has demonstrated, even works as a tool for sociopolitical change. Revolutionaries, who lack the virtue of patience, bring suffering on their fellow humans by wanting radical change immediately. They merely create the ground for equally rash and bloody counterrevolutions. Contrary to the American activist Ward LeRoy Churchill, author of *Pacifism as Pathology*, nonviolence in politics is *not* only not crazy but the only means of longer-term societal transformation.[14]

The strongest form of harming is killing another human being. I would like to briefly discuss this next in the contexts of the death penalty and euthanasia, before turning to the equally controversial subject of suicide. All mentally sane individuals would consider murder a vile and morally reprehensible act. Yet, every year, private citizens and governments deprive numerous fellow humans of their life. World statistics on homicide are unreliable and not easily available. It would appear, however, that homicide is extraordinarily high in a number of Latin American countries—with Columbia leading the field with c. 80 murders per 100,000 people. Compare this with Canada's average rate of 1.73 for 2003 and the United States' 7.4 for 2004. In other words, every year, tens of thousands of murders are committed around the world. Other violent crimes run into the tens of millions.

The U.S. government has congratulated itself for a decline in violent crime for several years in a row. But when we hear that in 2004 *only* 24 million violent crimes were committed—amounting to 21.4 per thousand people or one violent crime for every 47 residents—the picture still looks incredibly dismal and disturbing. Canada's violent crime rate for 2004 was 300,000—not an impressive figure either, given that country's much smaller population of 32 million. Statistics for the various European countries are also not encouraging. Violence seems to be an integral, if unhealthy, aspect of modern civilization.

One of the more morbid features of this trend is capital punishment, which today is still practiced by 75 nations.[15] The methods used are lethal injection, electrocution, gassing, hanging, beheading (in Saudi Arabia and Iraq), and even, in truly medieval fashion, stoning (in Iran and Afghanistan). According to Amnesty International, in 2004, at least 3,797 people were executed in 25 countries. In that year, China alone executed 3,400 criminals, which presumably included a significant number of political prisoners. Recently, in Nigeria, women have been executed whose only crime was abortion. Eight countries are known to have executed under-age prisoners in recent years, and the United States amended its laws on capital punishment for child offenders only in 2005.

The United Nations' Universal Declaration of Human Rights, which was ratified in 1948, guarantees all human beings the right to life. In direct response to this document, in whose creation the United States played a leading role, 118 member states abolished the death penalty. Not so the United States, which even ignores its own Declaration of Independence, which lists the right to life as the first of the natural rights guaranteed to an American citizen. Thirty-eight of its 50 states uphold the barbaric tradition of the death sentence, and in 2000 a total of 85 prisoners were executed. What makes this legal practice particularly shameful is that since 1973, as many as 121 felons who were condemned to death have been found innocent in the nick of time, and often after spending numerous years on death row. No one knows how many of those who have been executed were innocent after all. At least one inmate was executed even though he had been found innocent prior to his execution, and merely because his lawyer had missed a filing date. Nor can we tell how many of the 3,400 prisoners on death row in the United States today (in 2005) will die for crimes they did not commit. Since there is absolutely no evidence that capital punishment acts as a deterrent, this legal practice is both morally inexcusable and nonsensical. In 2005, California governor Arnold Schwarzenegger, lost voters by refusing to pardon Stanley Tookie Williams, even though he had reformed his character and for thirteen years had done his best to serve the youth of his country.

Capital punishment highlights the fact that the criminal justice systems of virtually all countries of the world are about punishment and vengeance rather than the rehabilitation of criminals. By and large, forgiveness and compassion are conspicuous by their absence. While some criminals are obvious psychopaths and should be restrained from doing further harm to others, many deserve a second chance and with appropriate help. In 2004, America's overcrowded federal prisons and local jails held 2,131,180 people, over 40 percent of which were African Americans, who make up only about 12 percent of the U.S. population (!). The national "war on drugs" and the "three-strikes" law have ensured a veritable explosion of the prison population in the United States. Apart from costing tax payers over $40 billion annually, the system is terribly flawed in a number of ways. Annually, some 600,000 inmates are released back into mainstream society without being given adequate assistance to rebuild their lives, so that within a couple of years, nearly half of them find themselves incarcerated again.

The high incidence of emotional and sexual abuse in prisons by both inmates and guards is responsible for rising suicide and AIDS rates among prisoners. Every year, some 90,000 male and 40,000 female prisoners are being raped. Guards tend to be indifferent toward these crimes and unsympathetic toward the victims. Prisons are inhumane factories, and their product is suffering. This has little to do with civilized humanity. I am reminded of one of Gandhi's ironic but deeply meaningful quips. When asked what he thought of Western civilization, he responded: "I think it would be a good idea."

When thinking about nonharming in the context of modern life, we must include at least a brief consideration of euthanasia, which made historical headlines at the end of World War II with the discovery that about four million Jews had died in the gas chambers of the Third Reich. In 1939, Hitler instituted his "euthanasia" initiative, which was to rid the country of the terminally sick, disabled, and insane—a horrible notion that, moreover, was quickly extended to those who were considered racially "inferior" like the Jews and Gypsies. After these shocking revelations, euthanasia understandably became a taboo subject. Not until the 1990s did some European countries dare legalize medical euthanasia for compassionate reasons. In 1998, the state of Oregon passed a law permitting assisted suicide in certain extreme cases.

But, then, only a year later the U.S. physician Jack Kevorkian, whom the media dubbed "Dr. Death," was found guilty of second-degree murder in the state of Michigan for giving a lethal injection to a patient suffering from Lou Gehrig's Disease. Tastelessly enough, the death was shown on *60 Minutes*, a CBS television program watched by millions. Kevorkian admitted to assisting 130 patients in committing suicide over the years and had been acquitted in four previous trials, one being a mistrial. He himself died in prison in 2005. His case polarized the medical and legal community. Some regarded him as a ghoul, while others saw in him a hero and pioneer, feeling that every person should have the right to determine his or her time of death, before illness makes it impossible to die with dignity.

Not a few physicians believe that it is better for a terminally ill or incapacitated patient who is enduring great suffering to die as peacefully as possible than to prolong his or her agony by medical intervention. The Dalai Lama and other high lamas of Tibetan Buddhism have expressed a similar view.[16] Existing laws, however, do not allow hospitals to disconnect such patients from life support systems, even when relatives and the patients themselves beg for it. From a yogic perspective, euthanasia and assisted suicide as conventionally practiced fall short of a good death, as they do not assist the person in what Yoga calls conscious dying—in which the mind is brought under control through meditation. Without this method, the sages maintain, suicide leads to undesirable mind forms in the post-mortem state. But the afterlife is generally not a matter of concern either to the suicides or the medical profession.

While voluntary suicide is known to traditional Yoga, it is permitted only to those adepts who, having fully overcome their attachment to the body-mind and feeling no further use for earthly existence, can enter an advanced state of meditation and simply drop their mortal coil at will.[17] In the Jaina tradition, the practice of *sallekhana* is allowed to those practitioners who are terminally ill or advanced in age. It essentially consists in fasting to death combined with meditation.[18]

Generally speaking, suicides have no spiritual practice associated with them but are committed out of sheer desperation.[19] Enough suicides are happening around the world to have given rise to a whole new academic discipline—suicidology. We can appreciate the seriousness of this problem when we look at U.S. statistics for 2002: 790,000 people attempted to commit suicide and over 31,000 succeeded at it. It is the third leading cause of death among young people between the ages of 15 and 24.

The suicide rate among the elderly—in the over-65 age group—also has been steadily climbing, possibly because of their experience of sickness, social isolation, and neglect. With the breakdown of the traditional extended family, our Western civilization has become callous toward its elderly. The abuse and neglect of older adults is one of the saddest aspects of "progressive" societies. According to the National Elder Abuse Incidence Study conducted in 1998 in twenty American counties, for every reported incident of elder abuse, five go unrecorded. Of the 44 million elderly, aged 60 and over, alive in 1996, as many as 450,000 were subjected to abuse or neglect in a domestic setting. These outrageous figures need no commentary but incisive preventive action.

For the spiritual practitioner, there is no dearth of social issues to be examined in the critical light of the great moral value of nonharming. Violence is all-pervasive. Report after report has shown that the portrayal of violence on television, in video games, and in films desensitizes our youth to violence.[20] Little has changed over the years. Personal freedom, even when it leads to bad and destructive choices, is sacrosanct in democratic societies, unless of course their respective governments feel the need to clip citizen's wings to promote nefarious agendas like the invasion of Afghanistan and Iraq. Then constitutional rights are unhesitatingly curtailed and trampled on.

In the midst of the moral swamp surrounding us, most people find it nearly impossible to make good moral judgments and choices. Many prefer to avoid the big issues and confine their interest to the limited arena of their own personal lives. The question is whether we can in fact live morally without bearing in mind the larger concerns of violence and injustice. If we are all interconnected and interdependent, as the spiritual traditions insist, we are our brother's keeper after all. Harming others is ultimately harming oneself. At the same time, nonharming begins at home—in regard to our own body-mind, our immediate relatives, and the animal friends for whom we are responsible. Next we can expand the practice of nonharming to our friends and coworkers, and finally to all sentient beings. If we cannot be kind and compassionate, we can always abstain from deliberately harming others. In his acceptance speech at the Nobel Prize ceremonies in Oslo in 1989, the Dalai Lama spoke these true and timely words:

> People inflict pain on others in the selfish pursuit of their happiness or satisfaction. Yet true happiness comes from a sense of brotherhood and sisterhood. We need to cultivate a universal responsibility for one another and the planet we share. Although I have found my own Buddhist religion helpful in generating love and com¬passion, even for those we consider our enemies, I am convinced that everyone can develop a good heart and a sense of universal responsibility with or without religion.[21]

ENDNOTES, CHAPTER 6

1   See Koshelya Walli, *The Conception of Ahimsā in Indian Thought Accord-ing to Sanskrit Sources* (Varanasi: Bharata Manisha, 1974) and Unto Tahtinen, *Ahimsā: Nonviolence in Indian Tradition* (London: Rider, 1976). See also Sethia Tara, ed., *Ahimsa, Anekanta and Jainism* (Delhi: Motilal Banarsidass, 2004).
2   On the history, culture, and philosophy of Jainism, see Peter Flugel, *Stud-ies in Jaina History And Culture: Doctrines And Dialogues* (London: Routledge, 2006). See also Chatterjee Asim Kumar, *A Comprehensive History of Jainism* (Calcutta: Firma KLM, 2003) and D. C. Jain and R. K. Sharma, *Jaina: Philosophy Art and Science in Indian Culture* (Delhi: Sharada, 2002), 2 vols.
3   Pyarelal, *Mahatma Gandhi: The Last Phase* (Ahmedabad, India: Navajivan Press, 1958), vol. 2, p. 681.
4   Ibid., p. 686.
5   Manubehn Gandhi, *Last Glimpses* (Agra, India: Shiva Lai Agarwala, 1962), p. 2. "Bapu" is the familiar Hindi honorific for father.
6   See Karen E. James, "From Mohandas to Mahatma: The spiritual metamor-phosis of Gandhi," Essays in *History*, vol. 28 (1984), pp. 5-20. This is a peer-re-viewed online journal. James's article contains much valuable information about Gandhi's mental life.
7   M. K. Gandhi, *Collected Works of Mahatma Gandhi* (New Delhi: Publica-tions Division, Ministry of Information and Broadcasting, Government of India, 1982), vol. 86, p. 302.
8   Sigmund Freud, *Civilization and Its Discontents*. Transl. and ed. by James Strachey, with a biographical introduction by Peter Gay (New York: W. W. Nor-ton, 2d. ed. 1989), p. 69.
9   Nafeez Mosaddeq Ahmed, *Behind the War on Terror: Western Secret Strat-egy and the Struggle for Iraq* (Gabriola Island, British Columbia: New Society Publishers, 2003), p. 302.
10 See the incisive and well-documented book by John Robbins, *Diet for a New America: How Your Food Choices Affect Your Health, Happiness and the Future of Life on Earth* (Tiburon, Calif.: H. J. Kramer, repr. 1998). See also his subse-quent book *The Food Revolution: How Your Diet Can Help Save Your Life and Our World* (Berkeley, Calif.: Conari Press, 2001). The literature on the important moral issue of animal rights is vast and steadily growing. The following books make a good starting-point. Michael Fox, *Returning to Eden: Animal Rights and Human Responsibility* (New York: Viking Press, 1980); Tom Regan, *The Case for Animal Rights* (Berkeley: University of California Press, 2004); Tom Regan and Peter Singer, eds., *Animal Rights and Human Obligations* (Englewood Cliffs, N.J.: Prentice-Hall, 1976); Peter Singer, *Animal Liberation* (New York: Harper-Collins, 2002); Peter Singer, ed., *In Defense Of Animals: The Second Wave* (Ox-ford: Blackwell, 2005), and Margaret Midgeley, *Beast and Man: The Roots of Hu-man Nature* (London: Routledge, rev. ed. 2002).
11 On vegetarianism, see Daniel A. Dombrowski, *The Philosophy of Vegetari-anism* (Amherst: University of Massachusetts Press, 1984); John Lawrence Hill,

The Case for Vegetarianism: Philosophy for a Small Planet (Lanham, Maryland: Rowman & Littlefield, 1996), and Colin Spencer, *Vegetarianism: A History* (New York: Four Walls Eight Windows, 2002), which was originally published under the title *The Heretic's Feast*. See also Shabkar Tsogdruk Rangdrol, *Food of Bodhisattvas: Buddhist Teachings on Abstaining from Meat* (Boston, Mass.: Shambhala Publications, 2004).

12   See Lynne U. Sneddon, V. A. Braithwaite, and M. J. Gentle, "Do fishes have nociceptors? Evidence for the evolution of a vertebrate sensory system," Proceedings of the Royal Society B: *Biological Sciences* (London 2003), no. 270, pp. 1115–1121.

13   See Gene Sharp, *The Politics of Nonviolence* (Manchester, Great Britain: Porter Sargent Publishers, 1973). 3 vols. See also Elise Boulding, *Cultures of Peace: The Hidden Side of History* (New York: Syracuse University Press, 2000) and Howard Zinn, *The Power of Nonviolence: Writings by Advocates of Peace* (Boston, Mass.: Beacon Press, 2002).

14   See Ward Churchill, *Pacifism as Pathology: Reflections on the Role of Armed Struggle in North America* (Arbeiter Ring, 1998).

15   See Roger Hood, *The Death Penalty: A World-Wide Perspective* (Oxford: Clarendon Press, 3d ed. 2002).

16   See the Dalai Lama's letter published in *Asiaweek* (November 1, 1985), p. 73.

17   See S. Settar, *Inviting Death: An Indian Attitude Towards the Ritual Death* (Leiden: Brill, 1989). See also Katherine K. Young, "Euthanasia: Tradition Hindu views and the contemporary debate," in Harold G. Coward, Julius J. Lipner and Katherine K. Young, eds., *Hindu Ethics: Purity, Abortion, and Euthanasia* (Albany, N.Y.: SUNY Press, 1989), pp. 71–130.

18   See T. K. Tukol, *Sallekhanā Is Not Suicide* (Ahmedabad: L. D. Institute of Indology, 1976).

19   For a psychiatric perspective on suicide, see the comprehensive monograph by Karl Menninger, *Man Against Himself* (New York: Harvest Books, 1938).

20   See, e.g., A. C. Huston et al., *Big World, Small Screen: The Role of Television in American Society* (Lincoln: University of Nebraska Press, 1992); Robert M. Liebert and Joyce Sprefkin, *The Early Window: Effects of Television on Children and Youth* (New York: Pergamon, 3d ed. 1988); Edward L. Palmer, *Television and America's Children: A Crisis of Neglect* (New York: Oxford University Press, 1988).

21   Cited after "The Government of Tibet in Exile" website at www.tibet.com maintained by The Office of Tibet, the official agency of His Holiness the Dalai Lama in London. See also Sidney Piburn, ed., *The Nobel Peace Prize and the Dalai Lama* (Ithaca, N.Y. Snow Lion, 1990).

CHAPTER 7

TRUTHFULNESS

Like nonharming, truthfulness is counted among the perennial virtues in Yoga and other spiritual traditions. Thus in the
Mahānirvāna-Tantra (4.75–77), composed several centuries ago,
we find the following declaration:

> There is no virtue greater than truth; there is no sin great-
> er than falsehood. Therefore a mortal being should take
> refuge in truth with his entire self.

> Worship without truth is futile. Recitation (*japa*) without
> truth is useless. Asceticism (*tapas*) without truth is as un-
> fruitful as seed on barren soil.

> The nature of truth is the supreme Absolute. Truth is the
> most asceticism. All actions should be rooted in truth.
> Nothing is superior to truth.[1]

The second-century adept Patanjali included truthfulness in
the five moral disciplines that make up the "great vow." As the
Sanskrit word *satya* suggests, truthfulness relates to *sat*, which
we can translate as "Reality" or "Being." Truthfulness brings forth
the truth, whereas "a lying mouth kills the soul," as we learn from
Proverbs (1:11). According to the *Yoga-Sūtra* (2.36), a Yoga prac-

titioner who is firmly grounded in this virtue is able to make whatever he says come true. This is no mere tautology. Rather, masters of Yoga have been known to utter statements that at the time seemed off the wall but that nonetheless came to pass exactly as predicted.

As in the case of nonharming, truthfulness must be practiced in regard to body, speech, and mind. Thus it entails closely related virtues like honesty, rectitude, integrity, sincerity, candor, openness, and guilelessness, which are meant to countermand lying, dishonesty, insincerity, fraudulence, pretension, duplicity, hypocrisy, affectation, posturing, and so on. Without truthfulness, human society would be virtually impossible. We can readily appreciate how the numerous lapses in truthfulness that mark our modern society needlessly complicate our lives.[2]

The ancients warned that one day a time would come when people would fail to respect the truth, and this would contribute to their ruin. Today we are literally surrounded by lies and pretense—from advertising and commerce to politics and interpersonal relationships. For many of us, truth is what is expedient in the moment. Morally, we almost enjoy inhabiting large gray areas where neither truth nor falsehood is thought to apply. While there is something appropriate about our having jettisoned the sometimes intolerant black-and-white morality of earlier eras, since life is a web of many colors, we tend to apply this newly found wisdom rather indiscriminately, usually with the intent to gain personal leverage. We have largely relativized moral behavior and often are frightfully uncertain of the moral choices before us.

Moral relativism has become a favorite philosophy. Since what is considered moral varies from culture to culture, there are, it is argued, no absolute moral values. That means, so the story goes, we are free to make up our own moral rules or even to subscribe to moral anarchism if it so pleases us. As I have explained in Chapter 5, moral relativism is based on half truths and is unviable as a philosophical stance. Virtues, in my view (which is the classical view), are intrinsic to our being. They are connected with Abraham Maslow's "being values."[3] At a certain point in a person's intellectual, moral, and spiritual development, what is felt to be virtuous can be expected to be similar between individuals of equivalent maturity. Thus spiritual virtuosos who are morally mature are in unanimous agreement that truthfulness is a highly desirable, life-enhancing and even liberating virtue, which should be seriously cultivated.

Before I discuss the virtue of truthfulness in more detail, I would like to take stock of the many ways in which our contemporary Western civilization, which is spreading its tentacles worldwide, is infringing this exceptional moral value. For the most obvious and grave failure in upholding the virtue of truthfulness, we must turn to the foundational ideological beliefs that most people in the so-called developed countries share either consciously or unconsciously. These beliefs, which are of a metaphysical nature, include the following ideas:

1. **There is an external, material reality, which is juxtaposed to a subjective mind or consciousness.** Secularists, moreover, maintain that mind or consciousness is an epiphenomenon of the brain (i.e., material reality). By contrast, the spiritual traditions give precedence to Mind, Awareness, or Self over objective existence, which leads to a morality that emphasizes personal responsibility for one's destiny.

2. **We live in the material world and must give preeminence to its demands.** Even those who consider themselves religious subscribe to this view at least in practice, although they may, in principle, know and

feel that—in the words of Jesus of Nazareth—one ought to aspire to the Kingdom of Heaven first and foremost. If they were to truly listen to the Nazarene's teaching, their religiosity would become converted to actual spiritual practice.

3. **Rigorous spiritual disciplines, as promoted by Yoga and other similar traditions, are not relevant because**
   (a) they are completely nonsensical since, as secularists assume, spiritual realities or dimensions do not exist; or
   (b) they are intended only for a select few (i.e., monastics), who have a capacity for contemplation; or
   (c) one's belief in religious doctrines (e.g., "Jesus will save me") is sufficient; or
   (d) leading a morally sound life is enough.

4. **We are embodied and hence appropriately identify with the body-mind at least while we are on Earth, which, for secularists, is in fact the only possible place to be.** In contradistinction, the spiritual traditions universally teach that the material body is not what it appears to be and that identification with the body is indeed a major error, because it involves a forgetting of our spiritual identity, however that may be conceived. Because of the close association of the mind with the body, we can speak of a body-mind. We consequently also identify with the various mental (or psychosomatic) processes that are associated with physical existence, notably negative emotions like fear, lust, and anger. In the extreme, we even identify with objective properties, such as one's

belongings, name, reputation, and so forth. A lot of drama (i.e., "karmic stuff") occurs around these diverse identifications.

5. **We have no control over the actual death process whenever death happens to occur.** Despite people's misidentification with the body-mind, they generally do not believe that the mind can have detailed control over bodily functions, particularly the processes involved in dying. The more sophisticated spiritual traditions consider control of the body-mind during death as crucial. They maintain that *how* we exit from embodied life, whether consciously or involuntarily, determines the quality of the state of disembodiment. A controlled exit ensures a positive aspect of the mental continuum in the hereafter. There is ample proof that the great adepts of Yoga enjoy such mastery.

There are several corollaries to the above premises, but itemizing them would go beyond the scope of the present discussion. Seen from a spiritual perspective, these five suppositions amount to a form of self-deception—a lie. Since these untrue beliefs are foundational, they inevitably affect our whole life, and they do so negatively. In fact, they disempower us by giving us the illusion— perhaps temporarily consoling but ultimately frustrating—that we are largely at the mercy of destiny, divine providence, or cosmic accident.

Once we see ourselves as basically helpless, we have all the excuse we need to indulge in blind faith in religious or scientific dogmas, as well as laziness, indifference, ennui, unresponsiveness, irresponsibility, and so on, which all are recognized as vices on the yogic path. What we have then is, pretty much, our everyday consensus reality—the dreamlike reality of sleepwalkers.

It is from within this consensus reality that many people allow things to happen, not because of some overwhelming mood of renunciation but out of sheer apathy: the unmitigated devastation of the environment; political machinations leading to injustice, discrimination, corruption, oppression, and war; the economic exploitation of Third World countries in the old colonial spirit and unbridled consumption at home; world hunger and poverty; runaway crime and juvenile delinquency rates; widespread alcoholism and drug addiction; elder neglect and abuse, and on and on.[4]

I would next like to address just three public areas in which the virtue of truthfulness is at an all-time low: politics, the corporate world (including advertising and marketing), and the media. First to politics, which has a particularly disastrous record when it comes to mendacity. Of course, it is always individual politicians rather than politics in the abstract who are perpetrating this particular vice.

In their bestselling book, Major Garrett and Timothy J. Penny identify fifteen whoppers that American politicians like to tell and that the media like to endorse.[5] They include "religion and politics don't mix," "immigration hurts America," "the budget will be balanced," and "social security is a sacred government trust." Anyone even a little bit familiar with U.S. politics knows that religious fundamentalism is an important feature of the contemporary American political landscape; immigrants are necessary to keep the economy going; the budget will never be balanced so long as politicians promise tax cuts and simultaneously grant upward of $400 billion to the military. As Vice President Dick Cheney has admitted, by 2018 social security will start to pay out more than is paid into it, and eventually the system will collapse. The above lies are routine for politicians, and they tell and often even get away with them, because most people seem to want to hear them. The American electorate is remarkably forgetful and oddly forgiving about being duped over and over again.

Who would not remember George Bush senior's infamous promise "Read my lips; no new taxes" reiterated *ad infinitum* during the 1988 presidential election and promptly broken upon his nomination. His filial successor in the White House appears to have an even greater aptitude for political dishonesty and prestidigitation.[6] Not a few independent political commentators have noted that the current U.S. regime is notorious for lying to the public on a grand scale. The unjustified and, according to international law illegal, attacks on Afghanistan and Iraq became possible only because of a whole series of lies, which are still being disentangled for eventual public reckoning. Perhaps the biggest contemporary political whopper is that the war on terrorism is winnable and is presently being won. The body bags containing U.S. soldiers on flights back home to grieving families tell a different tale, and for this reason are carefully kept out of the public limelight.

We also recall president Richard Nixon's insincere assurance "I'm not a crook" when the Watergate scandal hit the news in 1972 and subsequently led to his resignation under the threat of impeachment.[7] But for many, William (Bill) Jefferson Clinton epitomizes the political Pinocchio syndrome, though this might change after the current presidency has run its course. Former president Clinton repeatedly lied under solemn oath and was impeached on grounds of perjury and obstruction of justice but, amazingly, was acquitted and allowed to finish his second term in office.[8]

Political subterfuge, to be sure, is by no means unique to America. Scandals involving corruption, lying, and other vices are regular news items around the globe. To give just one example from Europe: In 1999, the North Atlantic Treaty Organization (NATO) warred against the former Yugoslavia, after that troubled country had been shaken by civil war for three years. For the first time since World War II, Germany, a member of NATO, committed its armed forces to war in an international cause. Understandably,

Germany's politicians were anxious to convince the public that the war was just and was intended to end a "humanitarian disaster" in Kosovo. But it appears, they were resorting to lies and exaggerations to win support for their commitment to military intervention. The lies are on record in the form of the former German defense minister Rudolf Scharping's widely circulated book on the Kosova war.[9]

At the beginning of 2001, the news media—in particular the program "Monitor" on the ARD television network—showed that the claims about a massacre in the town of Racak in Kosovo had been fabrications between the Kosova Liberation Army (KLA) and a US agent. The humanitarian crisis, in other words, began only with the bombing by NATO troupes. During its twenty-month-long occupation, NATO effectively displaced 200,000 civilians causing even more hardship than the country had experienced prior to the NATO intervention. Former president Slobodan Milošević, who is currently (2005) standing trial for war crimes at the International Criminal Tribunal for the Former Yugoslavia, should rightly be joined by his many accomplices—NATO officials and their political supporters in Germany, the United States, and elsewhere.

Among the skeptic observers of the political scene, an honest politician has almost become an oxymoron. Lust for power, approval from the public, and job security do not make good bedfellows for truthfulness. Already Confucius felt troubled by the collapse of the political institutions of his era and attributed it to the lack of virtue in politicians. This traditionalist sage believed that virtue (Chinese: *de*) was generated by the diligent observation of the prescribed rituals, which close the vital nexus between the living and the ancestral spirits. It is the kind of feedback loop that respects and even celebrates the interconnectedness of everything and, in turn, ennobles those who observe the ritual obligations. The absence of virtue in politicians, we could say, creates a vacuum that is then filled by corrupt intentions and actions, causing not only moral degradation in the political arena but also in the public. We find the same teaching in the *Bhagavad-Gītā*.

Today, whenever politicians do not indulge in outright lies, they demonstrate great skill in the art of evasiveness. Evasiveness can be and often is an essentially untruthful maneuver. Individuals, corporations, and governments frequently employ vagueness and elusiveness as ploys to conceal unpalatable truths, so that they can stay with their adopted programs, however foolish, reprehensible, or even illegal these may be.

Here is a good, if sad, example from Canadian politics. When, in 1987, the government signed a comprehensive "free trade" agreement with the United States, it failed to explain to the Canadian public exactly what this disastrous agreement involved. Instead, the government spent over CAN $25 million on printing and distributing oversimplified and essentially misleading summaries of a 300-page document. As the Canadian political gadfly David Orchard noted in his book *The Fight for Canada*, the trade agreement was a monumental mistake that favored only one of the trade partners—the United States.[10] As one U.S. government official gloated afterward: "We've signed a stunning new trade pact with Canada. The Canadians don't understand what they've signed. In twenty years, they will be sucked into the U.S. economy."[11]

In this particular instance, political watchdogs managed to mobilize the public to protest the legitimacy of the agreement. The Canadian government, however, opted to ignore the declared will of the people and went ahead with ratifying the treaty. As a result, Canada's economy was pushed into a recession, but more importantly the treaty, which is still in effect, represents the most serious challenge yet to its independence as a nation and culture.

When considering the vice of lying in politics, we cannot fail to also pay critical attention to the military and the secret service, which after all are branches of government. Angered by the war in

Afghanistan and not mincing words, Max Uechtritz, the director of news and current affairs at the Australian Broadcasting Corporation, remarked at a conference for news executives in Singapore: "We know for certain that only three things in life are certain—death, taxes and the fact the military are lying bastards."[12] In the United States the lies begin, it would appear, with military recruitment officers who, under pressure to procure new cannon fodder for the Iraq war, have taken to misrepresenting the kind of job training, education, veteran benefits, and "bonuses" the military has to offer. Of course, they also typically forget to mention the hazards and horrors of military service at a time of war or the hardship experienced by the recruits' families back home. In particular, they neglect to apprise their "victims" of the fact that a a high percentage of military personnel deployed in Iraq returns suffering from posttraumatic shock and strange physical symptoms that outside observers have attributed to depleted uranium exposure.

As the injustice and cruelty associated with the war in Iraq became better known, student organizations started to actively oppose the presence of recruitment officers at high school and university campuses around the country. Seeing the military trap into which uninformed students may fall, a growing number of educators also have sought to make schools into "demilitarized zones." Considering that the Pentagon employs some 15,000 recruitment officers, who in 2004 managed to hook over 200,000 recruits, there is a lot of lying or at least the sin of omission happening. The American Friends Service Committee (AFSC), an international social justice organization, has taken up the cause of exposing the confabulation tactics of military recruitment.

Yet, we must recognize that lying is probably as old as military conflict. From a military viewpoint, it may be foolish to let the enemy know the truth in every case. As the Greek dramatist Aeschylus observed 2,500 years ago, "Truth is the first casualty in war." Deception or trickery has long been a part of the martial game to gain advantage in a situation of conflict.[13] In wartimes, and if the war is just (and only if), we may find lying to the enemy—"war propaganda"—pardonable. But lying to the public at home, whether in war or peace, is a whole different matter. Lying consistently to "protect" nebulous military interests is simply a pathological trait.

That subterfuge and lying are part of any secret service organization should come as no great surprise. That they are also regularly subject to corruption should require no big leap of the imagination. Over the years, there have been a number of book-length exposés of the Central Intelligence Agency (CIA), which clearly suggest that such organizations are suffering from moral bankruptcy.[14] On numerous occasions, the CIA, which was created by President Harry S. Truman in 1947 as a cloak-and-dagger branch of the U.S. government, has been shown to be implicated in illegal activities—from simple theft and burglary to protecting Nazi war criminals, drug trafficking, toppling regimes, assassinating unwanted political or public figures, organizing military invasions, funding and arming rebels, and supporting dictators.[15] The Federal Bureau of Investigation (FBI), formed in 1908 during the Theodore Roosevelt regime, has a similarly mixed history.[16] Not unexpectedly, intelligence organizations in foreign countries have had comparable problems with integrity.[17]

Often closely associated with politics, the corporate world also appears to be a whole universe of massive public deception. The tobacco industry's lies are by now well known. In the 1999–2000 American election campaign, the all-powerful pharmaceutical industry spent over $260 million on influencing politicians through intensive lobbying, advertising, and campaign contributions. In return, elected officials continue to provide lavish subsidies at huge profits to drug companies, who then deceive the public by overcharging for prescription medicines under the pretext that research is expensive.

In 2004, the American billionaire Martha Stewart was found guilty by a grand jury of lying to investigators and was sentenced to a term of five months in prison and a further five months under house arrest. Stewart's transgressions were small fry by comparison with the Enron scandal in the opening year of the third millennium, which was the watershed of a whole line of corporate scandals that shook Wall Street in the following years.

Enron, once the world's leading electricity and natural gas corporation with an annual revenue of c. $100 billion, went bankrupt in 2001 thanks to fraudulent mismanagement. The company's chief financial officer ended up being sentenced for fraud, money laundering, and conspiracy, along with several other company officials. Investors were cheated out of their investments, and Enron's employees are unlikely to ever see a penny of their monthly contributions to the company's pension plan. Again, at the core of this major fiasco lay lying and cheating, prompted by indomitable greed.

The once prestigious Bank of England collapsed in 1991; in 1996, one of the bond traders of Japan's Daiwa Bank was sentenced to prison for fraudulent trading and the bank was ordered to pay fines of $340 million. In 2002, WorldCom admitted to making "account errors" of $7 billion. In the same year, the well-known investment bank Merrill Lynch was twice fined $100 million for engaging in questionable market analysis. In 2005, the insurance brokerage company Marsh & McLennan agreed to pay $850 million in restitution to policyholders after the company was found guilty of unlawful business practices. Also in 2005, Xerox corporation was fined $10 million by the Securities and Exchange Commission for overstating its profits by $3 billion. In the same year, in Europe, the fraud trials started against the dairy industry giant Parlamat.

In the meantime, back in the United States, President George Bush promised to clean house in the corporate sector to restore the public's confidence. Yet his own cabinet's affiliations especially with oil corporations have come under public scrutiny. The energy giant Halliburton, formerly run by Vice President Dick Cheney, was forced to repay the government $27.4 million for grossly overcharging meals delivered to the U.S. military in Iraq. More significantly, Cheney—a major shareholder of Halliburton—has been profiting on an $8 billion "no-bid" contract between the government and a Halliburton subsidiary (Kellogg, Brown & Root). This is just the tip of a huge iceberg of corporate corruption, cheating, and lying.

The mass media lie largely by omission. Never very accurate in news reporting to begin with, the major media have clearly fallen under the spell of the corporate world, which has a vested interest in politics. Naturally, the corporate oligarchs, like their political cronies, do not want the public to be in possession of accurate knowledge about the things that are vital to capitalist organizations. This has been ably presented by Robert W. McChesney and other writers.[18] The Universal Declaration of Human Rights guarantees that "[e]veryone has the right to freedom of opinion and expression" and that "this right includes freedom to hold opinions without interference and to seek, receive, and impart information and ideas through any media regardless of frontiers." Yet, the notion of "free press" has become something of an oxymoron, and critics have started to view the media as a branch of government.

Precisely because the mass media are in cahoots with politicians, it is difficult to get reliable and in-depth reporting about vitally important events like the Iraq war, the devastation of Yugoslavia by NATO forces, the continued use of depleted uranium in weapons, or the outrageous abuse of Iraqi prisoners of war. Were it not for the guts and determination of some risk-taking journalists, the public at large would remain ignorant of most of such political and military shenanigans, as well as of their equivalents in the corporate sector.

Because the mass media clamor for revenue from the corporate sector, they become vehicles for the inveterate public relations lies generated by corporations. Every year, corporations spend billions of dollars on cunning PR to project as angelic an image as circumstances will permit, while they continue to gouge the public, swindle the government, and pollute the environment. In private life, this obnoxious trait is known as hypocrisy. As the Australian sociologist Alex Carey put it: "The 20th century has been characterized by three developments of great political importance: the growth of democracy, the growth of corporate power, and the growth of corporate propaganda as a means of protecting corporate power against democracy."[19]

That even religious organizations are not immune to lying, especially when they are connected with politics, has been amply demonstrated in the case of American televangelism. The disgraceful scandals surrounding American TV evangelists of the ilk of Jim Bakker, Fred Price, W. V. Grant, Bob Larson, and Peter Popoff have driven home the lesson that religious leaders are not immune to corruption, tax fraud, lying, theft, money laundering, and embezzlement. Nor are men of the cloth in other religious traditions free from what their congregations would consider the cardinal sin of lying, never mind that of concupiscence.[20] Jim Bakker's religious empire was worth over $170 million when he was sent to prison in 1987.

In 2004, no less an august religious institution as the Vatican was caught in a whopping lie when Cardinal Alfonso López Trujillo, the Vatican's spokesperson on family affairs, stated that "relying on condoms is like betting on your own death." The Vatican's hardline stance on birth control is well known, but this time the World Health Organization (WHO) immediately stepped forward to condemn the cardinal's deceitful propaganda. WHO reminded the cardinal that in light of the AIDS epidemic, which is devastating Africa, even a method that is not altogether safe is better than none at all.

Obviously, people and organizations lie for various reasons, but usually it is out of self-interest and very rarely to protect or benefit someone else, as is the case with those "little white lies." While Aristotle maintained that lying is always unforgivable, Plato takes a slightly different view in his *Republic* when he allows statesmen and physicians to lie when it does no harm but actually benefits others. The *Tiru-Kural* (Saintly Aphorisms) of Tamilnadu, which is ascribed to the third-century South Indian saint Tiruvalluvar, expresses a similar sentiment: "Even falsehood is of the nature of truth, providing it yields faultless results" (verse 292). In the moral morass of contemporary civilization, such leniency toward politicians, is a prescription for disaster.

Even in private situations, when we subscribe to the view that the end justifies the means, lying for the "good" of others can backfire in many ways. It is clearly preferable to steer a course of honesty in all matters, unless an overwhelming sense of compassion prompts us to withhold the truth from someone who would otherwise be harmed. St. Augustine thought that even compassionate lying represents an unwarranted deviation from the truth and that it is better to remain silent than to succumb to any kind of lie. Only what Catholic theologians call a "jocose lie"—a lie that it is unequivocally intended as a joke—is not a violation of the truth.

Hypocrisy is feigning good qualities that we know we do not possess. It is definitely a form of lying. In October 2005, Pope Benedict XVI felt the need to address the hypocrisy of politicians who profess the Christian faith but often vote against Vatican rulings. In his opening sermon, the Pope remarked that "the type of tolerance which permits God as a private opinion but refuses to allow him in the public arena, is, in the reality of the world and our life, not tolerance but hypocrisy." The 250 bishops attending the synod were deliberating on whether political hypocrites ought to be denied communion. A typical example is afforded by Canadian Prime Minister Paul Martin, who voted in favor of same-sex marriage despite considering himself a devout Catholic. He protested that as a legislator, who respects the separation of Church and State, he must not allow his personal conscience interfere with the business of politics. Both the Pope's concerns and Martin's response highlight the fuzzy edges between private beliefs and public duties and loyalties, as well as between personal conscience and absolutist religious doctrine.

For decades the Papal See has turned a blind eye toward openly Catholic politicians who transgressed the sixth commandment, "Thou shalt not kill." Of course, there has long been a controversy over the correct translation of this commandment, with the Jews insisting that this divine ordinance addresses murder rather than killing in general. Nevertheless, the frequent infringement of this biblical law by Catholic politicians—as when they instigate or endorse war—seems far more significant than Martin's legislature on homosexual unions, which is reprobate from a Catholic perspective.

The moral frailty of hypocrisy sometimes beleaguers even those of whom one would expect better, such as philosophers. Thus the eighteenth-century philosopher and educator Jean-Jacques Rousseau placed all five of his children in a Paris orphanage as soon as they were weaned. He justified his action by saying that they would otherwise have been brought up in poverty. Francois Marie Arouet, who achieved fame under his pen name "Voltaire," despised Rousseau for this lapse in moral judgment, yet he himself was given to vices of his own, notably pronounced vanity and lying when it suited his purpose. In our own time, singular hypocrisy and lack of integrity were evinced by the renowned German philosopher Martin Heidegger who joined the Nazi party while simultaneously having an extramarital affair with the Jewish philosopher Hannah Arendt, who was then a student of his.

That hypocrisy has not been unknown in the world of traditional Yoga is evident from the fact that the eleventh- to twelfth-century *Kulārnava-Tantra* (13.107), for instance, refers to rogue teachers, who have no spiritual realization and merely mislead the unwary student. This unfortunate trend is also present in contemporary Yoga where female "Yoga" instructors have been found to be bulimic and male instructors have sexually harassed female students. In 2004, *Vogue* magazine brought an article about a former model, who, during a posture class, was suffering from a severe headache, which later turned about to be from a brain tumor. Her famous Yoga instructor, however, excitedly told her that she was simply experiencing a *kundalinī* awakening, feigning knowledge he obviously did not possess. Another world-renowned Yoga instructor unashamedly claims, in the manner of a snake oil salesman of the Wild West, that his system cures all diseases.

The exclusive focus on bodily fitness and trimness by many so-called Yoga instructors, who deliberately ignore the spiritual anchorage of this age-old discipline, could itself be classified as a form of pretense—hence lying. I have raised this controversial issue in public on a number of occasions, and each time there were surprisingly many students who found excuses for the moral lapses of their teachers. My observations about hypocrisy in the contemporary Yoga movement were seldom appreciated, though no one disputed my examples. It appears that moral relativism is as much at home in contemporary Yoga circles as it is elsewhere in our present-day society.

The purpose of this sorry catalogue of personal, governmental, and corporate moral transgressions is simply to refresh the reader's memory in order to underline the seriousness of the present-day breakdown of morality. When we see moral failure so consistently throughout the history of human civilization and especially in our modern age, we may be excused for thinking that human beings are inherently flawed. As Jeremy Campbell has argued in his thought-provoking book *The Liar's Tale*, human beings are hardwired for deception and Nature herself, as Charles

Darwin put it, is a liar.[21] To win at the mating ritual or achieve success at the hunting game, not a few animal and even plant species show remarkable deceptiveness. Think of the carnivorous Cobra Lily, the fraudulent cuckoo, or the camouflage of a stick insect. Homo sapiens, particularly of the modern variety, is reckoned among the big pretenders.

We live in a world of pretense or, as the yogic sages would say, illusion. But we ourselves are largely responsible for the world as we experience it. This is not mere wooly New-Ageism. As already Immanuel Kant insisted, every perception is colored by the concepts we carry around in our mind. The mind cocreates the universe that it believes is external to and independent of it. On the one side, we have Reality; on the other, we have appearance. But if the experiential world is essentially a lie, we are the liars. When we add to this philosophical viewpoint the psychological insights of Sigmund Freud into the role of the unconscious in everyday life, our human reality looks even more specious. However, to conclude from all this, as some people are wont to do, that genuine morality is impossible for our species would be absolutely myopic and ludicrous.

For, as the greatest representatives of the world's spiritual traditions have demonstrated over and over again, human beings also are fully capable of clarity and virtue. Their own exemplary moral conduct was honed by a lifetime of mental discipline. Vice is simply a habit arising from an undisciplined, uninspected mind. As the *Yoga-Bhāshya* (1.12), the oldest extant Sanskrit commentary on Patanjali's *Yoga-Sūtra*, puts it:

> The mind stream flows in two [directions]. It flows toward the good, and it flows toward the bad. [The direction] commencing with discernment and terminating in liberation flows toward the good. That commencing with lack of discernment and terminating in conditioned existence

flows toward the bad. Through dispassion the flowing toward [transient] sense objects is checked, while through
the practice of the vision of discernment, the stream of
discernment is laid bare.

The above passage articulates a tenet that is fundamental to
all spiritual traditions, which seek to transcend our mental conditioning. It shows that the self-transcending mind is, in the final
analysis, always a virtuous mind. Essential to the central task of
creating a virtuous mind that naturally tends toward transcending the ego is the cultivation of truthfulness. To quote again from
the *Tiru-Kural* (verse 298): "Water is used to cleanse the body, but
only truthfulness purifies the mind." A purified mind is a mind
that has no unconscious programs running, which could cause
harm to others or oneself and which spontaneously rests in Reality, or Truth.

ENDNOTES, CHAPTER 7

1 The authenticity of the *Mahānirvāna-Tantra* has been called into question by some scholars, but despite its relatively recent date this Sanskrit text is a genuine mouthpiece of the Tantric tradition. For a full English translation, see Arthur Avalon (Sir John Woodroffe), *Tantra of the Great Liberation (Mahānirvāna Tantra)* (New York: Dover Publications, repr. ed. 1972). This rendering was originally published in 1913.

2 See Evelin E. Sullivan, *The Concise Book of Lying* (New York: Picador, 2001); Charles V. Ford, *Lies! Lies!! Lies!!! The Psychology of Deceit* (Washington, D.C.: American Psychiatric Press, 1999); Michael Lewis and Carolyn Saarni, eds., *Lying and Deception in Everyday Life* (New York: The Guilford Press, 1993); J. A. Barnes, *A Pack of Lies: Towards a Sociology of Lying* (Cambridge: Cambridge University Press, 1994), and David Callahan, *The Cheating Culture: Why More Americans are Doing Wrong to Get Ahead* (Orlando, Fl.: Harvest Books/Harcourt, 2004).

3 See Abraham Maslow, *The Farther Reaches of Human Nature* (New York: Viking, 1971). See also *Toward a Psychology of Being* (New York: Van Nostrand, 2d ed. 1968).

4 For a good, if sobering, coverage of social problems, see the quarterly journal *Social Problems*, ed. by James A. Holstein and published by the University of California Press for the Society for the Study of Social Problems in Knoxville, Tennessee.

5 See, e.g., Major Garrett and Timothy J. Penny, *The Fifteen Biggest Lies in Politics* (New York: St. Martin's Press, 1998).

6 See David Corn, *The Lies of George W. Bush: Mastering the Politics of Deception* (New York: Crown, 2003).

7 See Richard Reeves, *President Nixon: Alone in the White House* (New York: Simon & Schuster, 2001). Reeves writes that under President Nixon, Washington had "a White House of lies," and this despite a presidential memo to himself written in 1972 in which Nixon declared "I have decided my major role is moral leadership."

8 See the damning book by Kenneth R. Becht, *Just the Facts – A Case for Impeachment: Over 200 Documented Lies, Misrepresentations & Contradictory Statements by William Jefferson Clinton* (Chula Vista, Calif.: Black Forest Press, 1997). See also John F. Harris, *The Survivor: Bill Clinton in the White House* (New York: Random House, 2005).

9 Rudolf Scharping, *Wir dürfen nicht wegsehen: Der Kosovo-Krieg und Europa [We Must Not Look Away: The Kosova War and Europe]* (Berlin: Ullstein, 1999).

10 David Orchard, *The Fight for Canada: Four Centuries of Resistance to American Expansionism* (Westmount, Calif.: Robert Davies Multimedia Publishing, 2d. ed. 1999).

11 Ibid., p. 176.

12 The comment was made at Newsworld Asia, a conference for news executives, held in Singapore in the summer of 2002.

13   Arthur Ponsonby, *Falsehood in Wartime: Propaganda Lies of the First World War* (Newport Beach, Calif.: Legion for the Survival of Freedom, Incorpora, repr. ed. 1991).

14   See, e.g., Melissa Boyle Mahle, *Denial and Deception: An Insider's View of the CIA from Iran-Contra to 9/11* (New York: Nation Books, 2004); Tom Gilligan, *CIA Life: 10,000 Days with the Agency* (n.p.: Intelligence E-Publishing Company, 2003), and Victor Marchetti and John D. Marks, *The CIA and the Cult of Intelligence* (New York: Knopf, 1974). These books were all authored by former CIA operatives.

15   See, e.g., William Blum, *Killing Hope: U.S. Military and CIA Interventions Since World War II*, revised edition (Monroe, Maine: Common Courage Press, 2003) and L. Fletcher Prouty, *Secret Team: The CIA and Its Allies in Control of the United States and the World* (Englewood Cliffs, N.J.: Prentice Hall, 1973).

16   See, e.g., David Burnham, *Above the Law: Secret Deals, Political Fixes, and Other Misadventures of the U.S. Department of Justice* (New York: Scribner, 1996).

17   See, e.g., Christopher Andrew, *The Sword and the Shield: The Mitrokhin Archive and the Secret History of the KGB* (New York: Basic Books, 2000); Christopher Andrew and Vasili Mitrokhin, *The World Was Going Our Way: The KGB and the Battle for the Third World* (New York: Basic Books, 2005); Victor Ostrovsky with Claire Hoy, *By Way of Deception: The Making of a Mossad Officer* (North Hollywood, Calif.: Wilshire Press, 2002); Gordon Thomas, *Gideon's Spies: The Secret History of the Mossad* (New York: Thomas Dunne Books/St. Martin's Griffin, 2000), and Mark Urban, *UK Eyes Alpha: The Inside Story of British Intelligence* (London: Faber & Faber, 1997).

18   See Robert W. McChesney, *The Problem of the Media: U.S. Communication Politics in the Twenty-First Century* (New York: Monthly Review Press, 2004) and *Rich Media, Poor Democracy: Communication Politics in Dubious Times* (New York: New Press, 2d ed. 2000). See also Ben H. Bagdikian, *The New Media Monopoly* (New York: Beacon Press, 2004).

19   Cited in John Stauber and Sheldon Rampton, "Deforming consent: The public relations industry's secret war on activists," *CovertAction Quarterly*, no. 55 (Winter 1995/1996).

20   See Quentin J. Schultze, *Televangelism and American Culture: The Business of Popular Religion* (Eugene, Ore.: Wipf & Stock Publishers, 2003).

21   See Jeremy Campbell, *The Liar's Tale: A History of Falsehood* (New York: W. W. Norton, 2001). This books is a wide-ranging and highly readable discussion of "truth" and "truthfulness," as well as "lie" and "deceit," in philosophy both in classical and modern times.

CHAPTER 8

NONSTEALING

Healthy tribal societies of the past were never plagued by an epidemic of theft as is the case with our modern civilization. Their essential egalitarianism, which frowned on individuals owning more than everyone else, made theft a relatively rare occurrence. If a person was found guilty of theft, he would most likely be cursed, but in some societies the offending hand would be cut off. It was, however, almost universally acceptable, if not heroic, to steal from another tribe, especially one that was deemed hostile. Among the Arabian Bedouins, for instance, raiding another tribe was a form of institutionalized thievery. Strangely, this practice had a certain survival value, and the Bedouins made sure that they did not apply excessive force during their raids to avoid suffering the same maltreatment in subsequent surprise raids.

Tribal egalitarianism changed, unfortunately, with the encroachment of modern consumerism into tribal cultures. For instance, the numerous gambling casinos owned by Native Americans, which cater to their greedy non-native fellow citizens, are a fitting example of what happens when tribal leaders adopt consumerist values and policies. Little of the profit seems to go toward helping the native population on the various reservations. Casinos and gambling in general are part of the get-rich-quick syndrome that bedevils modern society. Few gamblers, of course, ever walk away from a slot machine or roulette or poker table with a pocketful of winnings.

Let me stay with gambling a little longer, as it epitomizes an attitude that the spiritual traditions associate with greed on the one hand and self-centeredness on the other. Gambling is one of the vices mentioned already in the archaic *Rig-Veda* (10.146), which contains a hymn known as "Gambler's Lament." The Vedic people, it would seem, were fond of gambling, which was understood as an exercise in tempting fate. The dice, in an instant, could turn a man into a homeless pauper and bestow on him a life of fear and loneliness. Even responsible gambling, as it is called today, for the purpose of entertainment is frowned upon in the spiritual traditions, simply because it is self-indulgent. In bygone days, people foolishly wagered their most prized possessions, family members, and even entire kingdoms, but fortunately modern laws forbid this kind of excess.

From another perspective, gambling is a form of theft on the part of casinos, as the odds are never in favor of their customers. One could even argue that a winner steals from the numerous losers who contributed to the jackpot. In today's coinage, the riches desired from gambling and betting come in the form of money, which, all too many people believe, makes the world go round.[1] Yet money—the grist of the capitalist mill—causes us problems by its absence and even more difficulties by its surfeit in our lives.

With the emergence of more complex societies, which evince an unmistakable rift between the haves and the have-nots, theft also became ever more prominent. In our sprawling modern civilization, theft makes its appearance in many guises—from armed robbery, burglary, embezzlement, racketeering, shoplifting, tax evasion, exploitation of foreign labor, price gouging, and copyright infringement to ecological pillaging and overconsumption. Thus, at one end of the spectrum, theft has criminal implications; at the other end, we find behavior that is morally reprehensible but generally not illegal or punishable, including avarice and its ally—lack of generosity (or miserliness). I will deal with the greed component and overconsumption in Chapter 10 when discussing the virtue of greedlessness.

As Marxists are prone to point out, exploitative capitalism itself is institutionalized theft. The invention of money in the pre-Christian era introduced a sinister factor into history, which clearly has warped human minds and hearts. At first, money was a medium of exchange—whether a coin or cowrie shell—that possessed value in itself. A silver dollar at least had the value of its silver content. Then money became more abstract, and today coins and notes have no material value in themselves and are deemed "inconvertible." This type of money, known as "fiat money," is issued by a country's central bank; in the case of the United States this would be the Federal Reserve. The value of the issued money is determined by each central bank based on its assets in terms of treasury securities. Until 1933, the U.S. Federal Reserve had gold bullion backing up its "printed" money. Now the country's—any country's—monetary base is essentially a matter of credit—that is, an economic abstraction. This has made possible the United States' present enormous national debt of around $8,000,000,000,000 ($8 trillion), though no one knows how much debt a nation with a growing economy can accumulate before this becomes problematic.

With the U.S. government going deeper and deeper into debt, it is not surprising that individual citizens also should do the same. Unlike the Federal Reserve Bank, which can always sell more treasury bonds to generate income, an individual must sell concrete goods or services to make money. For many people in the low-to-middle-income bracket, there is a limit to the number of hours they can work in order to generate income. Credit cards have become an easy way to obtain money by creating debt. The average U.S. household is currently in debt by some $8,000 in credit cards alone. To this we must add the debt owed for mortgages, automobile and other loans for which the national average is over c. $140,000 per household. Little wonder that with this national and private disregard for financial debts, every year well over 1.5 million Americans declare bankruptcy to avoid having to pay off their financial debts. From a spiritual perspective, this is theft. While declaring bankruptcy may clean a person's financial slate, his or her karmic debt remains.

I believe there is something wrong with a nation that has piled up c. $1.7 trillion in consumer credit (a misleading euphemism if ever!) and with one-third of households being found *not* credit worthy. Put differently, 11 percent of credit card debts end up with collection agencies, and seven million Americans have to take a second job to make ends meet. While there is no shortage of money in the economy, most of it is hoarded by the super-wealthy and the multinational corporations. In 2001, 5 percent of the U.S. population owned 59 percent of the country's wealth, and the situation has not improved since then. In 2005, there were nearly 700 billionaires (in U.S. dollars) in the world, who between them had a net worth of c. $2.2 trillion. Half of them are American citizens. For the past eleven years, Bill Gates has held the top position, with a staggering sum of nearly $50 billion in his pockets. By contrast, the median U.S. household was able to save under $200 that year, and no fewer than forty million (!) households were below the government's official poverty level.

Inordinate wealth—hoarding at the expense of others—is undoubtedly a form of theft. Often the wealthy acquire their riches by questionable means, and *Forbes's* annual list of the super-wealthy has been called a list of the world's supercriminals. If they are not guilty of any illegalities in the acquisition of their wealth, they all too often resort to business practices that are morally blameworthy, such as the use of sweatshops and forced child labor that wickedly exploits those who are already underprivileged.

Spiritually, such loathsome practices are plain thievery. If corporations have no conscience, consumers must develop one, or they become morally liable conspirators.

Top-level executives making millions of dollars in bonuses and stock options while ordinary workers take home a pittance also is a form of theft. No amount of expertise, training, responsibility, pressure, or time invested on the part of executives justifies the outrageous disparity between their annual earnings and the marginal income of the labor force. In 2004, corporate "big dogs" earned c. 300 times the amount of a simple worker—a clear case of theft.

In view of the lack of financial incentive that workers face and the drudgery and stress of most jobs, many employees abuse their legal entitlement to sick leave in order to take care of family or other problems but also for more frivolous reasons. According to a 2004 survey, only 38% of unscheduled absences are actually due to personal ill health. The annual costs of absenteeism in the United States are reckoned to be over $50 billion in lost productivity. The Star Wars movie "Revenge of the Sith," released in 2005, has been calculated to end up costing US employers over $600 million in absenteeism. This widespread and growing practice of adult truancy involves two vices—lying and stealing. Clearly, the corporate world has to make reasonable adjustments to create better conditions to boost worker morale. An alienated, exploited worker is neither happy nor productive, though this is not intended to be an excuse for the current abuse of the system.

Sadly, it has become fashionable among a certain group of people to expect a great deal from life but for little or next to nothing in return. This attitude is found especially in socialist countries where people expect the State to take care of them. Low work morale in Great Britain, for instance, has led many warehouses to electronically tag employees to track their movements and performance. We can expect surveillance technology to be ever more widely used around the world, with Big Brother robbing us of our privacy inch by inch. There is no knowing how the lack of trust in the workplace will affect the mental health of workers, but one thing is sure: Given current trends, life in the future will be unlike anything past generations have witnessed, and George Orwell's *Nineteen Eighty-Four* scenario of a totalitarian dystopia is fast becoming our daily reality.

In their pursuit of One World, which is a homogenized consumer planet, political ideologues in cahoots with corporate leaders are busy stealing people's freedom. The most scary theft of this kind has occurred in recent years in the United States, where right under citizens' noses the Bush regime shredded major constitutional rights under the pretext of fighting terrorism.[2] Yet, few people are informed or alert enough to protect their constitutional rights vigorously, thinking that all democratic governments are by definition benign and that a Third Reich could never happen again.

The recent theft of Americans' constitutional rights must be viewed in conjunction with the United States' refusal to ratify the Kyoto Treaty in 2001. With America being the largest polluter in the world, contributing significantly to the huge problem of global warming, this refusal represents theft on a grand scale. It effectively deprives the other 180 nations that co-signed this decisive international agreement of a benign future. Global warming has conclusively been shown to be in effect and to affect our planet's weather patterns, giving rise, among other devastating phenomena, to hurricanes like Katrina.

Clearly, we need not only inspect our own individual consumption and contribution to world-wide pollution but also monitor the performance of our political leaders and the corporations we support through our purchases and investments. A great deal of information is available online and in printed books, and there is no excuse for not taking an active interest in how we inadvertently keep a whole system of thievery going that will have major adverse effects on us in our lifetime and on our children and their children in the future.[3] The yogic virtue of nonstealing must be viewed from this larger perspective along with the virtue of greedlessness, which is discussed in Chapter 10.

Another form of theft that easily and significantly can impinge on a person's life is what is known as "identity theft." In this crime, an imposter co-opts a person's name, social insurance number, credit card information, and so on. According to two separate studies done in July 2003, no fewer than seven million Americans had their identity stolen in the preceding year. In 2004, the number rose to 9 million victims. It took a person on average about 600 hours to clear their records and recover from this crime, but it can take up to ten years to straighten out everything.

This type of crime not only causes great havoc in the victims' life; it also has far-reaching social and economic implications. So does hacking, which has been calculated to cost U.S. corporations (and therefore the end consumer) some $10 billion annually. To this we must add many billions of dollars in welfare, insurance, internet, commerce, and tax fraud. The situation is similar in other parts of the world. Are we inhabiting a planet of liars and kleptomaniacs?

What makes matters complicated is that at times jurisprudence and public morality fail to match. A judge may find a person guilty of theft, while the jury does not. Or a superior court judge's verdict is overthrown by the supreme court of the United States. Or theft in one country is not regarded as such in another. In the sixteenth century, when Spain still ruled the oceans, the courts of England and France found it convenient to give a certain legitimacy to piracy, and in light of this, the British admiral Sir Francis Drake became a folk hero to his countrymen, including Queen Elizabeth I. Piracy, by the way, is still a problem especially in South Asian waters, with nearly 4000 cases reported to the

International Maritime Organization between January 2000 and mid-October 2005, and an annual loss of about $13 billion.

Another kind of piracy that has been in the news in recent years is copyright theft, with millions of pirated music downloads from the Internet—the illegal duplication of copyrighted music. Most people see nothing wrong with this, though the affected companies and most of their artists do. The video industry is facing the same challenge and is losing millions from illegal copying of tapes and CDs. Few Internet users know that articles, poems, and art found on the Internet are typically copyright protected and that their unauthorized use is not only illegal but subject to heavy fines. From a legal angle, we know that ignorance of the law is no excuse. And yet, jurisprudence has become so comprehensive and complicated that even legal experts often argue over which laws apply in a given situation. In most cases, however, we can tell when we ourselves have stolen something or indulged in some other vice.

This is where a fine-tuned conscience comes in. Some individuals have one, others do not. With the exception of pathological thieves (i.e., kleptomaniacs in the clinical sense), everyone can acquire a well-honed conscience if they do not have one already. This does, however, require much personal work, which begins with respecting others and oneself. We adopt a moral way of life not because we want to win someone's affections (as with a toddler) or avoid punishment (as with a school child), but because we wish to harm no one and promote goodness in the world.

In his *Yoga-Sūtra* (2.30), Patanjali lists nonstealing (*asteya*) among the five aspects of a yogin's "great vow," and as such this virtue is meant to be practiced in body, speech, and mind at all times and under all circumstances. In the oldest extant Sanskrit commentary on this text, stealing is defined as "the unauthorized appropriation of things belonging to another person."[4] Nonstealing is said to be the exact opposite, and it is also circumscribed as noncoveting. In Yoga, this virtue is clearly related to the injunction against greed (*lobha*), which is considered one of the three root vices, together with ignorance and anger.

To live conscientiously in a world that has such a surfeit of thievery, racketeering, and fraud, we must first of all become fully aware of all the nuances of the vice of theft—from deliberate stealing and defaulting on payment of debts to being chronically late to work and stealing attention away from others because of a neurotic need to be the perpetual focus. What has been called passive stealing includes usury (or unfair exchange of goods and labor), the abuse of legal rights (a popular vice in America's litigious society), acts of negligence that harm another person and, most importantly, habitual overconsumption. The last-mentioned pattern must be treated as theft simply because it takes energy and opportunity away from those who are underprivileged and disenfranchised, notably fellow humans in the Third World, but also from nonhuman beings and future generations.

As St. Paul reminded the reprobate Corinthians in one of his admonitions (I Corinthians 6:10), written in c. 57 A.D., the sin of theft, like that of greed, is a transgression that prevents the offender from entering the heavenly kingdom. Not least, it violates the two great virtues of justice and charity. In his *Confessions* (2.4ff.), St. Augustine recollects his childhood prank of stealing pears from a neighbor's orchard, not because he was hungry but just for fun. This incident, which most modern readers of his work would dismiss as fairly innocent, St. Augustine judged to be a grievous sin. As a boy, the saintly churchman argued, he had the gift of reason and also knew that stealing was wrong. More than that, however, St. Augustine felt that his real sin was pride—the notion that he was above God's law.

Looking at the pear theft from a non-theological perspective, we could argue that it represents a slip in moral judgment, which might set the stage for further similar transgressions. We know that bad habits are easily formed but difficult to break. While in this case, self-chastisement seems hardly appropriate, self-inspection and a commitment to greater mindfulness can be encouraged. If we do not learn to pay attention to our small slip-ups early on, we are bound not to notice our big blunders later.

For practitioners of Yoga, even the seemingly simple act of claiming an undue amount of space for one's exercise mat in a class is, strictly speaking, a kind of theft. So is talking overly much, which steals others' time. The yogins and yoginīs of ancient times were quite sensitive to the virtue of nonstealing, which they extended even to the realm of thoughts: The mere thought of coveting someone else's possessions would qualify as theft. The Judeo-Christian tradition has a similar injunction against coveting one's neighbor's wife (at a time when women were still regarded as property). The virtue of nonstealing, as mentioned previously, is closely connected with nongrasping whose converse is voluntary simplicity.

When we practice voluntary simplicity, we also practice contentment—a virtue that Patanjali lists under the five self-restraints (*niyama*). A contended person has no need of more, and thus the thought of stealing does not even enter into his or her mind. We only resort to stealing when we feel we do not otherwise have enough. Manifestly, our modern Western civilization has a problem with contentment. Already as children, we learn to want more. In fact, entire industries go out of their way to indoctrinate children to become inveterate consumers.

If we want to discover who we are beyond prescribed social roles and adopted behaviors and consumption patterns, we would do well to enter into a period of retreat where we can encounter the true needs of our body and mind. To be sure, we can live healthily and sanely on very much less food and stimulation than the average person believes possible. Much of what we ordinarily do is mere distraction by which we steal time from ourselves and the primary work of mindful living. The true yogin is a "miser": He does not squander his or others' energy or resources but freely gives his love, compassion, and kindness, and gladly shares any surplus material goods. The only thing he steals is others' inner darkness by creating in them the space or light to engage the spiritual path.

Because the yogin is content with little and is firmly rooted in the virtue of nonstealing, he, as the *Yoga-Sūtra* (2.37) affirms, is apt to attract all sorts of riches. We can understand this literally or metaphorically. There are many stories—often demoted to mere legendary status—of masters of Yoga who received large sums of money whenever they were in need of it to create a hospital, temple, or hermitage benefiting others. Those preferring a metaphoric interpretation of Patanjali's statement can think of the virtue of nonstealing as a cornucopia of spiritual riches. But all these effects resulting from the dedicated practice of nonstealing are of course not the reason for cultivating this virtue. As a virtue, nonstealing is good in itself—a goodness that transforms not only the yogin's life but also the world around him, at least at the subtle (energetic) level of existence. Virtuous conduct ennobles the universe by transmuting chaos into cosmos.

ENDNOTES, CHAPTER 8

1   See Jacob Needleman, *Money and the Meaning of Life* (New York: Currency Paperbacks/Doubleday, 1994). See also Geoffrey K. Ingham, *The Nature of Money* (Malden, Mass.: Polity Press, 2004).

2   See Elaine Cassel, *The War on Civil Liberties: How Bush and Ashcroft Have Dismantled the Bill of Rights* (Chicago, Ill.: Lawrence Hill Books, 2004).

3   For bibliographic references, see Chapter 10.

4   *Yoga-Bhāshya* (2.30), which is traditionally ascribed to a certain *Vyāsa*. This name, however, appears to be a professional function rather than a personal name, as it means "collator."

CHAPTER 9

CHASTITY

In our era, no classical virtue has been surrounded with more controversy than chastity, which may be defined as the voluntary control of the so-called sex instinct, ranging from complete abstinence to moderation in sexual self-expression. Like nonhuman animals, our biological instincts are basic programs that allow us to relate to the stimuli of our environment swiftly and efficiently, without having to first think things through. These DNA habits are generally life preserving. Our body has all kinds of reactive mechanisms by which it seeks to sustain itself in its natural environment. For instance, we breathe automatically, and our blood carries oxygen automatically to the various organs to maintain their optimal functioning. Our eyes' irises involuntarily contract when they encounter bright light and widen when our surroundings become darker. These are physiological reflexes without which our body would not survive for long.

Instincts are reflexes that are mediated by the brain, and that is where the problem starts, as I will discuss. The survival instinct, which is known in Yoga as *abhinivesha*, is a master program that informs all our behavior and is cross-linked with all other instincts. Yet, it too is subject to the mind: We can consciously direct and even suspend this particular instinct. Thus, a mother seeing her baby in great danger will risk her own life to save the neonate, thereby overriding the survival instinct. Another powerful instinct is the sex drive, which, perhaps more than any other instinct, has been culturally modulated. As Sigmund Freud argued in *Civilization and Its Discontents* (1930), human civilization has always tampered with the instincts and thus has systematically frustrated our human quest for happiness, which he tied to the fulfillment of our instinctual needs.[1] In its repressiveness, to put it more bluntly, civilization has been a source of suffering for human beings, though we have by and large turned a blind eye to this fact. We must remember that Freud worked on this particular book during twentieth-century Europe's darkest hours, but it is impossible to dismiss his observations altogether.

Freud felt that civilization works especially against what he called the "death instinct" (*thanatos*) and also the libidinal urge. The two urges are in constant combat with each other. While the former is inherently destructive, the latter can be converted—sublimated—into creative love. By fostering the ideal of universal love, civilization suspends, as Freud saw it, genital sexuality. Sublimation is at the base of all the great cultural achievements but leaves plenty of sexual energy (*libido*) unexpressed, which is then stuffed down into the unconscious where it lives a shadow existence that, at a moment of unwariness, can emerge as a neurotic thought, emotion, or action.

From a spiritual point of view, libido is life energy expressed at the level of sexuality, that is, energy flowing out through the portals of our genitals. Life energy itself, however, is not intrinsically limited to either procreation or the experience of pleasurable sensations. In fact, it is thought to have the higher purpose of self-actualization culminating in the realization of our transcendental nature, or essential being. Thus from a broad evolutionary perspective, the expenditure of life energy at the sexual level amounts to a fateful diversion. It perpetuates our species but also our peculiar human destiny (karma), with its ego-fixation, instinctual drivenness, lack of true wisdom, and suffering.

Throughout the ages, men and women in pursuit of religious or spiritual goals have felt it necessary to control their instincts, especially the sex drive. Certainly in religious circles, they often succeeded only in repressing rather than sublimating or constructively utilizing the available life energy. The recent spate of Church scandals involving Catholic priests who seduced and raped children of both genders speaks for itself. Any consideration of yogic morality would be meaningless apart from a consideration of this unsavory state of affairs.

Since the early 1980s, dozens of Catholic clergymen, including bishops, have been forced to resign over heavy accusations of sexual abuse in the United States, Canada, Great Britain, and Ireland. Father Bryant, a former director of the in-patient clinical services at the St. Luke Institute in Silver Spring, Maryland, admitted in *America* magazine that between 1985 and 1995, some 450 priests were treated for sexual "disorders" at the Institute.

The Vatican is guilty of having protected such predatory pedophiles not only for decades but for whole centuries, thereby creating an insidious culture of deception and secrecy.[2] In the tenth century, the incestuous Pope John XII operated a brothel out of the Lateran Palace, while the fourteenth-century antipope John XXIII confessed to having raped over 200 women, including nuns.[3] At one time, the Catholic priests of Spain had sired almost as many bastard children as there were children from legitimate unions among the laity. The hundreds of millions of dollars paid out so far in restitutional fines of the recent pedophile transgressions do not make up for the emotional damage done to the abused children. The ecclesiastic cover-up of essentially criminal behavior, which the Church viewed merely as being sinful, evinces an exceptional degree of callousness toward the suffering of those children.

In 1992, Church investigators extended their inquiry to the sexual abuse of women not only in the United States but also

African countries. They found that the sexual victims of priests have included nuns, some of whom were even urged to have abortions. According to a 1996 survey by the Jesuit St. Louis University, one in eight American nuns claimed to have been sexually exploited. The Doyle-Moulton-Peterson Report, which became public knowledge during the trial of the Boston Archdiocese in 2002, states that of the 47,000 Catholic priests living in America, some 12,000 admitted to having had sexual relationships with adult women, c. 6,000 with adult men, and c. 3,000 with minors. Of the 195 Catholic dioceses in the United States, over 100 reported incidents of sexual abuse of minors. These are staggering and damning figures.

Sexual abuse on the part of clergy—Catholics and others—is of course not a recent development. It occurred in diverse religions and cultures of the past. Hiding behind the mask of their vocation's respectability, religious authorities have long been able to exploit the defenseless in this way. It is tempting to speculate that sexually repressive doctrines, particularly those demanding complete abstinence from members of the clergy, cause them to engage in pathological and criminal acts. Whether or not this is the case, however, it would still not excuse their misconduct.

Sexual abuse, unfortunately, is not confined to the religious sector. It seems to crop up like weed wherever people—especially men—have authority over others: fathers, physicians, psychiatrists, teachers, caregivers for the elderly, policemen, and not least United Nations peacekeepers. In March 2005, another scandal rocked an already troubled United Nations. This time, fifty soldiers and U.N. civilians were implicated in the sexual abuse or exploitation of war refugees in the Democratic Republic of Congo. The c. 150 allegations of misconduct, supported by videotaped evidence, included rape, prostitution, and especially pedophilia. Thus far, only one of the U.N. culprits involved has been charged with sexual abuse. Similar serious allegations had been brought against U.N. officials during the preceding decade. An independent report released in October 2005 revealed that the regulations put in place to stop such grievous wrongdoing were simply not implemented at the local level. The lack of initiative by the United Nations to stomp out this callous and criminal misconduct is symptomatic of that corrupt, bumbling international organization, which should have been disbanded long ago.[4]

Because the victims of sex crimes are understandably reticent to step forward, it is difficult to gauge how widespread sexual abuse actually is. Statistics differ widely and of course fail to convey the victim's fear, shame, guilt, confusion, sadness, or anger. Apparently, in the United States, one in four girls will have experienced some kind of sexual abuse by the age of fourteen, while one in six boys will have experienced sexual abuse by the age of sixteen. One in nine children falls victim to sexual abuse during his or her educational career. Only one in ten children is thought to tell of his or her abuse. These figures for the United States match those for other countries.

According to official U.S. statistics, in 2001 as many as 248,250 rapes and sexual assaults were reported to law enforcement.[5] But this figure is only a pale echo of the actual situation. One of the saddest aspects of the reality of sexual abuse concerns the vulnerable 1.6 million residents of American nursing homes. As has come to light in recent years, a large percentage of these elderly people is subjected not only to emotional, verbal, and physical abuse but, unbelievably, even to sexual assault. In the two-year period of 1999 to 2001, one third of America's 17,000 nursing homes were cited for almost 9,000 instances of elder abuse.

The serious social problem of sexual abuse is not unique to America, and in some countries it appears to be even worse, which is hard to imagine. As a form of violence, sexual abuse not only represents a failure to live up to the traditional ideal of a chaste life but involves a more serious moral bankruptcy in regard to the root virtue of nonharming. As human beings, the perpetrators of sexual abuse—unless mentally truly deranged—are in principle capable of controlling their instincts and cultivating a virtuous life. While self-interest—under the impetus of the survival instinct—is indeed a key factor in our behavior, it does not exhaust our behavioral repertoire. Rather, we clearly also have a self-transcending capacity, which has made the emergence of civilization possible, however shaky its foundations may be.[6]

Lamentably, the so-called sexual revolution of the 1960s and 1970s, which aimed to liberate people *from* the puritanical shackles supposedly inherited from the nineteenth century, failed to create in them the wisdom and responsibility *for* a mature moral stance.[7] Rather, the invention of the birth control pill in 1960 made casual and irresponsible sex possible on a large scale. After the brief Hippie phenomenon of "free love," sexual permissiveness increasingly assumed epidemic proportions, experiencing a temporary lull in the 1980s with the advent of AIDS. This liberal trend in sexual mores has led to the kind of uninhibited promiscuity we are witnessing today, especially among the youth.

In 2004, the British magazine *Bliss*, which is geared toward fourteen-year-old girls, conducted a survey among its young readers and discovered that one fourth of them had engaged in sexual activity, averaging three partners. A landmark report published by San Diego State University in 2005 showed that teenage sex in America follows similar patterns. This report, based on an analysis of 530 studies spanning five decades and involving nearly 270,000 respondents, revealed that teenagers are having sex more frequently and with more partners than in previous decades, and apparently with far fewer restraints.[8]

Teenage behavior unquestionably reflects the sexual conduct—or, as some would argue, misconduct—of adult society. The hypersexualization of modern culture began with the "Roaring

Twenties," the era of post-war prosperity, hedonism, movies, the prohibition, illegal "speakeasies," bootleggers, gangsters, knee-high hemlines, fashionable European lesbianism, and jazz.[9] Sex went underground after the stockmarket crash of 1929 and re-resurfaced after World War II in the Rhythm and Blues era, which witnessed a change in sexual mores, chronicled in the two Kinsey reports, *Sexual Behavior in the Human Male* (1948) and *Sexual Behavior in the Human Female* (1953). Stimulated by the Kinsey reports, Rock and Roll, the Bohemian libertinism of the Beat Generation, *Playboy* magazine, subliminal sexual advertising, and not least the sexually ever more explicit Hollywood movies, this underground or "silent" phase of the Sexual Revolution exploded into a loud cacophony in the 1960s.

It has been estimated that, today, a *tween*—a child between the ages of eight and twelve—is exposed to some 300 sexual images per day. Of course, the kids are reacting, as hoped for by the marketplace, notably the fashion industry, which finds nothing wrong with selling sexy lingerie, "Porn Star" T-shirts, and "Follow Me Boy" body lotion to them. American tweens represent a spending power of $1.7 billion, and they are superlative consumers. They also can be easily manipulated.[10] Their prepubescent sexuality, shaped by their dominant need to fit in with their peers, includes sexual self-advertising in the form of color-coded bracelets that announce the tween's preferred type of sexual activity. Lacking proper direction, they are given to a shallow body narcissism, which prepares them for subsequent breast augmentations, liposuction, and serious dieting to attain the perfect body that will make them more attractive.

We must see this deplorable development in the context of the breakdown of the nuclear family. In the period from 1900 to 1970, the divorce rate increased by 700 percent, and single-parent families are becoming more and more common. Parents are overworked and stressed out and do not have the energy to pay adequate attention to their children. "Things"—consumer goods—often take the place of parental love and care.

Part of the general hypersexualization is the invasion of public space, especially the Internet, by pornography. Cyberporn is omnipresent and huge business.[11] By 2003, there were some 260 million pages on the Internet that had pornographic content, with cybersex fast becoming a popular pastime. Many people—both men and women—apparently see nothing wrong with having an "online affair." To say that the traditional virtue of chastity has become obsolete would be an understatement; it has been utterly forgotten. So have the poignant words of the fourth-century Roman emperor and Neoplatonist Julian, who remarked: "Never think that you are free while your belly and the part below the belly rule you, since you will then have masters who can furnish you with pleasures or deprive you of them."

Where religious folk have frequently gone wrong is in underestimating the power of the instincts and the feebleness of good intentions backed only by dogmas and beliefs. A somewhat different spirit tends to prevail in those circles—call them spiritual or mystical—which see personal transformation as a life-long, intensive project and which tackle it with more sophisticated tools than are available to conventional religious folk.

Yoga can look back upon a protracted history of wrestling with the issue of chastity. First mentioned in the *Atharva-Veda*, which may be dated back to c. 3000 B.C., the ideal of chastity is embodied in the Sanskrit concept of *brahmacarya*. The word means literally "brahmic conduct," *brahma* standing here for "spiritual," "holy," or "divine." *Brahmacarya* denotes the discipline proper to a Brahmin, a member of the priestly class, who seeks to imitate in his life the purity of the transcendental Reality (called *brahman*). It also refers, more specifically, to a student of the sacred Vedic lore. The chaste practitioner, or *brahmacarin*, is guided by the ideal of abstinence from sensuality, especially but not only of the sexual variety.

We may relate *brahmacarya* to the "conduct" of the ultimate Reality, or *brahman*, which transcends all gender distinctions. The spiritual aspirant is asked to emulate that genderless condition so as to preserve and cultivate the great power of the sexual urge. In Hinduism, the term came to stand for the traditional period of pupilage in general but also denotes the actual practice of chastity among householders and ascetics alike. This brings me to the important distinction between those spiritual practitioners who are married, have children, and engage in worldly business on the one side and those who seek out the solitude of forests and mountain caves for intensive Yoga practice on the other side: householders vis-à-vis ascetics. While the former are generally expected to practice chastity by voluntarily limiting and regulating their sexual activity within a committed relationship, the latter are for the most part supposed to follow a life of celibacy, that is, chastity in the unmarried state. In the Christian tradition, this distinction is that between layperson and priest.

The Catholic Church, which (probably incorrectly) claims a membership of over one billion worldwide, has from the beginning taken chastity very seriously. In the past, and with all religious traditions, punishment for various breaches of this virtue were typically rather severe. Ever since the fourth century, the Roman Catholic clergy has been expected to practice celibacy, which has historically been attendant with numerous psychological and social problems. Any teaching that regards sexual activity as innately sinful and looks upon marriage as a second-best option opens the floodgate to morbidity. Many of the so-called Church Fathers afford ample illustration of a perverted libido. Thus the fourth-to-fifth-century Alexandrian anchorite Arsenius, who was later canonized, is said to have rebuffed a Roman girl when she implored him to remember and pray for her. He indignantly yelled to the young pilgrim: "It shall be the prayer of my life that I may forget you!"

Other pious but troubled ascetics flagellated and castrated themselves and even lopped off their genitals to "mortify the flesh." St. Benedict of Nursia threw himself into a thicket of brambles and nettles to stop impure thoughts and unwanted hallucinations; the Ursuline sister superior Jeanne des Anges went one step further by throwing herself upon a brazier of hot coal and spending an entire night naked in ice and snow, while others, like St. Ammon, would dress and undress only in the dark to avoid seeing their own naked body.

The *Agni-Purāna* (372.9), a late Sanskrit text, understands "brahmic conduct" in the strict sense of the term as the renunciation of the eight aspects of sexual activity: fantasizing, glorifying the sex act or the opposite gender, dalliance, "making eyes," secret love talk, longing, the resolution to break one's vow of chastity, and the consummation of the sex act. According to other texts, such as the *Linga-Purāna* (1.8.17), this definition of chastity applies only to anchorites, forest dwellers, and widowed people, whereas householders may have sexual intercourse with their marriage partner but must abstain from the eight aspects of sexual activity in regard to everyone else.

The object of the virtue of chastity is lust—more precisely, its control in body, thought, and speech. As Jesus is reported to have said: "Whosoever shall look on a woman with lust has already committed adultery with her in his heart" (Matthew 5:28). Mind matters. As an urban legend would have it, men think about sex every seven seconds, but such degree of monoideism would had landed everyone of the male gender in a psychiatric ward long ago. Whatever the actual statistics may be, sex is undoubtedly frequently on the mind of both men and women who are in their prime and feel the call of the mating game. But, then, it all depends on what we do when this biological urge wells up in our body and presents itself to our awareness. Do we simply take note of it or do we allow the mind to wander and indulge in sexual fantasies and intentions? Our contemporary society offers plenty of stimuli that trigger sexual thoughts but little wisdom about the destructiveness of sexual obsessions.

Conventional speech is increasingly littered with obscenities, which merely reinforce people's sexual thoughts. Hence there is great merit in the traditional practice of guarding both speech and mind. The constitutionally guaranteed right of the freedom of speech has guaranteed a luxuriant growth of all manners of verbal vulgarities. Language itself—this most powerful form of human communication—has been trivialized. The unenviable record for obscenities on screen seems to be held by the Broadway musical "Jerry Springer—The Opera," which was screened on BBC television in 2005. No fewer than 50,000 viewers in Great Britain contacted the BBC mainly to voice their objection to the musical's inordinate amount of blaspheming and swearing—apparently some 300 occasions in the span of two hours. This particular production suggests an all-time low in the performing arts and in television.

Turning to the contemporary "Yoga scene," we find little evidence of the virtue of chastity either in the married or unmarried state. Sexy outfits for women and men are common in so-called Yoga classes. Modesty, once a highly valued yogic virtue, is considered old-fashioned. There are even public classes in "nude Yoga," and a fashionable coterie of Yoga practitioners indulge in sexual free-for-alls under the pretext of practicing Tantra-Yoga. Centuries ago, the Tantric tradition fell into ill repute in India owing to the same erroneous interpretation. Today, this kind of distorted Tantra is an underground movement in India and part of the New Age movement in the Western hemisphere. As an authentic tradition, however, Tantra thrives largely only in the sophisticated form of Tibetan or Vajrayana Buddhism. Here the emphasis is on ritualism, insight, renunciation, and compassion rather than sensual or sexual practices.

At advanced levels of practice, Tibetan Buddhist adepts are indeed customarily permitted to take a flesh-and-blood consort for the sacred ritual of sexual congress in order to facilitate the spiritual process. Some Western Vajrayana practitioners have eagerly, if prematurely, embraced this ritual practice, and to nip this unsurprising trend in the bud, the Dalai Lama felt obliged to make the following clarifying remarks: "Unless we have reached a stage where we have completely developed the power to control all our energy and have gained the correct understanding of shūnya (emptiness, reality), unless we truly possess all the faculties through which those negative emotions can be transformed into positive energy, we never implement practice with an actual consort."[12] Even few Tibetan veteran teachers could claim to "truly possess all the faculties," never mind Westerners, who are rarely exposed to intensive discipline. Vajrayana is no "California Tantra," as one lama once commented to me, humorously but pointedly.

Lest any doubts remain, contemporary Yoga is morally lax, matching the permissiveness of our contemporary society in general. For instance, seldom do Western Yoga "instructors" or "teachers" ask their students to wear modest outfits to class in order to avoid a sexy fashion parade and inappropriate behavior between students. Over the years, not a few of these teachers (especially men) have been found flirting during class or afterward, and some of the best known teachers have become notorious for their affairs with students.

The Yoga Alliance, an organization registering teachers at the 200-hour and 500-hour level of training, has a code of professional conduct comprising eight rules. Rule 6, as published on the Yoga Alliance website, explicitly relates to the practice of avoiding words and actions that constitute sexual harassment. This, however, is a curious way of phrasing an important moral discipline. While another rule admittedly deals with respecting the rights, dignity, and privacy of all students, the formulation of Rule 6 focuses on what appears to "constitute" the legal threat of sexual harassment that should be "avoided" rather than the positive virtue of *brahmacarya* that should be cultivated. Be that as it may, Rule 6 was included for a good reason, namely the frequent infringement of the virtue it seeks to protect.

While, in my view, the religious language of "sin" is indeed outmoded, there undoubtedly is conduct that is unbecoming, nonvirtuous, or detrimental to a person's spiritual wellbeing. Our behavior is "sinful" when it takes us away from our true nature, or authentic spiritual core. Many religious traditions are uneasy about sex, and some traditions even regard sex as the "original sin." This attitude has led to an artificial divide between supposed saints, who go to heaven, and alleged sinners, who are doomed to go to hell. As a result, the conscience of the average believer, who cannot live up to the proposed ideal of moral perfection, is riddled with unhealthy guilt and shame, or self-deception or hypocrisy.

More sophisticated spiritual paths, notably authentic Tantra, make it clear that sexual activity and pleasure are not inherently sinful. Liberation, or enlightenment, does not depend on sexual or any other kind of repression. On the contrary, individuals suffering from repression will disqualify for heaven, or spiritual realization. More likely, they will be condemned to dwell in a painful mental hell of their own making. Instead of suppression, repression, regression, or any other neurotic manipulation of reality, Tantra and similar life-positive traditions, ask us to understand and exercise our instincts in their proper contexts.

As embodied beings, we are inevitably endowed with genitals and are subject to their hormone-driven biological processes. Under normal circumstances, we also are capable of experiencing sexual sensations and feelings, and those sensations are typically the most intensely pleasurable of which the human body is capable—short of a blissful mystical experience that ripples through every cell. The life-positive spiritual traditions do not seek to dampen or eradicate the body's innate psychosomatic energy but to *harness* it, so that it can become useful for a higher purpose. That purpose is to realize our true nature, which all spiritual traditions assure us, is supremely blissful or, at least, utterly free from physical, emotional, or mental suffering.

Thus, the reason for regulating the sex drive is to be able to tap into an even greater "pleasure." If we habitually allow our psychosomatic energy to spend itself at the level of the genitals, we will never discover its higher potential. The ordinary person behaves like someone who reads about a far-away tropical paradise without ever actually swimming in a crystal-clear emerald lagoon surrounded by white sandy beaches, or like someone who enjoys reading romance novels without ever experiencing a genuine love relationship.

To be sure, there is nothing wrong with sex if we desire children, want to enjoy our partner's intimate company, or are satisfied with the momentary thrill of orgasm. If our sights are set higher, however, we must be willing to take a closer look at how our sex life may bind our attention, limit or prop us up emotionally, or enslave us to a mere physical habit. On the spiritual path, we must bring deep understanding to all aspects of our life, especially those dark, neglected niches like sex.

While chastity is a virtue that helps regulate our interpersonal behavior, it also has a very personal aspect to it. For, through the practice of sexual economy or, in the case of ascetics, even complete sexual abstinence, which is part of the discipline of chastity, we can "store" the body's psychosomatic energy and deploy it for spiritual purposes. The yogins and yoginīs knew long ago that when the libido is raised above the genitals, it becomes fuel for the process of spiritual transformation. This is more than the Freudian process of sublimation by which libidinous energy is channeled into cultural creativity. Elsewhere I spoke of this as "superlimation," or literally, "going beyond the lintel," that is, beyond the threshold of the conventional mind and hence also the conventional Freudian point of view.[13] Superlimation is a higher-octave sublimation, which allows the mind to liberate itself from its bondage to the habit of conceptualization. It leads to true transcendence, or enlightenment.

Yogically, this process even entails a biological component, which is captured in the Sanskrit term *ūrdhva-retas* meaning "up-ward-[flowing] semen." This concept refers to the curious psychosomatic experience of the "seminal" life energy, or libido, flowing out of the genital area into the brain. This subjective experience is accompanied by a progressive loss of interest in sex and bodily pleasure in general without, however, falling prey to repression and its unwelcome symptoms. The loss of interest in sex is set off by an augmented interest in spiritual experiences and realizations and, in the end, the complete transcendence of the body-mind first in the advanced but temporary state of transconceptual ecstasy (*nirvikalpa-samādhi*) and then in the unebbing condition of enlightenment.

When the esoteric process of *ūrdhva-retas* has completed itself, perfect chastity comes naturally and easily to the ascetic. But already prior to this event, in which the higher psychosomatic centers (*cakra*) are activated, the ascetic will have gradually brought his sexual drive under control. At more advanced stages of practice, he or she may even have done so by means of ritualized sexual activity à la Tantra. This goes to show that what matters in all this is the mind and whether it can control the body or is controlled by it. In the post-enlightenment state, adepts are typically not sexually active, but there have been cases of masters who chose to engage in sexual intercourse, but a discussion of this controversial subject lies beyond the scope of the present work.[14]

When considering Yoga, we must always bear in mind that it comprises two great factions. One faction emphasizes a more ascetical and often life-denying approach; the other, notably in its Tantric form, is more life-embracing. Elsewhere I made a distinction between verticalism and integralism. The verticalist, or ascetical, faction has "up and out" for its motto, focusing on the gradual ascent of attention and life energy toward the esoteric centers in the brain and beyond. It sees the world, the body, sex, women, food, and money as evils to be overcome. By contrast, the integralist schools, which regard the verticalist approach as one-sided, see no intrinsic danger in embodiment but appreciate the body as a platform for spiritual realization.

"Mahatma" Gandhi articulated the puritanical, verticalist camp of Hinduism well when he wrote: "I can affirm, without the slightest hesitation, from my own experience as well as that of others, that sexual enjoyment is not only not necessary for, but is positively injurious to health. All the strength of body and mind that has taken long to acquire is lost all at once by a single dissipation of the vital energy. It takes a long time to regain this lost vitality, and even then there is no saying that it can be thoroughly recovered. A broken mirror may be mended and made to do its work, but it can never be anything but a broken mirror."[15]

Gandhi clearly had a problem with sexuality, food, and the body. He confused Yoga with self-denial. By his own admission, he greatly struggled with chastity. In order to prove to himself that he had mastered or could master this virtue, he regularly shared his bed with his grand niece and other maidens, with both parties often being naked. There is no reason to doubt Gandhi's testimony, or that of his grandniece Manu, that strictest chastity was observed on all occasions.[16] When news of this eccentric practice surfaced in 1947, some of his contemporaries did, however, consider it exploitative of the females involved.

While Gandhi championed women's cause and was eager to support and motivate their struggle for social liberation and equality, he remained firmly lodged in India's patriarchal system.

As a householder, should he not have shared his marital bed with his self-effacing wife and unsung heroine Kastur ("Ba")?[17] In many ways, he behaved like an ascetic, yet enjoyed the unquestioned loyalty and support of his wife in addition to the caring attentions of his many female admirers. Gandhi's neglect of his own body is self-evident from his famous emaciated look and his well-known obsession with dieting and fasting. He felt elevated while fasting but often would succumb to depression when he had to resume eating.

A concern with the loss of life energy through intentional or accidental seminal discharge is always a major concern of ascetical traditions. As India's psychiatrists have learned, this is a key motif in the dynamics of the Hindu psyche in general. While some Western neurotics also harbor a fear that orgasm drains them of vitality, our modern Western culture tends to associate asceticism with physical feebleness rather than strength. As Patanjali made clear in his *Yoga-Sūtra* (2.38), however, chastity vitalizes the practitioner's body.

The integralist orientation was beautifully epitomized by the twentieth-century philosopher-sage Sri Aurobindo, whose Integral Yoga sought to replace the traditional "life-killing" asceticism, as he called it. He believed in the inner conquest of all egoic desires but insisted that this did not require any external techniques and certainly no detour into self-torture. Rather, Aurobindo maintained that by radically opening the mind to "Truth-Consciousness," the required transmutation of the human personality would occur spontaneously and gracefully.

Integral Yoga, which can almost be regarded as a modern restatement of the key principles of Tantra, favors a positive attitude toward life, body, sexuality, and the female gender. Yet, like any authentic spirituality, it does not dismiss the virtue of chastity. The proper management of all our energies is vital to the success of spiritual transformation to the point of enlightenment.

There are no shortcuts to inner freedom. We cannot indulge in sex and hope to liberate ourselves from the shackles of the unconscious and the instinctual habits it favors. So long as we bow to the consensus reality that is the artifact of our collective will, we unavoidably also bow to the unconscious and thus to instinctive life. When, however, we are eager to raise our sight higher, we must come to honor the value of reason, wisdom, and virtue.

ENDNOTES, CHAPTER 9

1   Sigmund Freud, *Civilization and Its Discontents*. Trans. and ed. by James Strachey, with a biographical introduction by Peter Gay (New York: W. W. Norton, 2d. ed. 1989). This book was first published in German in 1930.

2   See Jason Berry, *Lead Us Not Into Temptation: Catholic Priests and the Sexual Abuse of Children*. Foreword by Andrew M. Greeley (New York: Doubleday, 1992); Elinor Burkett and Frank Bruni, *A Gospel of Shame: Children, Sexual Abuse, and the Catholic Church* (New York: Viking / Penguin Books, 1993), and Marie M. Fortune and W. Merle Longwood, eds., *Sexual Abuse in the Catholic Church: Trusting the Clergy?* (Binghamton, N.Y.: Haworth Pastoral Press, 2003).

3   The twentieth-century Pope John XXIII, who was a truly saintly man, deliberately adopted his regnal name, perhaps to expunge the bad memory left by his fourteenth-century antipapal namesake.

4   On the corruption of the United Nations, see Jed Babbin, *Inside the Asylum: Why the United Nations and Old Europe Are Worse Than You Think* (Washington, D.C.: Regnery Publishing, 2004). Babbin is a former U.S. deputy undersecretary of defense, and his indictment of the United Nations is weighty. See also Dore Gold, *Tower of Babble: How the United Nations Has Fueled Global Chaos* (New York: Crown Forum, 2004).

5   See the U.S. Department of Justice's *Sourcebook of Criminal Justice Statistics* 2002.

6   See Matt Ridley, *The Origins of Virtue: Human Instincts and the Evolution of Cooperation* (New York: Penguin, 1996).

7   See David Allyn, *Make Love, Not War: The Sexual Revolution—An Unfettered History* (New York: Little, Brown, 2000); John Heidenry, *What Wild Ecstasy: The Rise and Fall of the Sexual Revolution* (New York: Simon & Schuster, 1997); George Leonard, *The End of Sex* (Los Angeles, Calif.: J. P. Tarcher, 1983); Lillian B. Rubin, *Erotic Wars: What Happened to the Sexual Revolution?* (New York: HarperCollins, repr. 1991), and Mary E. Williams, *The Sexual Revolution* (Framington Hills, Mich.: Greenhaven Press, 2002). See also Sharon R. Ullman, *Sex Seen: The Emergence of Modern Sexuality in America* (Berkeley: University of California Press, 1997).

8   See Brooke E. Wells and Jean M. Twenge, "Changes in young people's sexual behavior and attitudes, 1943-1999: A cross-temporal meta-analysis," *Review of General Psychology*, no. 9 (2005), pp. 249–261.

9   See Frederick L. Allen, *Only Yesterday: An Informal History of the 1920's* (New York: Harper Perennial Modern Classics, 2000).

10   See David Siegel, Timothy Coffey, and Gregory Livingston, *The Great Tween Buying Machine: Marketing to Today's Tweens* (Ithaca, N.Y.: Paramount Market Publishing, 2001). See also D. Elkind, *All Grown Up And No Place to Go: Teenagers in Crisis* (Reading, Mass.: Perseus Books, 1998) and K. S. Hymowitz, *Ready or Not: Why Treating Children As Small Adults Endangers Their Future - And Ours* (New York: Simon & Schuster, 1999).

11   See B. McNair, *Mediated Sex: Pornography and Post-Modern Culture* (London: Hodder & Stoughton, 1996).

12   Excerpted from "H. H. Dalai Lama answers questions at Life as a Western Buddhist Nun" featured on www.thubtenchodron.org/publications/preparing-forordination/PFO_Q&AWithHHDL.html.

13   See Georg Feuerstein, *Sacred Sexuality: The Erotic Spirit in the World's Great Religions* (Rochester, Vt.: Inner Traditions, repr. ed. 2003), p. 151.

14   Some highly realized adepts have used sexuality as a means of initiation, while any number of would-be and fake gurus have used initiation as an excuse for exercising their sexual appetite. See my book *Holy Madness: Spirituality, Crazy-Wise Teachers and Enlightenment* (Prescott, Ariz.: Hohm Press, rev. enl. ed. 2006).

15   Mohandas K. Gandhi, *Gandhi's Health Guide* (Freedom, Calif.: Crossing Press, 2000), p. 145.

16   See Manubehn Gandhi, *The End of an Epoch* (Ahmedabad: Navajivan Publishing House, 1962).

17   See Arun Gandhi and Sunanda Gandhi, *The Forgotten Woman: The Untold Story of Kastur Gandhi, Wife of Mahatma Gandhi* (Huntsville, Ark.: Ozark Mountain Publishing, 1997).

CHAPTER 10

GREEDLESSNESS

The principle of what happens to the undisciplined human mind when it encounters surplus was graphically depicted in the 1980 movie *The Gods Must Be Crazy*, which was filmed among the Bushmen of the Kalahari Desert in Botswana. In this case, an empty Coca Cola bottle, discarded from an airplane, becomes a major irritant in the village of the Bushman who found it. In the end, in order to restore harmony between his fellow villagers, he sensibly returns it to the Creator at the edge of his tribe's universe.

Our own overconsuming, avaricious civilization, littered with billions of metaphoric and actual Coca Cola bottles, has not been so fortunate. No one has been able to put a stop to all the social irritants that cause strife and unhappiness in our midst. Indeed, the all-pervasive capitalist system itself, for which there is no antipodean Creator, does not permit such undoing. Greed—the impulse to want ever more—is self perpetuating. It also is potentially highly destructive. The 1924 silent movie *Greed* captures this syndrome well. It depicts three close friends whose lives are devastated by a lottery win, primarily because the winner becomes neurotically miserly and forces herself and her husband into poverty, while her ex-boyfriend is greedily pursuing the unused wealth. Greed and retentiveness are closely connected; a greedy spendthrift does not exist. The avaricious individual is motivated by the magic notion of "more": more money, more material goods, more desirable experiences, more power, more influence.

One cannot think of greed without thinking of the icon of greed—gold. Who would not know of the Gold Rush of 1849, which brought thousands of impoverished prospectors to California and exploded the local population from 13,000 to 300,000 within a few years? Driven by covetousness, the gold miners in California shifted no fewer than 12 billion (!) tons of soil to get their hands at the yellow metal. They also thought nothing of driving Native Americans off their homeland and killing and enslaving them by the thousands. Few miners ever saw their hopes for "the good life" come true.[1] Perhaps only the most ruthless walked away with millions of dollars in gold.

It is not widely known that in the 1960s, a second Gold Rush happened in California and Nevada, again with disastrous consequences for the native population of the areas involved. New technology, using giant excavators and deadly cyanide, made the extraction of gold possible and profitable again. Mining, as Native Americans see it, is raping Mother Earth, but this thought is alien to industrialists and their engineers. Gold mining is still a worldwide industry, which is environmentally destructive and also continues to jeopardize the health of indigenous peoples apart from often infringing on their land rights. All this seems particularly callous when one knows that nowadays most of the gold is used only for jewelry.

To see greed in action, however, we do not need to single out the corporate world. It is in plentiful evidence in our own modern households. Our science- and technology-driven civilization is a perpetuum mobile of overconsumption. To put it more directly, we—you and me—are overconsuming. Effectively, we are habitually stealing from future generations by condoning and supporting all those corporations that are rapaciously stripping the Earth of its natural resources to meet our ever-growing demand for consumer goods. We also contribute to injustice on a global scale, because our unthinking overconsumption takes away from others even now.[2] The money we pay for importing and exporting food-stuffs and other goods disappears down the seemingly infinite plughole of commerce, and thus it cannot go toward feeding and supporting other, poorer nations and less fortunate individuals.

Strangely, even the law-makers see nothing wrong with this disastrous attitude. If anything, they preserve a legal climate that permits multinational corporations to continue to ransack our planet and preach their insidious gospel of "Thou shalt consume ever more!" Because we cannot meaningfully discuss the virtues of greedlessness and nonstealing apart from the present-day con-text of capitalism and consumerism, I will begin with a précis of the catastrophic reality of modern avarice and its consequences. In doing so, I will focus on the United States, which in many ways leads the world in fateful patterns of consumption and for which statistics are readily available.

First of all, the current US budget deficit, as previously men-tioned, stands at nearly $8 trillion, and every year another $400 billion are added to this horrific figure. With no "victory" in sight, the so-called war on terrorism—at the moment played out mostly in Iraq—is expected to cost the United States over $600 billion over the next decade.[3] If, as can reasonably be expected, America will make war elsewhere in the world as well, this figure and the corresponding national debt will escalate appreciably. This liabil-ity is not merely the business of American citizens, but the U.S. government's fiscal policy has far-reaching repercussions that af-fect the rest of the world.

When we speak of capitalism and debt, we inevitably speak not only of governments but banking, and when we speak of banking, we speak of usury. This is how it works, the central bank of a nation fixes a prime lending rate, and individual banks then charge lenders that rate plus so many percent on top. The current U.S.

federal funds rate, which banks are forced by the Federal Reserve to charge one another, happens to be 3.75 percent. The prime rate, which is the minimum banks charge their best corporate lenders, is generally 3 percent above the federal funds rate. But individual consumers are charged yet more, depending on the occasion. Thus mortgage lending rates currently hover under the 5 percent mark, but your credit card bank may still charge a whopping 18 percent. In the olden days, bank "interest" used to be called "usury," which rightly has an unsavory ring to it.

Bank interest is really an arithmetic abstraction, because banks do not actually give a lender anything concrete. Simply slips of paper—cheques, receipts, ledgers—are shuffled around at the bank and between you and the bank, and the work involved seldom justifies the interest paid. We all have come to accept this system unquestioningly. While we are struggling to stay out of debt or pay back loans plus the interest on them, the banks are making billions of dollars for their directors and stockholders. In 2003, the top 1000 banks in the world raked in over $400 billion in pre-tax profits. Citicorp, the largest banking conglomerate, by itself claimed nearly $70 billion of this staggering sum. Now you know where your money goes!

Today, even non-capitalist political systems participate in and depend on the capitalism of the world economy. Thus, capitalism rules the world. If we do not aspire to political correctness, we may simply equate capitalism, as practiced, with greed: A few private individuals control the lion share of a nation's wealth.[4] They are the celebrated or envied multibillionaires behind the largest transnational corporations, notably General Electric (with $647 billion in total assets), General Motors ($448 billion), Ford Motor Co. ($304 billion), Vodaphone Group ($262 billion), and Daimler/Chrysler ($225 billion, all according to 2003 figures). The "globalization" program pursued so vigorously by the U.S. government in cahoots with the corporate giants is an all-too-transparent attempt to convert the entire planet into a controllable market for the exploitation of greedy and unsuspecting consumers around the world. Whichever way we look at the economic reality of our lives, we see avarice and the profit motive.

As I mentioned before, we must not blame the current state of affairs on the corporate world alone. Every single consumer is co-responsible for creating, maintaining, and worsening the situation. This becomes very obvious when we look at the Walmart phenomenon. This $100-billion corporation was founded in 1962 and by 2004 had over 1400 discount stores and more than 1400 supercenters worldwide. In the same year, its annual sales exceeded $256 billion. Although the company donates over $150 million to charitable organizations every year and has made juicy profits for its stockholders, it has a history of exploiting and discriminating against employees and especially bankrupting small locally owned businesses. Also, Walmart shamefully accepted $1 billion in government subsidies! Without the ongoing support of shoppers looking for "a deal," Walmart would not be possible. One man's profit is another man's loss.

The magnitude of the vice of consumerist greed can readily be gauged from our civilization's mounting garbage dumps.[5] Every day, 50,000 tons of trash are hauled from New York alone to various landfills. The annual total domestic and commercial garbage produced in the United States is fast approaching 300 million tons! That amounts to a staggering one ton per person. To this we must add c. 14 billion gallons of sewage per day. At least 10 per cent of the sewage and waste water—only partially treated or completely raw—still ends up in rivers, lakes, and oceans. According to the Organic Consumers Association, farms and industry dump annually c. 860 billion gallons of untreated sewage into America's waterways. To give a specific example: Every year, New York City's combined sewage overflow system is known to discharge some 27 billion gallons of raw, sewage into the Long Island

Sound estuary, a feeding and breeding place for numerous species of fish, birds, and land animals. Besides, New York's antiquated network of sewers spills its pathogenic contents onto the streets every time there is a downpour of rain.

The worst kind of "garbage" is radioactive waste from spent fuel rods in nuclear reactors, which is buried underground without clear understanding of the possibly disastrous effects of this practice, such as leakage into aquifers and contamination caused by future geological events (notably earthquakes).[6] Large amounts of radioactivity have already been released into water and air, accidentally or by poor design, with little concern about the long-term consequences to the health of humans, animals, and plants. Other nuclear nations seem to have even fewer safeguards to protect the world's biosphere from baneful radioactivity. There simply is no absolutely safe method of disposing of radioactive waste. The U.S. National Academy of Sciences calculated that it will take three million years for the existing nuclear waste in the United States to decay to the level of background radiation. What makes this problem particularly urgent is the fact that the effects of radioactive contamination are not merely local but through water and air reach all corners of our planet. We are busy fouling our own nest.

It is easy to lay the blame for this enormous problem on science, technology, the need for non-fuel energy, short-sighted legislation, and so forth. But at the bottom, I propose, lie human ignorance and greed—the psychological engines of our consumer society. In our voracious need for plenty of cheap power, we as citizens allow our respective governments to take the necessary shortcuts. It would not be wrong to say that we even expect them to do so, because raising taxes to pay for safer alternative methods is never our first choice. In the democratic nations of the world, where at least in principle the population could have a say in the political process, we find an extraordinarily lethargic citizenry.

We simply do not think of future generations as long as our every want is met, and as quickly as possible.

Our lives are full of "stuff." The comedian George Carlin has a provocative routine about "stuff," and one of his punchlines is that "A house is just a pile of stuff with a cover on it." His listeners laugh, but they also know he is pointing out an unpleasant truth. The stuff in our homes includes all the food we stuff into cupboards, refrigerators, freezers, and not least our growing bellies. A sub-form of greed is indeed gluttony, which is reckoned among the seven deadly sins in Christianity. Francine Prose, in her book *Gluttony*, observed how this vice is no longer deemed a cardinal sin but thrives luxuriantly in the "developed" countries where food and dieting have become a neurotic obsession.[7] It is estimated that between 5 and 10 million American women are suffering from bulimia—gorging and vomiting. Bulimia is recognized as a disease but in the religious traditions would be considered a version of the vice of gluttony.

About 2 million American women are compulsively dieting, that is, starving themselves to lose weight or stay thin. Forty percent of first-, second-, and third-grade American schoolgirls responded to a survey that they would like to be thinner, and many older girls resort to diet pills and other means to achieve their goal of looking like Barbie. This has nothing to do with the spiritual disciplines of fasting and dietary moderation. According to the National Center for Health Statistics, 64 per cent of American adults aged 20 or over are considered overweight or obese. The U.S. Surgeon General declared 2005 to be the Year of the Healthy Child, and in his report released on Father's Day (June 17) encouraged fathers to take an active interest in their children's physical health, including teaching them healthy eating habits. Problems with overweight are manifesting in ever younger populations and are costing the nation hundreds of millions of dollars, not counting the suffering in the form of ill health and decreased vitality.

Writing in the Chicago *Sun Times* (August 20, 2004), the widely read theologian and novelist Andrew Greeley called greed "America's disease." But with consumerism (read: materialism) rapidly spreading like a wildfire around the globe, this disease is cropping up everywhere. Greeley concluded: "Don't let anyone tell you that lust is the most deadly of the deadly sins." Even the otherwise highly conservative economist Alan Greenspan, U.S. Federal Reserve chairman, felt called to speak of an "infectious greed" back in 1996 when the great corporate scandals were rocking Wall Street.[8]

One of the malevolent and potentially fatal aspects of America's avarice is the tie-in with the government's military imperialism, which most recently has devastated Afghanistan and Iraq. In order to maintain America's overconsuming habits, the U.S. government has systematically pursued an interventionist foreign policy, backed by the world's most sophisticated military technology. This has allowed America to exploit other countries on a large scale, if need be by force and against all U.N. rules and generally under the banner of spreading democracy.[9] The American public tends to be both politically naïve and passive, and it does not even seem to be overly alarmed by the recent erosion of major freedoms guaranteed by the Constitution. This topic exceeds the compass of the present work, although from a yogic perspective, each citizen ought to assume moral responsibility also in the political arena.

It is no accident that in the spiritual traditions of India, greed (*lobha*) is regarded as one of the three poisons, together with anger (*krodha*) and delusion (*moha*). Especially Buddhism pays this unholy triad much attention, holding it responsible for the prevalence of suffering in the world. The three are depicted in graphic form at the center of the wheel of life, which is a favorite teaching device. The rooster stands for avarice, the snake for anger, and the pig for ignorance. These three are thought to poison our life, individually and collectively, and therefore they must be uprooted.

Ignorance, or delusion, is the breeding ground of the other two poisons. It is, in fact, traditionally considered to be the source of all evil, that is, the bedrock of all obstructions to spiritual realization. After all, it is out of ignorance that we succumb to anger, greed, and other vices. Would we become angry, for instance, if we remembered in the moment that things go wrong and people make mistakes and that anger reduces our wellbeing and lifespan by flooding our body with stress chemistry, never mind the harmful effect it has on others? Or would we indulge in avarice if we were fully aware of the brevity of our human life and the fact that we cannot take a single possession with us beyond the grave?

The yogic traditions are not alone in nominating greed as a cardinal vice. In Christianity, it figures as one of the seven deadly sins—"deadly," because each sin, or vice,[10] harms others and leads to the perpetrator's spiritual demise. The fact that the great religious traditions have moral injunctions against greed and the other major vices tells us that these were indulged in even by premodern humanity. This, of course, does not excuse any of them. The motto "There is strength in numbers" does not apply in this particular situation, and having avarice as an entire lifestyle, as is the case with the United States and other developed nations, makes this vice only more reprehensible. We must bear in mind that greed is always at the expense of other people. Simpler societies knew this instinctively, but our own enormously complex society has clearly lost sight of the manifold and baneful repercussions of avarice. We no longer even consider our lifestyle as covetous. Overconsumption has become an unconscious habit, and we take all the little and big luxuries afforded to us by our modern society for granted.

Individual and collective wealth is not inherently wrong, providing it is obtained in a lawful manner and also is used to benefit others. There is, however, something terribly awry with simply sitting on million and billions of dollars in the miserly fashion of a Dagobert Duck, one of Walt Disney's memorable creations: He had a nose for gold and loved to bathe in mountains of money and to regularly count his piled-up riches. His idol was King Midas, and what he hated to do most was to pay for things or give away even a single cent of his fortune. When I was a young boy, I found the greedy antics of this proverbial scrooge particularly amusing, because his behavior seemed so irrational to me. Today I am no longer amused but still flabbergasted by the stinginess of so many affluent people. Some multimillionaires even worry about the day that their money will run out, and perhaps this is a common symptom among the rich. Why else would philanthropy be so rare? Also, I have yet to meet a rich individual whose wealth does not exacerbate his or her negative emotions.

The combined personal fortune of the Waltons, the heirs to Walmart and the richest family of the United States, is estimated to be around 100 billion dollars. Yet, since 1998, they have given only some $700 million to charitable causes. While their philanthropic work is laudable, it amounts to less than one per cent of the family's net worth. Perhaps because of public criticism, the family recently indicated that it is considering upping the ante in the future. Bill Gates, who with over $40 billion in his pockets, is the richest individual in the world, has been far less tightfisted. His charitable foundation has an endowment of $27 billion of which over $7 billion have been donated thus far. Nevertheless, we may ask: how many billions, or even millions of dollars, does one need to live comfortably?

In the spiritual traditions that favor an ascetical lifestyle, wealth or even more than a handful of possessions has always been problematic. It is considered a form of theft and thus a vice. More integral approaches, however, do not regard wealth as a spiritual impediment. This includes the teaching of Gautama the

Buddha. He recognized that for householders, poverty and debt are a great bane and are not conducive to their spiritual wellbeing either. Indeed, the Buddha praised some of his well-to-do disciples because of their generosity and charitable activities. The wealthy merchant Anathapindika was one of them. He is remembered in the Buddhist scriptures as someone who generously fed hundreds of monks every day and also bought the original monastic community a large plot of land. The story has it that the prince who owned the land asked for an exorbitant amount, and Anathapindika ended up placing gold coins next to each other filling the entire acreage in order to acquire it for the Sangha.

One of Anathapindika's nephews, who likewise is remembered in the Pali canon, embodied the opposite spirit. He had come into a huge fortune but had quickly squandered it on partying. He asked his uncle for more money and was given a thousand gold pieces to rebuild his life. Instead of investing this generous gift wisely, he again wasted it. He returned to Anathapindika a second time and received five thousand gold pieces with the stipulation to never return. Not long after his dead body was found, after a brief spell of debauchery followed by abject wretchedness.

According to the Buddha, monastics ought to limit themselves to just a few essential possessions, but he applauded those who attracted more substantial donations, that they were then expected to hand over to the monastic community. Possessions over and above the items allowed by the Buddhist canon—a robe and a begging bowl—were seen as a possible sign of greed on the part of individual monks and nuns. In the popular *Dhamma-Pada* (v. 75), we can read of a road to wealth and a road to *nibbāna* (*nirvāna*), which distinction summarizes well the Buddhist view in general. Buddhism regards wealth as the result of "good karma." It should be properly used for the benefit of oneself, one's family, and one's community. Only wealth obtained by harmful means is deemed blameworthy, as is hanging on to or squandering it. The Buddhist middle path favors balance in all things, and greed is clearly an imbalance, which is best corrected.

Hindu and Jaina Yoga uphold the same truth. In his *Yoga-Sūtra*, Patanjali employs the word *aparigraha* to denote "greed-lessness." The antonym *parigraha* stands for "grasping at," the stem *graha* meaning "grasping." In other texts, the synonym *alobha*, or freedom from greed, is used. But "grasping" gives us a better sense of this curious action of reaching out for something and claiming it for oneself. According to a somewhat enigmatic aphorism in the *Yoga-Sūtra* (2.39), the yogin who has mastered the virtue of greedlessness comes to understand the wherefore of his birth. This statement implies an important insight: Avarice extends not only to external objects but also to our own person—our body and mind. When our mastery of greedlessness has become stable, we begin to understand the mechanism of grasping by which we hold onto our body and mind, especially the notion of selfhood, or "I am." By loosening the hold on who we think we are, we can discover the secret of our present birth and all our incarnations (since Yoga maintains that the present life is only one in a sequence of embodiments).

Greedlessness is radical nonattachment, and this is where the ascetical orientation stops. From a more integral perspective, this attitude looks bland and limited, and it could easily be mistaken for self-centeredness. But the dispassionate yogin simply wants to avoid generating new karmic debts and therefore his greedlessness is anchored in a feeling of neutrality toward everyone and everything.

But, as I have pointed out on a number of occasions already, a more positive approach is possible, which combines dispassion with social engagement—the typical tactic of the householder yogin, who, while practicing inward renunciation, fulfills his external obligations. His greedlessness has a positive aspect to it, namely that of generosity, which I will discuss in Chapter 13.

Integral greedlessness, like any other virtue that is understood in an integral manner, reaches out to others without seeking to acquire and retain anything. It is a generous self-sharing on one level and conscious participation in the nexus of life on another level. Since we are an inalienable aspect of life, we already "have" everything we need and therefore have no cause to anxiously cling to anyone and anything. Greedlessness spells inner freedom, which the yogin endeavors to pursue under all circumstances. Another name for it—or aspect of it—is contentment.

When Alexander the Great visited Diogenes living in a large barrel under the open sky, the emperor asked that great Greek yogin what he could do for the ascetic. Indifferent to Alexander's fame and power, Diogenes simply but with symbolical poignancy requested that he move to the side a little so as not to block the sunlight. If only the emperor had understood the deeper meaning of Diogenes' words.

ENDNOTES, CHAPTER 10

1 See the online report *Gold, Greed and Genocide* (www.1849.org/ggg/before. html), which talks about the plight of the Pomo and Paiute Indians during and after the Gold Rush era and its revival in the 1960s. See also Peter L. Bernstein, *The Power of Gold: The History of an Obsession* (New York: Wiley, 2001).

2 For a religious perspective on the injustice caused by our consumer society, see Paul F. Knitter and Chandra Muzaffar, eds., *Subverting Greed: Religious Perspectives on the Global Economy* (Maryknoll, N.Y.: Orbis Books, 2002).

3 See Michel Chossudovsky, *America's "War on Terrorism": In the Wake of 9/11* (Pincourt, Canada: CRG, 2003); Richard A. Clarke, *Against All Enemies: Inside America's War on Terror* (New York: Free Press; 2004), and Steven Emerson, *American Jihad: The Terrorists Living Among Us* (New York: Free Press, 2003).

4 There are those who believe that capitalism can overcome the avarice that has been almost universally associated with it. See, e.g., Marc Benioff and Karen Southwick, *Compassionate Capitalism: How Corporations Can Make Doing Good an Integral Part of Doing Well* (Franklin Lakes, N.J.: Career Press, 2004).

5 See Elizabeth Royte, *Garbage Land: On the Secret Trail of Trash* (New York: Little, Brown, and Co., 2005); Susan Strasser, *Waste and Want: A Social History of Trash* (New York: Owl Books, 2000), and Porter C. Richard, *The Economics of Waste* (Washington, D.C.: Resources for the Future, 2002).

6 See K. S. Shrader-Frechette, *Burying Uncertainty: Risk and the Case Against Geological Disposal of Nuclear Waste* (Berkeley: University of California Press, 2003) and Michael B. Gerrard, *Whose Backyard, Whose Risk: Fear and Fairness in Toxic and Nuclear Waste Siting* (Cambridge, Mass.: MIT Press, 1996).

7 See Francine Prose, *Gluttony: The Seven Deadly Sins* (New York: Oxford University Press, 2003).

8 See, e.g., Kenneth R. Gray, Larry A. Frieder, and George W. Clark, *Corporate Scandals: The Many Faces of Greed* (New York: Paragon House, 2005); Philip Augar, *The Greed Merchants: How the Investment Banks Played the Free Market Game* (London: Penguin, 2005), and John Perkins, *Confessions of an Economic Hit Man* (San Francisco: Berrett-Koehler, 2004).

9 America's imperialism is ably discussed in a good many publications. See particularly V. G. Kiernan, *America: The New Imperialism: From White Settlement to World Hegemony* (New York: Verso, 2005), Andrew J. Bacevich, *The New American Militarism: How Americans Are Seduced By War* (New York: Oxford University Press, 2005), and, by the same author, *American Empire : The Realities and Consequences of U.S. Diplomacy* (Cambridge, Mass.: Harvard University Press, 2004).

10 See Henry Fairlie, *The Seven Deadly Sins Today* (Notre Dame, Ind.: University of Notre Dame Press, 1979); Solomon Schimmel, *The Seven Deadly Sins: Jewish, Christian, and Classical Reflections on Human Psychology* (New York: Oxford University Press, new ed., 1997); Phyllis Tickle, *Greed: The Seven Deadly Sins* (New York: Oxford University Press, 2004).

CHAPTER 11

COMPASSION

A neonate does not feel compassion but is "hardwired" for it. His or her basic needs are met by food, warmth, and physical comfort. In other words, the newborn child's cosmos is still entirely "biocentric." There is not even an ego yet to call his or her life egocentric. Slowly, as the mind constellates itself, the baby also begins to have social needs and, hopefully, comes to be the recipient of love, kindness, and caring, so that later on he or she can lavish the same on others. Psychologists tell us that our basic emotions as human beings are fear, anger, disgust, sadness, happiness, and surprise.[1] Some researchers add to this list also shame, guilt, and contempt. These are reflected in corresponding facial expressions and bodily poses, and are found across cultures. Significantly, happiness is the only positive emotion of the lot. The emotion of surprise hovers somewhere between the positive pole of happiness and the negative pole occupied by all the other basic emotions.

Feelings like compassion, love, or kindness belong to the desirable variety of the so-called social emotions.[2] They are often said to be learned responses, but we can learn only what we are potentially capable of learning. Also, we know from research on animals like monkeys, dolphins, and dogs that they have all sorts of social emotions, including empathy, which appear to be innate rather than painstakingly learned responses. *Readers Digest* is well known for frequently featuring stories of animals who go beyond their instinct of self-preservation to aid a human being in danger or distress. Lassie of movie and television fame delightfully illustrates the aptitude for compassion in the canine species.

A single trigger event is often all it takes for a social emotion such as caring to be activated and become part of a human individual's horizon of experience and repertoire of behavior. We learn compassion by flexing the compassion muscle with which we all are born. As the American writer Eric Hoffer, famous for his book *The True Believer*, observed: "We are made kind by being kind."[3] Unborn children are known to react to disharmonious sounds and energies with stressful behavior. Young children experience compassion or kindness through a soothing voice and gentle touch. As Ashley Montagu showed in his 1971 book, touch is all important in human development.[4] The skin is hungry for touch, and in all-too-many cultures—including America—people are touch starved, which has a detrimental effect on body and mind.

The compassionate individual is, as it were, "touched" at the heart and then extends himself or herself by reaching out to others. Without compassion, mothers would abandon their children at birth. Compassion, in a way, can be seen as an extension of this maternal "instinct." Hence the Mahayana Buddhists speak of all sentient beings as "mothers," whom we ought to treat with great respect and loving kindness. Some mothers, who lack this psychological attribute, do in fact abandon their newborn child or criminally neglect him or her later on.

If we find this reprehensible, what about the numerous people who turn a blind eye to the misfortune and suffering of others? A person might show great considerateness, which they call love, toward their own kind, but have absolutely no time for an "outsider"—be it a member of another ethnic or religious group, an immigrant, or a beggar. In such cases, compassion has not been generalized as a conscious virtue. The capacity for empathy, which is a vital ingredient of all caring behavior, is underdeveloped. The Japanese society apparently works along these lines. Peter Tasker, in his book *Inside Japan*, characterizes the Japanese as the "kindest, cruelest" people on Earth, because their altruism tends to be limited to "insiders."[5] Remnants of the caste system of feudal Japan persist beyond the suburbs of Tokyo, and a certain group of villagers are brutally labeled *burakumin*, or "filth." The workplace, too, has its outcaste—the *madogiwa-zoku* or "window-side people," elderly employees who are given humiliating jobs close to a window, which assumes that they wile away their time gazing out the window rather than being productive.

The word "compassion" means literally to "suffer with." This hints at the fact that compassion is a response to seeing someone suffer or experience misfortune. Empathy allows us to put ourselves in another's place. As we can read in the biblical book Romans (12:15), "Rejoice with them that do rejoice and weep with them that weep." Without the ability to empathize, there could be no mature moral response to life. In that case, if a person had any morality at all, it would be built merely on the basis of avoiding punishment for transgressing established rules. This, in fact, marks the moral development of a typical child prior to the age of nine or ten. Unfortunately, it is this kind of morality that we often witness also in adults.

We can see this immature moral response at work even in the American criminal system, which is fixated on punishment rather than prevention and rehabilitation. Since the late 1980s, juvenile criminals in America increasingly have been tried as adults. We are talking some 200,000 children every year! In 2001, a fourteen-year-old boy was sentenced to life imprisonment without the possibility of parole for a murder committed when he was only twelve years old. Even though the child's slaughter of a six-year-old was a heinous crime, the question of rehabilitation was never an issue. Until March 2005, only five countries in the world meted out the death sentence to juveniles, and the United States was among them. Finally, in a 5-to-4 vote, the Supreme Court abolished this practice and, by rights, should have outlawed the barbaric tradition of capital punishment altogether.[6]

In 1994, the governor of California signed into law the infamous "Three Strikes and You're Out" initiative, which allows judges to give life sentences to criminals who have committed a total of three crimes even when these are nonviolent in nature, such as shoplifting. What makes this law particularly brutal is the fact that it has been used as a weapon of oppression against African Americans, who now make up 44 percent of prison inmates, even though they represent only about 13 percent of the total population of the United States. American law seems to favor Old-Testament-style justice and callousness.

There are no areas of interpersonal life to which compassion cannot or ought not to be applied. It is not surprising, therefore, that the various religious traditions of the world should have given this virtue, along with love, a key position in their moral teachings. Compassion, unlike other acts of caring, specifically aims at the alleviation of suffering and thus we find it noticeably active in charitable work, including voluntary relief during disasters, epidemics, famine, and so forth. The International Committee of the Red Cross, the International Federation of the Red Cross and the Red Crescent Societies have become symbols of compassion and charity, which are recognized worldwide. These two international organizations, as well as the national Red Cross organizations in 181 nations, rely on some 300,000 full-time employees and 97 million volunteers to do their charitable work.

While observing impartiality, neutrality, and independence, these organizations monitor warring nations to ensure compliance with the Geneva Conventions; arbitrate between warring nations; organize care for the wounded, sick, and homeless; assist with the search for missing persons in times of war, and organize measures of protection and care for civilians both in situations of armed conflict and disaster. The Red Cross movement was launched in 1862 by the Swiss humanitarian Jean Henri Dunant after he witnessed the atrocities at the decisive battle of Solférino in the Austro-Sardinian war of 1859. His efforts also led to the Geneva Conventions, which have been ratified by almost all nations of the world, although they are frequently being broken by the signatory states, notably America.

While compassion is often understood in a general way, mercy or charity (*caritas*) is specifically immediate assistance to someone in need because of injustice or calamity. In the Judeo-Christian tradition, the Good Samaritan exemplifies the attitude of mercy. Today it consists of running shelters and food pantries for the homeless or organizing clothing drives and emergency services. Charity emphasizes giving, and I will deal with this aspect of compassion separately in Chapter 13. Mercy is prompt assistance, which may or may not involve material giving. Mercy comes in many forms. Often it is rendered as timely nursing and healing, but sometimes it simply takes the shape of a kind word.

Throughout the ages, human beings have had to face the uncertainties caused by inadequate income, unemployment, illness, disability, death, and old age.[7] In the past, the extended family and perhaps friendly neighbors helped alleviate situations of need, distress, and suffering. In the Middle Ages, feudal lords stepped in to ensure the welfare of their serfs at a minimal level, and merchants and craftsmen guilds assumed a similar role for their members. The guilds, in turn, led to the friendly societies, the forerunners of fraternal organizations and trade unions. The English "Poor Law" of 1601 was a major step toward nationalizing the concern for the welfare of citizens, and with the Industrial Revolution and increased productivity in the mid-eighteenth century, this trend became firmly established and led directly to the modern welfare system.

The United States spends annually nearly $900 billion on welfare programs, notably social security (c. 86%), which comprises old-age pensions, disability grants, child and family maintenance grants, and grants for relief of distress, and so forth. The government also makes grants to nongovernmental organizations, which then cater to the needs of individual citizens. The combined expenditure for the welfare programs of Social Security (21%), Medicare (13%), and Medicaid (8%), amounts to 42% of the total U.S. budget. Compare this to the 48% allocated for military expenditures (including veteran pensions) amounting to $1,027 billion (1) in 2006. In other words, the American government spends more money on harming non-Americans and destroying their property than on caring for its own people. This schizophrenic mindset is intolerable and, from a spiritual standpoint, entirely immoral and unjustifiable.

The American welfare system has come under attack for just doling out money to the poor without bureaucrats becoming personally engaged.[8] It would be unrealistic to hope for a bureaucracy with a human face. Instead, we ought to clearly understand the roots of poverty, which spring from an inequality that is built into the capitalist system. Given the complexity of our modern "developed" society, the state's involvement in the welfare of citizens is irreplaceable. At the same time, however, we would do well to teach our children early on about altruism, compassion, and charity, so that these virtues do not become extinct or are reduced to a mere bureaucratic formula.

Altruism is found in numerous animal species. The animal kingdom is not only about competition but also about cooperation. Sometimes it seems that only human beings find it hard to shelve the competitive spirit and instead exercise altruism. Under Darwin's influence, it was thought for a long time that war was natural. In the meantime, we have learned, however, that evolution would not be possible without a great deal of cooperation.

Even at the bodily level, the cooperation between trillions of cells makes the human organism a functional whole. Even at the cellular levels, tens of thousands of proteins in a given cell fulfill their specialized tasks cooperatively. We could understand all this cooperation as a form of biological altruism.

At the social level, this cooperation becomes a matter of choice. Yet, upon closer analysis, cooperation ends up serving our self-interest, as Ayn-Rand saw more clearly than others.[9] The purest form of cooperation hails from compassion, which has no deliberate self-interest in it. The French philosopher Auguste Comte, who founded positivism, recognized that human beings are implicated in a web of obligations. He disliked the notion of moral rights, as it implies an emphasis on the individual. Rather, as he saw it, our happiness depends on altruistically serving the human community. Hindu, Jain, and Buddhist teachers would insist that this altruism or compassion must be extended beyond the human family to all sentient species.

Even as individual animals have shown extraordinary compassion toward humans, collectively we humans have a miserable record when it comes to compassion for animals. The brutality of the meat industry with its reprehensible practice of "factory farming" is well documented but not yet widely enough known.[10] Every year, with predictable monotony, we inflict enormous suffering on literally billions of animals. Only very slowly are people beginning to take note of humanitarian pioneers like Peter Singer, Tom Regan, and Richard D. Ryder, who have for decades argued in favor of animal rights. The ground for their work was prepared in the nineteenth century by the German philosopher Arthur Schopenhauer and the British writer Henry Stephens Salt.

Many people do not even believe that animals can experience pain—a truly absurd position, which is easily contradicted by experience. This notion derives, historically speaking, from the so-called Enlightenment idea that animals are things. Even though this erroneous belief was beginning to be undermined in the nineteenth century, it still makes its appearance today, presumably out of sheer convenience. Yet, as I mentioned in Chapter 6, research has shown that even fish have pain receptors and deserve compassionate treatment. The widely publicized study by James D. Rose, a professor of zoology at the University of Wyoming, prematurely reassured anglers and sports fishers that they do not cause pain to fish.[11] A study conducted by a team at Edinburgh University and the Roslin Institute in Scotland in 2003 conclusively demonstrated that at least rainbow trout, but more likely all fish, react to exposure to noxious substances, which they interpret as signaling the experience pain.[12] While Professor Rose and others have contested this interpretation, People for the Ethical Treatment of Animals (PETA) anyway has decided to follow the latter conclusion in their activist campaigns.

If, as seems plausible, fish experience pain, commercial fishing is one of the more brutal industries. Every year, literally billions of fish are condemned to die a slow and painful death on the decks of trawlers and purse seiners or in the bloody nets of gill netters. The world's oceans have become a $70-billion-a-year slaughterhouse, with the fish population declining rapidly. In 2003, 130 million tons of fish were harvested worldwide in oceans and rivers, including aquaculture. Perhaps as many as 100 billion individual fish are involved in this massacre. Fish farms have their own cruel practices, which no compassionate person could support in all good conscience. Aquaculture is a culture of violence.[13]

Even though one may want to object to PETA's often overly aggressive approach, this organization has contributed greatly to the public awareness of the plight of animals. We certainly cannot find fault with PETA's Fish Amnesty Day, which is observed on the fourth Saturday in September—a day on which anglers should, as PETA suggests, toss their tackles and try something else for fun.

Practitioners of Yoga, who are dedicated to the virtue of compassion, would not deliberately engage in a harmful activity, and certainly not for the purpose of mere entertainment.

Compassion in World Farming (CIWF), now an international organization, was started in England in 1967 by dairy farmer Peter Roberts. It achieved wide public recognition in 1984 via a high-profile court case against a veal crate farm in Sussex. This led to the abolition of the horrendous practice of veal crates in Great Britain by 1990. The activist work of the same organization also led to the abolition of sow stalls (gestation crates) and sow tethers by 1999 in the U.K. and by 2006 on the European mainland. In 1997, after a ten-year campaign, CIWF succeeded in having animals recognized as sentient beings by the European Union, which added an animal welfare protocol to the European Treaty. As a result of CIWF's, the European Union also agreed to ban battery cages for laying hens by 2012. In 1992, in landmark legislation, Switzerland was the first nation to recognize animals as sentient beings rather than things. Thus the groundwork has been laid for other nations to follow suit.

But such gains in social awareness and conscience are fragile achievements. Conservative forces are forever seeking to undermine the advanced made in the animal rights movement. For instance, the British Royal Society for the Prevention of Cruelty to Animals (RSPCA), which is hugely popular, not long ago had to modify its campaign against vivisection. The Charity Commission deemed the charity's stance on this crucial issue as illegal and, in so many words, dictated to the RSPCA that it must put human need before animal pain.[14] Human need is indeed great around the world, and there is much room for compassion among our own kind. However, a traditional yogin or yoginī would argue that human happiness or comfort should not be purchased by causing harm and suffering to other species. Vivisection is definitely not a yogic concept.

Because of social injustice, hunger and homelessness haunt even the wealthiest nations. Particularly in the United States, the disparity between the poor and the rich has grown ever more acute since the 1980s. There has been a twenty-fold increase of emergency requests for food in medium to large cities in the period from 1984 to 2002. According to the U.S. Department of Agriculture, in 2001 over 33 million Americans experienced "food insecurity," that is, they were unsure whether they had adequate resources to acquire food sometime during the year. What is more, the *Hunger and Homelessness Survey* conducted and published by the United States Conference of Mayors-Sodexho in 2004 reported that the 27 cities involved in the survey had been unable to meet 20 percent of the requests for food by impoverished citizens. Considering America is the richest nation on Earth, this is a shocking and disgraceful fact.

Homelessness is another big and shameful problem in many of the developed countries, but especially in the United States. In 2004, there were an estimated 3.5 million homeless people. According to the above-mentioned survey, the same 27 cities have had to turn away 23 percent of these underprivileged members of the affluent American society, including families with children, who requested emergency shelter. The homeless and hungry Americans do not necessarily fit the stereotype of "down and out" people, who are lazy, drunk, or drugged. In fact, c. 30 percent of these unfortunates hold down a job and receive wages, but their income simply does not earn them enough to feed themselves and their families and provide a roof over their heads.

Numerous charitable organizations endeavor to help feed the poor. In the United States, the largest organization of this type is America's Second Harvest, founded in 1979 and maintained by donations from the public and corporations. It distributes about 2.5 million pounds of food to a network of 200 regional food banks and food-rescue organizations in all 50 states, as well as the District of Columbia and Puerto Rico. Thus, while the U.S. government cannot claim to be particularly compassionate, compassion and giving are still part of the American way of life.

If there were a public compassion index, however, Canadians would likely be at the top. Canada spends more on healthcare than any other industrialized nation. Adrienne Clarkson, a former Governor General of Canada, said: "For all and everyone we must have compassion because it is in compassion that life consists."[15] This sentiment seems to be echoed in the annual donations to charities. In 2004, Canadians gave no less than CAN $6.9 billion, with a record $743 million going to the victims of the Indian Ocean earthquake. The Canadian government also offered prompt and generous assistance when hurricane Katrina devastated New Orleans, but was repeatedly turned down by the U.S.

It is sometimes said that compassion is strikingly absent from big urban centers, and New York is frequently singled out for its callousness. Yet, this impression is not altogether correct. Metropolises are potentially hostile environments, and violent criminality has become part of the daily experience of city dwellers. Their residents understandably tend to be on the wary side when dealing with strangers or street people asking for (or demanding) handouts. However, New Yorkers generously extended compassionate help, for instance, to the victims of the September 11 terrorist attack on their city, which clearly showed that the spirit of kindness is far from extinct in that city.

For a yogin or yoginī, the modern notion of compassion fatigue is unthinkable.[16] Genuine compassion, in which we put others before our own comfort and concerns, is thought to generate energy and strength rather than deplete us. Of course, different people have a varying capacity for virtue, and it would be uncompassionate to ignore this. Caring for the wounded, sick, insane, and infirm—especially when this is done professionally—can be exceedingly demanding and draining. Compassion fatigue among caregivers is today a recognized symptom, which itself needs a compassionate response.

From a broader spiritual perspective, compassion must become a 24-7 attitude, which embraces all beings. Just before the death of Bhīsma, the great hero of the Bharata war, he and those assembled around him were visited by Brihaspati, the preceptor of the deities. He passed on valuable wisdom to them and, among other things, extolled compassion as the greatest virtue, because it treats all beings as one's self.

Lao Tzu spoke of "three treasures": compassion, moderation, and humility. The same wisdom is mirrored in the words of the Dalai Lama:

> In terms of training the mind, all major religions are the same. They all have the same potential to transform the human mind. A clear indication of this is that all major religious traditions carry the message of love, compassion, forgiveness, contentment, and self-discipline.[17]

In Buddhism, caring concern for others comes in two forms: general kindness—*maitrī* in Sanskrit or *mettā* in Pali—and deep empathy, or compassion, for all suffering beings, which is called *karunā*. These two can be practiced as part of a fourfold spiritual discipline known as *brahma-vihāra*, or "brahmic dwelling." This meditation/visualization practice also includes empathetic joy (*muditā*) for others and profound equanimity (*upekshā*) in all circumstances. This ancient discipline, which is widely used in Buddhism, is also mentioned in the *Yoga-Sūtra* (1.33).

To be able to cultivate compassion, we must allow our self-sense to recede. As Albert Einstein expressed it trenchantly:

> A human being is part of the whole called by us universe,
> a part limited in time and space. We experience ourselves,

our thoughts and feelings as something separate from the rest. A kind of optical delusion of consciousness. This delusion is a kind of prison for us, restricting us to our personal desires and to affection for a few persons nearest to us. Our task must be to free ourselves from the prison by widening our circle of compassion to embrace all living creatures and the whole of nature in its beauty. The true value of a human being is determined by the measure and the sense in which they have obtained liberation from the self. We shall require a substantially new manner of thinking if humanity is to survive.[18]

ENDNOTES, CHAPTER 11

1   The psychological concept of "basic emotion" is not without controversy, and diverse researchers have compiled different lists, and some psychologists have dismissed this notion altogether. See, e.g., Andrew Ortony and Terence J. Turner, "What's basic about basic emotions?," *Psychological Review*, no. 97 (1990), pp. 315–331.

2   See Marc Ian Barasch, *Field Notes on the Compassionate Life: A Search for the Soul of Kindness* (Rodale Press, 2005); Dalai Lama, *An Open Heart: Practicing Compassion in Everyday Life*. Foreword by Nicholas Vreeland (New York: Adult Books/Time Warner, 2001); Lorne Ladner, *The Lost Art of Compassion: Discovering the Practice of Happiness in the Meeting of Buddhism and Psychology* (New York: HarperCollins, 2004); Jeffrey Hopkings, *Cultivating Compassion: A Buddhist Perspective* (New York: Broadway Books, 2001), and Lauren Gail Berlant, ed., *Compassion: The Culture and Politics of an Emotion* (London: Routledge, 2004).

3   Eric Hoffer, *The Passionate State of Mind: And Other Essays* (Cutchogue, N.Y.: Buccaneer Books, 1998), p. 494. See also *The True Believer: Thoughts on the Nature of Mass Movements* (New York: Harper & Row, 1951).

4   See Ashley Montague, *Touching: The Human Significance of the Skin* (New York: Harper & Row, 1971). See also Phyllis Davis, *The Power of Touch: The Basis for Survival, Health, Intimacy, and Emotional Well-Being* (Carlsbad, Calif.: Hay House, 1999).

5   See Peter Tasker, *Inside Japan: Wealth, Work and Power in the New Japanese Empire* (Harmondsworth, England: Penguin Books, 1988).

6   For a Christian viewpoint on capital punishment and the quest for dignity and meaning among death row inmates, see Randolph Loney, *A Dream of the Tattered Man: Stories from Georgia's Death Row* (Grand Rapids, Mich.: Eerdmans, 2001).

7   See Phyllis J. Day, *New History of Social Welfare* (Boston, Mass.: Allyn & Bacon, 2003).

8   See Marvin Olasky, *The Tragedy of American Compassion* (Washington, D.C.: Regnery, reprint ed. 1992); by the same author, *Renewing American Compassion: How Compassion for the Needy Can Turn Ordinary Citizens into Heroes* (Washington, D.C.: Regnery, 1997).

9   See Ayn Rand, *The Virtue of Selfishness* (New York: Signet Books, reissue ed. 1964).

10   See, e.g., John Robbins, *Diet for a New America: How Your Food Choices Affect Your Health, Happiness and the Future of Life on Earth* (Tiburon, Calif.: H. J. Kramer, repr. 1998); Gail A. Eisnitz, *Slaughterhouse: The Shocking Story of Greed, Neglect, and Inhumane Treatment Inside the U.S. Meat Industry* (Amherst, N.Y.: Prometheus Books, 1997), and Matthew Scully, *Dominion: The Power of Man, the Suffering of Animals, and the Call to Mercy* (St. Martin's Griffin, 2003).

11   See James D. Rose, "The neurobehavioral nature of fishes and the question of awareness and pain,"*Reviews in Fisheries Science*, no. 10 (2002), pp. 1–38.

12   See Lynne U. Sneddon, V. A. Braithwaite, and M. J. Gentle, "Do fish have nociceptors: Evidence for the evolution of a vertebrate sensory system," Proceedings of the Royal Society B: *Biological Sciences* (London 2003), no. 270, pp. 1115–1121.

13   See Anne Mossnes, "Fish farms are biological time bombs," Mangrove Action Project, September 12, 2001 (www.earthisland.org/news/new_news.cfm?newsID=74). See also the booklet by Philip Lymbery, *In Too Deep: The Welfare of Intensively Farmed Fish* (Petersfield, England: Compassion in World Farming, 2002).

14   Bernard E. Rollin, *The Unheeded Cry: Animal Consciousness, Animal Pain, and Science* (Iowa State Press, 1998), M. Rose et al., *Animal Pain: Ethical & Scientific Perspectives* (Hyperion Books, 1992), Allen Warner, *Dogs Don't Cry Tears: Understanding the Emotional Pain of Animals* (Big Apple Vision Publishing, 2005), and James C. Turner, *Reckoning with the Beast: Animals, Pain, and Humanity in the Victorian Mind* (Baltimore, Md.: Johns Hopkins University Press, repr. 2000).

15   From Adrienne Clarkson's acceptance speech on being awarded an honorary doctorate by the University of Ottawa in 2003.

16   See Charles R. Figley, ed., *Treating Compassion Fatigue* (New York: Brunner-Routledge, 2002) and Christina Maslach, *Burnout: The Cost of Caring* (Cambridge, Mass.: Malor Books, 2003).

17   Dalai Lama, *Many Ways to Nirvana: Reflections and Advice on Right Living.* Ed. by Renuka Singh (Toronto: Penguin Canada, 2004), p. 5. See also Dalai Lama, *Ethics for the New Millennium* (New York: Riverhead Books, 1999).

18   Thomas F. Burke, *Einstein: A Potrait,* (Petaluma, Calif.: Pomegranate Communications, 1984), p. 46.

CHAPTER 12

LOVE

As psychoanalyst Erich Fromm astutely observed in his essay "Love in America," the American obsession with symbols of love suggests that the reality of the situation is that there is a lack of genuine love.[1] We only need to look at the statistics for divorce, single-parent families, and latchkey children, as well as juvenile crime and elder abuse to see the truth of Fromm's observation.[2]

Of course, America is not the only country experiencing love-lessness on a large scale. Modern civilization itself is largely unloving and unkind. We have become confused about the nature and role of love and are starved for real love in our lives. This is why writer and public speaker Leo Buscaglia was so hugely successful.[3] By the end of the twentieth century, his books had sold 18 million copies worldwide. He untiringly worked for a more loving world by showing his readers and listeners practical steps to overcoming the psychological and social barriers to love.

Others, especially from within the fold of Christianity, are similarly dedicated to spreading the virtue of love. The greatest example of Christian love in recent times, of course, is Mother Teresa, a Macedonian-born nun, who was sent to India in 1934 and from 1948 until her death in 1997 worked indefatigably for the poorest of Calcutta. Her charitable labors not only brought relief and hope to countless Indians, they also inspired 4,000 nuns of her new order to dedicate themselves to the same noble goal in 123 countries.

Many Westerners, who are familiar with the Judeo-Christian religion, do not associate the virtue of love with any of India's religio-spiritual traditions. Especially Christian theologians have tended to naïvely assume that love is a peculiarly Christian quality. Yet, love is a key element also in the devotional traditions of Hinduism, which are far more prominent than is generally thought.[4] The term *bhakti-yoga* is a catch phrase for these traditions. *Bhakti* or devotion/love comprises love for God, God's love for devotees, and love for fellow beings. This Sanskrit term stems from the verbal root *bhaj*, which means "to participate in." Love, then, is a form of participation in another's being. A further Sanskrit term used to denote love is *preman* or *premā*, which is derived from the verbal root *prī*, "to please, gladden, delight in." Both *bhakti* and *preman* must be carefully distinguished from common love, which is shot through with passion and attachment. The Sanskrit language has numerous words that express the nuances of erotic love or emotional attachment—*kāma, rati, rāga, anurakti, prīti, bhāva, sneha, madana*, and *sambhoga.*

Christianity similarly distinguishes between *agape* and *eros*—two Greek words—which respectively stand for unselfish, spiritual love and physical love or attachment. While the more ascetical wing of Christianity sees *agape* and *eros* as being mutually exclusive, a more moderate contingent considers love without passion as bloodless and abstract. In this second interpretation, *eros* is not inherently self-centered and deficient. The Protestant theologian Paul Tillich, for instance, observed: "An *agape* in which there is no *eros* has no warmth. *Eros* without *agape* lacks discrimination. They belong together and cannot be severed."[5] This, incidentally, also epitomizes the body- and life-positive approach of Tantra, which in my view is India's most advanced spiritual tradition.[6] The Tantric tradition acknowledges that body and world are manifestations of the ultimate Reality and thus need not be anxiously rejected or ignored. On the contrary, the omnipresent Reality must be found here and now in order to avoid the fallacy of philosophical separatism.

The Christian ideal of love builds upon the bedrock of Old Testament morality. According to Deuteronomy (6:5), to love God is the very first of the Ten Commandments: "You must love the Lord your God with all your heart, all your soul, and all your might." This rule is reiterated *verbatim* in the New Testament in the Gospel of Matthew (22:37) and the Gospel of Luke (10:27), and it is a sentiment shared by the devotional traditions of India. There the supreme Being is called Vishnu, Krishna, Shiva, Kālī, and so forth. If a faithful individual cannot come to love God first and foremost, he or she is thought to never be able to love other beings either. Love of God is deemed the purest form of love. This idea is universal among the great monotheistic traditions of Judaism, Christianity, and Islam.

According to the above-mentioned verse from the Gospel of Luke, the first commandment includes the qualifying phrase "and [love] your neighbor as yourself." While the first biblical commandment does not actually contain this stipulation, the principle "love your neighbor as yourself" is unquestionably part of Old Testament religion (see Leviticus 19:18). Jesus, however, focused his disciples' attention on loving one another, as well as loving all other fellow beings. If a Christian's love for God is not also expressed in his or her love for others, it is deemed insincere. Jesus taught that his own presence (as God "made flesh") and his teaching of universal compassion has made following the Old Testament rule of divine and neighborly love truly possible. He preached against the kind of parochial love and compassion that excludes one's enemy. As reported in the Gospel of Matthew (5:43), Jesus insisted that his followers love their enemies, bless those who curse them, do good to those who hate them, and pray for those who exploit them.

Many Christian theologians who are familiar with Eastern traditions have uncritically believed that statements about love and compassion in Hinduism and Mahayana Buddhism were inspired by Christian missionaries. This, however, is mistaken. The *Bhagavad-Gītā*, one of the first Sanskrit scriptures to explicitly teach the path of devotion, and certainly the early Mahayana *Sūtras* were definitely composed prior to the rise of Christianity. Today, some researchers even believe that historically the opposite was true: Christianity, a highly syncretistic religion by any standards, bears the stamp of Buddhist influence.[7] Be that as it may, already the Vedic (ancient Hindu) and Pali Buddhist teachings prior to Christianity emphasized the importance of loving kindness and other similar virtues.[8]

There is no question about the Buddha's compassionate nature. In his own words, as recorded in the *Anguttara-Nikāya* (1.22), he resolved to embark on his teaching career out of sympathy for the world, "for the welfare and happiness of the multitudes." The Buddha's sympathy ought not to be confused with sentimentalism. Rather it was a loving concern for the spiritual well-being and wholeness of others, which transcended conventional emotions. He was neither attached to others nor attached to his teaching role. The impulse to teach arose in him spontaneously after his enlightenment, and because there was a corresponding response from fellow humans and nonhuman beings, he persisted in this altruistic endeavor until he drew his last breath c. 2,500 years ago.

As far as Hinduism is concerned, devotionalism was present already in the ritualism of the *Vedas*, the earliest portion of India's revelatory literature. Many of the hymns of the archaic *Rig-Veda* ("Knowledge of Praise") were composed in adoration of specific deities, such as the male gods Agni, Indra, Soma, Varuna, Vāyu, and Sūrya, as well as the female deities Prithivī and Sarasvatī. Just as the composers of these hymns were assumed to chant them with love, so also the deities were said to draw close to their devotees out of love for them.[9] The visionary bard, whose spontaneous compositions so delighted the deities, also showed utmost diligence in the performance of rituals. His mind was firmly yoked in prayer; he was clearly a yogin and a forerunner of the later devotional mystics of Hinduism.

Bhakti-Yoga undoubtedly had its origins in the devotionalism of the Vedic seer-bards (*rishi*). For centuries, priests followed this age-old path, though at times their strict ritualism stifled the devotional heart and degenerated into the routine performance of sacrificial magic. Scriptures like the *Bhagavad-Gītā* and the *Shvetāshvatara-Upanishad*—both belonging to the early Buddhist or even pre-Buddhist era—were the products of a monotheistic revival, favoring the practice of heartfelt devotionalism. In the *Shvetāshvatara-Upanishad*, this devotionalism focused on God Shiva, while the *Gītā* is the earliest extant document of Krishna worship, which was destined to become the single most outstanding devotional tradition of India.

The former text, which is usually assigned to the third or fourth century B.C. but is probably many centuries older, for the first time mentions the word *bhakti*, or "love/devotion." This scripture foreshadowed devotionalist developments within the camp of those who worshiped God in the form of Shiva—a minor deity in the *Rig-Veda* but in medieval times one of the three aspects of the Hindu trinity, the other two being Vishnu and Brahma. While Brahma never had much of a cult associated with him, Vishnu (especially in the incarnational form of Krishna) appealed to an ever-growing mass of people. Today Vaishnavism—the devotional religious culture focusing on Vishnu—is widespread throughout the Indian subcontinent. A school of this proliferating tradition even made its way to occidental shores in the form of Bhaktivedanta Swami's Krishna Consciousness movement, which in 1969 was made famous by

George Harrison's song "Hare Krishna." This hit, which made the top-ten charts in America and Europe, is based on a traditional *mantra* in praise of God Krishna, the most beloved of Vishnu's ten incarnations.

What many people in the West who witnessed the rise and decline of the Krishna Consciousness movement never knew was that this school has its legitimate roots in the teachings of the fifteenth-century saint Caitanya, one of the great preceptors of Bhakti-Yoga. Caitanya, in turn, stood on the shoulders of illustrious predecessors all the way back to Vedic times.

If we want to understand Bhakti-Yoga, we only need to examine the teachings of the God-man Krishna, as they are enshrined in the *Bhagavad-Gītā*, a didactic poem comprising a mere 700 verses. Here are two of Krishna's statements, which can serve as a convenient starting-point for the present consideration:

Of all yogins, he who loves Me with faith and whose inner self is absorbed in Me—him I deem to be most yoked. (6.47)

Be Me-minded, be devoted to Me, sacrifice to Me, salute Me. Thus you will come to Me. I promise you truly, for you are dear to Me. (18.64)

Because Krishna spoke the above utterances as an incarnation (*avatāra*) of the Divine itself, and to avoid confusion, I have opted to capitalize all references to himself. In the first quoted verse, we learn that those yogins who love Krishna and meditatively immerse themselves into him, he considers the most disciplined and self-controlled. Others may reach extraordinary spiritual heights, and even attain liberation, but they remain inferior to the true devotee of the divine Being. Relatively speaking, they are not as "yoked," not as accomplished in their yogic practice.

As Krishna himself reassures his readers, he extends his sublime love equally to all. Yet, there is a special chemistry between him and those who are devoted to him. Like Jesus after him, Krishna wanted to serve others as the portal to the Divine. Hence his admonition to be "Me-minded," that is, to be focused not on the ego but entirely on him as a full incarnation of Vishnu. He solemnly promised that by placing their attention with deep faith on him alone, yogins would come to participate in his divine nature. In other words, they would find themselves in his transcendental company, embraced by his eternal love and free from all karma and suffering.

The relationship between Krishna and his devotees is highly personal and intimate and yet simultaneously suprapersonal. When this God-man says "you are dear to Me," he does not mean that he cherishes the false self-sense, the ego personality, of devotees, but that he treasures every being in his or her divine essence. When a person turns his or her attention to Krishna in voluntary devotion, there is a ready response, which is of the nature of loving grace (*prasāda*). Here we have the old paradox of theistic grace: In order to receive it, a person must somehow be open to it. God cannot or will not force his love or grace upon anyone. Everyone is free to choose or reject the Divine. Translated to the level of interpersonal relationships this means: We are free to love and be loved, but in order to be loved, we must first want to be loved.

At the level of spiritual discipline, of course, the challenge is more one of loving than being loved. Bhakti-Yoga is the path of active love. This love has a strong ingredient of faith—faith in the liberating grace of the Divine, faith in the teachings, and also faith in oneself as an inalienable particle (*amsha*) of the supreme Person. In the context of Buddhism, this last type of faith manifests as one's recognition that every single being contains the seed of Buddhahood, which, when appropriately nurtured, will blossom into actual Buddhahood.

The classical form of the devotional path can be found outlined in the ninth-to-tenth-century *Bhāgavata-Purāna*, an encyclopedic work of the Vaishnava tradition. Here the following nine stages of devotion are described:

1. Listening (*shravana*) to the sacred names of the Divine.
2. Chanting (*kīrtana*) songs of praise or mantras in honor of the Divine.
3. Remembrance (*smarana*) of the Divine, which is the contemplative exercise of recalling the attributes of the supreme Person.
4. "Service at the feet" (*pāda-sevana*), which consists in ceremonial worship of the Divine in the form of a suitable icon.
5. Ritual (*arcanā*), which stands for the performance of the prescribed religious rites, as codified in the sacred literature.
6. Prostration (*vandana*), which is generally done in front of an iconic representation of the Divine.
7. "Slavish devotion" (*dāsya*) toward the Divine, which manifests in the devotee as a profound yearning to be in God's visionary or transcendental presence.
8. Feeling of friendship (*sākhya*) for the Divine, which represents a more intimate, mystical way of relating to God.
9. Self-offering (*ātma-nivedana*), which is the spontaneous self-transcendence that occurs upon merging with the Divine in the state of ecstasy (*samādhi*).

These nine stages form, as it were, a ladder of devotional perfection—a *scala mystica* by which the devotee draws ever closer to the divine Beloved until his or her being is entirely eclipsed by the Divine. The monotheistic traditions, however, insist that even in the most perfect merging with the Divine, the being of God infinitely exceeds the being of the devotee. However sublime the realization may be, the devotee remains always a devotee; God is always God.

On the devotional path, love for God is the primary motivation, while love for others may be regarded as a "spillover" of the devotee's love for God. When the heart is exuberant with devotional love it sees God in everyone and everything and easily extends itself to all others. As Nārada states in his *Bhakti-Sūtra* (4.55): "Having realized that [love], he sees only that, he hears only that, he ponders only that." This unqualified love is rare, however, and the schools of Bhakti-Yoga have had their share of narrow-minded zealousness and bigotry.

At the same time, we must not forget that the *bhakti* movement, which swept across India in medieval times, opened its doors to all sections of society. Many of its greatest representatives hailed from the lower social strata and even included outcastes. The famous mystic Kabīr was a weaver, while the celebrated Tukārām belonged to the shūdra caste, as did the woman saint Janabāī. This wonderful spirit of tolerance is captured already in the *Bhagavad-Gītā* (13.27) where Krishna affirms:

He who sees the Supreme Lord abiding equally in all beings, not becoming lost when they are lost, he sees; he indeed sees.

In its highest articulation, Bhakti-Yoga is far removed from uncontrolled emotionalism. Like all authentic yogic teachings, it values harmony and balance, and is solidly based on the spiritual ideal of seeing the "sameness" of all things. This is known as "equal vision" (*sama-darshana*), that is, regarding a piece of gold and a lump of grass with equal dispassion. The devotee, or *bhakta*, makes the Divine his or her "ultimate concern," and regards everything *sub specie aeternitatis*, "under the aspect of eternity."

As is evident from various virtues recommended in the *Gītā*, the mood of love must find expression in the devotee's interpersonal relationships. This is borne out by the insistence to relinquish self-centeredness and evil deeds and instead cultivate the spirit of goodness (*sattva*) in the form of purity, integrity, truthfulness, generosity, and the will to promote the welfare of all beings. The last-mentioned virtue is embodied in the phrase *loka-samgraha*, or "uniting the world." This, of course, has absolutely nothing to do with the economic-political concept of One World, which is the target that the American neoconservatives and their cronies have for years been selling to an unsuspecting public. There is nothing charitable about political leaders and multinational corporations wanting to install a One World government, which would effectively amount to a tyranny that silences dissent and levels cultural differences—all in the interest of economic profit for the select few.

The *Gītā's* idea of "uniting the world" has a sound spiritual anchorage, and the associated notion of social equality must be understood as an aspect of a larger equality by which every individual is given equal access to divine grace and help. Here the goal is a just society in the broadest sense possible: a society of just, virtuous people whose hearts are on fire with love and compassion.

ENDNOTES, CHAPTER 12

1   Erich Fromm, "Love in America," in H. Smith, ed., *The Search for America*, (Englewood Cliffs, N.J.: Prentice Hall, 1959), pp. 123–131.

2   See my comments in Chapter 11.

3   See, e.g., Leo Buscaglia, *Love: What Life Is All About* (New York: Ballantine Books, 1996).

4   See R. G. Bhandarkar, *Vaiṣṇavism, Śaivism and Minor Religious Systems* (Varanasi, India: Indological Book House, repr. 1965); Jan Gonda, *Viṣṇuism and Śivaism: A Comparison* (London: Athlone Press, 1970); Friedhelm Hardy, *Virāha-Bhakti: The Early History of Kṛṣṇa Devotion in South India* (New York: Oxford University Press, 1983). On the *bhakti* ideal in India's Middle Ages, see N. N. Bhattacharyya, *The Medieval Bhakti Movements of India* (New Delhi: Munshiram Manoharlal, 1989).

5   Paul Tillich, "The importance of new being," *Man and Transformation: Papers from the Eranos Yearbooks*, ed. Joseph Campbell (Princeton, N.J.: Princeton University Press, 1964), p. 174.

6   See Georg Feuerstein, *Tantra: The Path of Ecstasy* (Boston, Mass.: Shambhala Publications, 1998). See also my *Sacred Sexuality: The Erotic Spirit in the World's Great Religions* (Rochester, Vt.: Inner Traditions, repr. 2003).

7   See, e.g., Marcus J. Borg and Ray Riegert, eds., *Jesus and Buddha: The Parallel Sayings* (Berkeley, Calif.: Ulysses Books, repr. 1999) and John P. Keenan, *The Wisdom Of James: Parallels With Mahayana Buddhism* (Newman Press, 2005).

8   See Harvey B. Aronson, *Love and Sympathy in Theravāda Buddhism* (Delhi: Motilal Banarsidass, repr. 1996).

9   See *Rig-Veda* 10.7.89, 16–17.

CHAPTER 13

GENEROSITY

Charles Dickens' popular work *A Christmas Carol* (1843) celebrates the conversion of Ebenezer Scrooge, "a squeezing, wrenching, grasping, scraping, clutching, covetous old sinner," into a kind, generous, and benevolent human being. Converted by the ghost of his former business partner, the niggardly Scrooge mends his ways and becomes "as good a friend, as good a master, and as good a man, as the good old city [of London] knew." The poor and downtrodden people of nineteenth-century England had in this great novelist a stalwart spokesperson against social injustice and hypocrisy. Dickens paid for the printing of the book himself and then fixed a price low enough so that as many as possible could afford it—a fitting gesture for a novel that sought to condemn miserliness. Dickens' compassion and generosity were especially stirred by the plight of the uneducated, victimized street urchins who were forced into child labor, who feature prominently in his books.

The vice of miserliness is condemned in the literatures of all great cultures, and each country has its own "counter hero" of stinginess—from the Indian Illisa the Cheap, the Greek Euclio in Plautus's *Pot of Gold*, and the Lady of Stavoren in a well-known Dutch legend to Shakespeare's Shylock in *The Merchant of Venice*, Molière's Harpagon in *The Miser*, and Charles Montgomery "Monty" Burns in the popular television series *The Simpsons*. The figure of the miser has also been immortalized in the fine arts—from Donatello's early-fifteenth-century sculpture depicting the so-called "heart miracle" according to which a miser's heart was found not in his coffin but in his coffer to Hieronymus Bosch's painting "Death and the Miser."

Practically all cultures deem miserliness an unenviable character trait and favor its opposite: generosity, hospitality, charity, benevolence.[1] Yet, stinginess and avarice have nowhere been completely eradicated. As I have argued in Chapter 10, greed has become systemic in the developed nations of the world, which are driven by consumerism, and therefore we can expect to also find a degree of miserliness in them. To a homeless beggar struggling to stay alive, any person with a roof over his head and a hot meal on the table will seem incredibly rich and fortunate. Wealth is relative, and so is generosity. We ought to bear this in mind when pondering the following facts and figures.

In 2004, there were nearly 1.4 million tax-exempt charitable organizations in the United States alone. Institutionalized philanthropy has unquestionably been an important aspect of American life ever since the nation's birth.[2] It replaced to a certain extent the simple personal charity of earlier ages, which was motivated by piety. The U.S. tax system, we must remember, favors the wealthy, and their greater affluence allows them to be generous. In fact, philanthropy pays, because prosperous individuals and corporations receive generous tax incentives for their charitable donations. The situation is different in Great Britain, for instance, where the rich are taxed more and consequently do not tend to be as giving as their American counterparts. In the United States, philanthropy could be said to be very big business, involving c. $240 billion a year.

Since 1994, American philanthropists have the benefit of a comprehensive online database that lists all charitable organizations registered with the Inland Revenue Service. The database was created by GuideStar, a registered nonprofit, to provide accurate information about charities, and some 20,000 people make use of it every day.

A very revealing feature is the online Generosity Index, compiled by the Catalogue for Philanthropy, which shows the relative generosity of the fifty states in the union. The index is calculated per state on the basis of a person's average adjusted gross income and the tax-deductible charitable contribution made. In 2004, Mississippi ranked first on the Generosity Index, while California was in twenty-ninth place and New Hampshire came last. As is evident from this compilation, the wealthy are personally tightfisted. They obviously do not know or heed Jesus' words, as recorded in the Gospel of Luke (6:38):

> Give to others, and God will give to you. Indeed, you will receive a full measure, a generous helping, poured into your hands—all that you can hold. The measure you use for others is the one that God will use for you.

This statement expresses a sentiment that is basic to all religio-spiritual traditions. Because of the tolerant social values of Jesus' teachings, the Christian tradition particularly appealed to the underprivileged and grew rapidly into a world religion. Immense civilizations—like Pharaonic Egypt, Rome, and the United States—have always attracted large numbers of people in search of a better life. Often these unfortunates have had to migrate from their homelands only to be condemned to a life of possibly even more abject destitution, if not slavery. Christianity, with its focus on a post-mortem paradise, at least provided them with an ideology of hope, while the practical charity of Christians often helped to alleviate the worst material distress.

Poverty was virtually omnipresent in the Middle Ages, and there was plenty of opportunity for Christians to exercise charity.[3]

Jesus had imbibed this great virtue from his Jewish faith and made it a pivotal aspect of his own teachings. Deuteronomy (15:11) extols charity as follows:

> There will never cease to be poor people in your land; therefore I command you: Open your hand to your kinsman, the needy, and the poor in your land.

The same passage (15:1ff.) directs the faithful to forgive all debt every seventh year—a munificent injunction that, however, applied only to the Israelites, not foreigners. If an indigent person was forced to enslave himself to a wealthy man, he or she would have to be set free in the seventh year and bid good-bye "weighed down" with gifts. Jesus expanded this Old Testament morality into a more comprehensive "brotherly" sentiment. To practice charity/justice (Hebrew: *tsedaqah*) is a fundamental duty of the "righteous" Jew, who is expected to give away ten percent of his or her income. This is not so much a matter of feeling charitable as a time-honored obligation. To simplify somewhat, Jesus emphasized the feeling of compassionate love over obedience to the law.

According to Rabbi Moshe ben Maimon, who is better known as Maimonides, charity comes in eight degrees of virtuousness: (1) giving begrudgingly, (2) giving cheerfully but less than one ought, (3) giving only after being asked, (4) giving before being asked, (5) giving without knowing the recipient's identity but with the recipient knowing the identity of the donor, (6) giving when both donor and recipient know each other's identity, (7) giving when neither party is cognizant of the other's identity, and (8) giving so that the recipient becomes self-reliant.

Tithing is also a solemn obligation for Muslims. Alms-giving (Arabic: *zakat*) is not a substitute for compassion but rather an expression of it. Originally, Christianity did not adopt the practice of tithing but emphasize *caritas*—giving freely and joyously "from the heart." This changed in the sixth century when tithing was instituted to finance the clergy, and a version of obligatory payment still exists in some Christian countries, such as Austria and Germany. In most countries, however, Christian churches rely on the spirit of *caritas*. Modern philanthropy, by contrast, frequently is little more than a commercial transaction that lacks any sense of compassion.

The early Christian Church expressed its symbiotic ideals of charity and equality in the so-called "love feasts," or *agapae*, in which rich and poor gathered for a common meal to which everyone, each according to his or her means, had contributed. Today we would call this a potluck dinner. As the congregations grew larger, these love feasts degraded into lavish banquets financed by the rich and serving more their own self-importance than any spiritual need or communal living. Fortunately, they became unfashionable, and today we can only see pale echoes of them in the shelters and "soup kitchens" catering to the hungry. The one important difference between the original *agapae* and modern soup kitchens is that the latter's meals are shared only by the poor without the "brotherly" presence of the rich many of whom, I daresay, would find the company of the homeless and impoverished unnerving or embarrassing. The caste system is not unique to India!

The resentment that many indigent homeless in developed nations seem to feel is at least partly due to this cultural barrier between the haves and the have-nots. They regard the handouts they are given as an easy way out, with no one actively championing their cause. All too many people blame the homeless for not reintegrating into the larger society, as if this were inevitably a matter of choice. The fact is that it is extremely difficult for an impoverished and homeless person to climb back up the socio-economic ladder.

Then again, the feeling that everyone "deserves" a comfortable or successful life is a modern-day error, which calls for deeper inspection. From the viewpoint of Hinduism and Buddhism, for instance, while we are in principle free to make choices, our choices are enfolded in karmic factors. Thus, we may choose to respond to a job offer and do our utmost to obtain a particular job, whether we will in fact get it depends on our prospective employer. In turn, whether an employer will hire a particular applicant depends on factors that exceed the rationality of the situation. For instance, a person may be well qualified, even ideally suited, for a job, but because the employer feels a certain obligation to someone else or has an ethnic bias opts to give the same job to a lesser qualified individual. Or, perhaps, on the day of the job interview, the applicant has a harmless cold; the employer, who has had a lot of problems with employee absenteeism, quietly and unreasonably starts to wonder about the applicant's health and ends up not hiring the person.

From a traditional perspective, it is absolutely legitimate to aspire to an equitable life, but it would be wrong to consider such a life as an entitlement, a "birthright." Such an assumption merely paves the way to frustration and disappointment. In every life there are causes and conditions that are beyond our control, even beyond our cognizance. The Indians call this *karma*, which is the causal nexus between action—the literal meaning of this Sanskrit word—and its effects. What makes this nexus so largely unpredictable is that, according to the Indian sages, it extends beyond our present lifetime to untold numbers of previous lifetimes.

Instead of feeling envious or resentful, it is therefore best to cultivate patience and equanimity. Life is an unpredictable series of good (enjoyable) and bad (unenjoyable) events. Even the rich are exposed to misfortune, illness, and death. As a Yiddish saying has it, "If the rich could hire people to die for them, the poor could make a nice living." A beggar might find a winning lottery ticket and become incredibly wealthy overnight. A well-to-do company executive might be laid off and fail to find another job—any job—

and within a couple of years lose his home, car, bank savings, and wife, and depend on handouts. In case this sounds far fetched, there are literally thousands of former executives on the streets of America and Japan.

As India's sages assure us, life is full of suffering. Poverty and wealth bring their own challenges. Spiritually speaking, affluence is a far greater obstacle, for it gives us the illusion of security. In Jesus' words, "It is easier for a camel to pass through the eye of a needle than for a rich man to enter the kingdom of God."[4] Wealth tends to fatten and buffer rather than overcome the ego. Therefore we would do well to remember the wisdom of the fifth-century Tamil sage Tiruvalluvar, who wrote in his famous *Tiru-Kural* (4.2) that the greatest wealth is a virtuous mind. It is, after all, the only possession that we will take with us upon the demise of the body.[5] A mind suffused with virtues, as the Indian sages insist, is the best possible condition for a meaningful and satisfying life in the future. For, a virtuous mind will inevitably tend to be karmically drawn toward the right circumstance for further moral and spiritual growth.

In India, the cardinal virtue of generosity, or charity, was advocated already in the 5,000-year-old *Rig-Veda*. The Sanskrit word for charity is *dāna*, literally "giving," and the *Rig-Veda* (10.117) includes an entire hymn dedicated to this sublime virtue:[6]

1. The deities did not ordain hunger as our [inevitable cause of] death. Even to the well-fed comes death in various forms. The riches of the magnanimous never dwindle, while the miser gains nothing to comfort him [in his hour of need].

2. The man with food in store who hardens his heart against the pauper in dire straits begging for food, even when previously he rendered him service, will find no one to comfort him.

3. He who gives to a feeble beggar who comes to him in want of food is bounteous, and success attends him in the battle [of life]. He makes a friend for future troubles.

4. He is no friend who offers nothing to a friend and comrade who comes asking for food. Having no home to rest in, let him depart and rather seek out a stranger for support.

5. Let the rich satisfy the destitute beggar and fix his sight upon the long stretch. Wealth comes now to one, now to another, and like the wheels of a cart is ever rolling on.

6. The foolish man wins food with fruitless labor: that food—I speak the truth—shall be his ruin. He feeds no trusty friend, and has no one to love him. All guilt belongs to him who eats with no one to share.

7. The plowshare digging down makes the food that feeds us, and with its edge cuts through the path it follows. Better a speaking [i.e., teaching] than a silent Brahmin. A generous friend is worth more than a miser.[7]

The emphasis on generosity, or charity, in the Vedic civilization was carried over into Hinduism, Buddhism, and Jainism. Thus the Hindu moral literature has extensive regulations for the institution of giving (*dāna*) relative to each social class, which are codified in the *Dharma-Shāstras* and the *Dāna-Nibandhas* (compendiums on giving). This may sound like a legalistic form of charity, but we must understand such rules in conjunction with other moral virtues, including compassion, which are not merely of a religious nature but are spiritual disciplines. Generosity is not merely a prescribed duty, which the pious Hindu must religiously observe. This becomes clear when we learn that gift-giving must not be mechanical and, in fact, ought to increase both the recipient's and the donor's delight. Thus the Hindu notion of generosity entails an important subjective or feeling quality, which is absent in mere rule-obeying forms of charity.

In particular, in our assessment of Hindu charity, we must not allow ourselves to be misled by questionable applications, such as competitive gift-giving in order to gain merit (*punya*) in the karmic game, which on occasion can also be found among Buddhists. While giving is indeed said to be a meritorious activity that benefits the donor spiritually, the Sanskrit texts are very clear that this positive side effect must not be made the motivation for charitable giving, as this would in fact obliterate its spiritual merit. The basic philosophy of charity within Hinduism is epitomized in the following stanzas from the *Bhagavad-Gītā* (17.20–22):

A gift given because it ought to be given to a worthy recipient at the proper place and time and without [expecting any] reward—that is known as *sattva*-natured.

A gift given reluctantly and aiming at a reward or at [spiritual] merit—that gift is known as *rajas*-natured.

A gift given unkindly or contemptuously at the wrong place and time and to an unworthy recipient—that is named *tamas*-natured.

Sattva, *rajas*, and *tamas* are the three fundamental qualities of cosmic existence, standing respectively for lucidity/goodness, dynamism/agitation, and lethargy/darkness. A virtuous gift has the quality of *sattva*, which promotes goodness, virtue, joy, and spiritual transparency in both the recipient and the donor. The kind of gift that is partially flawed is thought to contain an abundance of *rajas*, and while still being at least potentially helpful to the recipient is not really meritorious. The "throw-away" sort of gift is burdened by the quality of *tamas*; it certainly is of no spiritual benefit to the donor and may even harm the recipient. Clearly, the conscientious donor is expected to be responsible for the quality of his or her charity, which lifts the act of giving out of mere obedience to some moral rule. Proper gift-giving is thus inevitably mindful and compassionate. The donor imbues the gift with the aroma of his or her virtuousness.

The above notions also prevail in Jainism and Buddhism, and the centrality of gift-giving in these two spiritual cultures can be gauged from the fact that without this custom, their respective monastic traditions would be impossible. Jainism recognizes the following five factors involved in any charitable act: (1) recipient, (2) donor, (3) the gift, (4) the manner of giving, and (5) the result. The result, or outcome, depends on the quality of the other four factors. Ideally, charity should be liberating for both donor and recipient, with the best recipient being an ascetic whose life is utterly dedicated to the grand ideal of spiritual liberation.

The *Shvetāmbara* branch of Jainism additionally lists the following five factors, which need to be considered when a charitable gift is made: (1) place, (2) time, (3) the donor's faith, (4) respect for the recipient, and (5) proper sequence. Factors 3 and 5 deserve some elaboration. By "faith" (*shraddhā*) here is meant the donor's state of mind, which must be virtuous and based on a proper understanding of the nature of gift-giving in the context of a spiritual view of the world. "Proper sequence" refers to the appropriate order in which alms are to be distributed, which perhaps has more to do with social customs than spiritual considerations. All these stipulations go to show how for charity to be truly virtuous, the donor must be caring and mindful.

According to the Digambara school of Jainism, the donor's mind, which is crucial in gift-giving, must have the following seven qualities: (1) faith (as explained above), (2) devotion (*bhakti*), (3) contentment, (4), luminous energy (*sattva*), (5) discernment, (6) renunciation, and (7) patience. The gift itself, according to the Digambaras, can consist in shelter, food, medication, or knowledge. These and other similar categories of gift-giving are discussed at great length in Jaina literature. Of special interest here is the gift of knowledge, which has its equivalent in Buddhism, where the gift of the Buddha's teaching (*dharma*) is deemed the highest form of charity, because it removes a person's ignorance, the root cause of all karmic conditioning and lack of inner freedom. When the gift of the Buddha's teaching is accepted, it will in due course liberate the recipient from all those physical, verbal, and mental actions that are inherently demeritorious and not conducive to liberation. As we find stated in the *Dhamma-Pada* (354): "The gift of the Teaching surpasses all gifts."

The Buddha often talked about charity and praised it as a superlative virtue. He considered it one of the three types of meritorious activity, the other two being the cultivation of virtue and contemplation (see, e.g., *Anguttara-Nikāya* (4.241). As he put it:

> Some provide from what little they have, while others who are affluent don't like to give. An offering given from what little one has is worth a thousand times its value.[8]

At one point, the Buddha even encouraged a recent convert from the Jainism, a certain Upāli, to continue to give alms to the Jaina monastics who were accustomed to begging at Upāli's house (see *Majjhima-Nikāya* 1.371). This exemplary tolerance was characteristic of the Buddha and indirectly served to strengthen Upāli's faith in him as an enlightened teacher.

In his discourses, which have been preserved in the Pali language, Gautama the Buddha would often begin with explaining the merit of giving. Not surprisingly, *dāna* is also the first of the ten stages of virtue perfection on the path of the *bodhisattva* at the heart of Mahayana Buddhism. Charity must be extended to all sentient beings. The *bodhisattva* offers protection even to the least insect, and the Mahayana literature is full of touching examples of such compassion and generosity.

A particular aspect of generosity, or charitable friendliness, which deserves to be singled out, is hospitality. Since our modern gregariousness lacks a spiritual ingredient, we generally limit our entertainment of guests to what is "reasonable" and see it as a favor to them rather than a sacred obligation. The phrase "entertainment of guests" in itself is indicative of how we regard this social act: While we entertain our guests, we also very much would like to be entertained by them, and we generally dodge those whom we judge to be "boring people." We might even consider inviting a bore if we can see an advantage in doing so. Thus our hospitality is all too often heavily self-motivated.

Contrast this with the Vedic attitude, which regards any guest as a deity (or angel). The Sanskrit adage *atithi devo bhava* found in the *Taittirīya-Upanishad* (1.11.4) is well known throughout India and in 2005 was even made into a political slogan by India's Ministry of Tourism. The Muslims of the Republic of Azerbaijan (which achieved independence from the Soviet Union in 1991) have a proverb that goes "A guest in the home is a light." When we know that the Sanskrit word *deva* ("deity") applied to a guest means literally "shining one," we can see the connection even better.

Yet, admittedly, Hindu folk wisdom also has a saying that goes "First day, a guest. Second day, a guest. Third day, a calamity." The Sanskrit word for "guest" is *atithi*, which means something like "one who does not (*a-*) [stay more than] a lunar day (*tithi*)." Proper behavior is obviously incumbent not only on the host but also on the guest. Muhammad, founder of Islam, knew of the three-day rule for hospitality, and he belonged to a culture that greatly valued hospitality. The Arabian desert is a desolate, inhospitable place, and in the days of makeshift tents, hospitality had a life-saving function. This probably held true of other regions as well.

In the case of India's spiritual culture, however, we must look beyond the survival value of a custom like hospitality, which offers food and shelter to a stranger. It also is a practical application of the Vedic notion of the interconnectedness and interdependence (*bandhu*) and thus respect or, as Albert Schweitzer would say, reverence for all beings. This is captured in a verse from the *Mahābhārata* (12.374):

> Just as a tree does not deny its shade even to the wood-cutter, so proper hospitality must be offered even to an enemy who comes calling at one's home.

Even an enemy is part of the nexus of life. The Indian way of thinking is that in one lifetime or another, we all have been friends and enemies to all others. Whatever role a person may have in a given lifetime—enemy or friend—if he or she is in need of help, we must never withhold our charity. We can understand the virtue (*dharma*) of hospitality as mirroring the cosmic law (*rita*) in the context of the human microcosm. We can further regard it as an instance of the kind of generosity (*dāna*) that implies an uplifting self-offering, which is like the gift of breath to a suffocating person. For now, suffice it to say that generosity toward a guest is a moral virtue that enhances life for both guest and host.

Life itself is a great gift, and its giver—in the case of our planet—is the Sun. Hence since Vedic times, the Sun has been hailed as the most generous being of the cosmos. This is a fundamental notion in the Solar Yoga of the Vedic seers.[9] The *gāyatrī-mantra*, the most sacred Hindu *mantra*, is in praise of the solar deity:

Om bhūr bhuvar svar, tat savitur varenyam bhargo devasya dhīmahi dhiyo yo nah pracodayāt.

Om. Earth. Midspace. Heaven. May we contemplate that most excellent splendor of God Savitri, so that He may inspire our visions.

We might do well to follow the self-less example of the life-giving star that is at the center of our solar system.

ENDNOTES, CHAPTER 13

1   The warped recommendations of Niccolò Machiavelli in *The Prince* (1505) are a cheerless exception to the rule. He advised power-hungry rulers to be ruthless and give generously of what is not theirs but never to indulge in giving liberally of their own wealth.

2   See Susan U. Raymond, *The Future of Philanthropy: Economics, Ethics, and Management* (New York: John Wiley, 2004); Claire Gaudiani, *The Greater Good: How Philanthropy Drives the American Economy and Can Save Capitalism* (New York: Henry Holt, 2003); Lawrence J. Friedman and Mark D. McGarvie, eds., *Charity, Philanthropy, and Civility in American History* (New York: Cambridge University Press, 2003), and Kathleen D. McCarthy, *American Creed: Philanthropy and the Rise of Civil Society, 1700-1865* (Chicago, Ill.: University of Chicago Press, 2003).

3   See Michel Mollat, *The Poor in the Middle Ages: An Essay in Social History* (New Haven, Conn.: Yale University Press, 1986).

4   See, e.g., Gospel of Mark (10:25).

5   See the user-friendly English translation of the *Tirukkural* by Sivaya Subramuniyaswami, which is available online at various locations, including www.mountainman.com.au/kural/index.htm.

6   The following rendering leans heavily on the 1896 translation by R. Th. Griffith, *Hymns of the Rig Veda* (New Delhi: Munshiram Manoharlal, repr. 1987), 2 vols.

7   There are two more verses to this hymn, which I have left untranslated, as they would require lengthy exposition.

8   *Samyutta-Nikāya* 1.107.

9   For a modern version of this Solar Yoga, see teachings of the Bulgarian Gnostic Omraam Mikhaël Aïvanhov. See, e.g., his book *Toward a Solar Civilisation* (Frejus, France: Prosveta, 1982). See also my book *The Mystery of Light: The Life and Teaching of Omraam Mikhaël Aïvanhov* (Lower Lake, Calif.: Integral Publishing, 1998).

CHAPTER 14

MISCELLANEOUS YOGIC VIRTUES

The average person does not lack virtues altogether, but these tend to be inadequately, unevenly, and unstably developed. Thus, someone might be generous by nature but suffer from anger. Or someone might have a well-developed sense of justice but lack equanimity. Another individual might be naturally frugal but prone to jealousy. Or a person might possess great courage but have little sense of responsibility. And so on. From a yogic perspective, such virtue specializations are the product of positive but lopsided habit patterns cultivated over many lifetimes. While these moral qualities are desirable in themselves, they do not amount to a virtuous character from which virtues flow naturally like the beautiful scent of a flower. In other words, just as a good memory does not mean someone possesses a great intellect, the presence of a single virtue does not make a virtuous character. With compartmentalized rather than integrated virtues, moral backsliding is always a possibility. Moreover, as long as virtues are not accompanied by understanding, they can easily become imbalanced and neurotic. A generous individual can become an insufferable do-gooder and a courageous person a mere fool who "rushes in where others fear to tread."

As Plato knew, a truly virtuous character is a harmonious character. Virtues "click into place" naturally when we voluntarily polish the mirror of the mind. In yogic terms, our behavior becomes virtuous when we magnify the quality of lucidity (*sattva*)—

or what Socrates called the beauty—within us. Yoga proceeds with this noble work by various psychophysiological means, notably meditation, but also by way of abstaining from negative thoughts, emotions, words, and actions and consciously fostering their opposites. Thus the yogic path comprises the two aspects of mental training and ethical discipline. The former deconstructs the ego-illusion and its dependent psychomental habit patterns; the latter reinforces the newly emerging personality ("the new Adam") by meritorious social action.

In the beginning, the Yoga practitioner is apt to pay self-conscious attention to his or her newly gained understanding and ability to behave in more meritorious ways. The predictable feedback from others serves the beginner as a yardstick for gauging the degree of his or her mental and moral transformation. Thus behaving virtuously is a kind of virtue training. The guru, who is typically highly sensitive to the disciple's inner state, also may at decisive moments hold up a mirror in which the beginner can see his or her hidden motivations and true state of mind. This typically gruelling and long-drawn-out process of self-transformation must be expected to contain periods in which the disciple experiences self-doubt, confusion, and discouragement, as well as moral failure. In those moments, the teacher and the teaching, as well as a supportive community of like-minded practitioners, will prove invaluable. By noticing his or her moral missteps, the beginner can reorient himself to the guiding ideals of a virtuous life.

In the long run, however, the Yoga practitioner will stop all neurotic self-watching and self-censoring and simply and naturally engage the program of self-transformation on a day-to-day basis. As Lao Tzu observes in his *Tao Te Ching* (38):

> The man of superior virtue is not deliberately virtuous and thus indeed is virtuous. The man of inferior virtue never forgets he is virtuous and thus forfeits virtue.[1]

The creation of a virtuous character is never accidental, however. As the wise Roman statesman Lucius Annaeus Seneca expressed it in his work *De Beneficiis*, "Nature does not bestow virtue; to be good is an art." Yoga is the art of conscious self-transcendence and self-transformation, which promotes the development of virtuous qualities. Thus virtue crystallizes in us through much deliberate and intelligent work on ourselves. While Yoga's final aim is to create a free rather than merely good person, goodness is understood to be the underpinning of a greater freedom. For the yogin, virtue manifests as part of a far more comprehensive program of personal deconstruction and reconstruction. On the road to inner freedom—equated with spiritual enlightenment—the Yoga practitioner must traverse the path of virtue lest he should become tripped up by karmic actions, notably those that cause harm to other beings.

Virtue theorists have identified over one hundred individual virtues. If we had to cultivate them one by one, we would never be able to see the fruit of our labors in a single lifetime. Benjamin Franklin singled out the following thirteen virtues for systematic cultivation: temperance, silence, order, resolution, frugality, industry, sincerity, justice, moderation, cleanliness, tranquility, justice, and humility. The last virtue he added on the recommendation of a Quaker friend, who gently pointed out to Franklin that pride was one of the moral flaws from which the inventor and statesman suffered. Franklin, who compiled this baker's dozen when he was in his twenties, dedicated a certain amount of time to cultivating each virtue. He even kept a chart to mark his progress but by his own admission failed at his naïve goal of achieving moral perfection. His contemporaries would probably have wholeheartedly agreed with him; they were well aware of his various moral shortcomings. Nevertheless, Franklin's effort is commendable.

Luckily, virtues are interconnected in our own psyche, and as we "purify" our inner life by our sincere intentions, contemplation, and conduct, we simultaneously allow all virtues to emerge. As the Latin word *virtus* suggests, virtues are inner strengths. Virtues are the good qualities that we possess whenever self-centeredness has been suspended and the mind's characteristic turmoil has been properly pacified.

In earlier chapters, I discussed the major virtues that form the backbone of the moral teachings of Yoga in their Hindu, Buddhist, and Jaina variations. These do not, of course, exhaust the repertoire of meritorious attitudes and actions that are available to the yogin. Numerous other virtues are mentioned in the yogic literature, such as Patanjali's five self-restraints (*niyama*) consisting of purity/cleanliness, contentment, asceticism, self-study, and devotion to the Lord with which I will begin the present consideration.

It was the Methodist bishop John Wesley who in the late eighteenth century said in one of his sermons that "cleanliness is indeed next to godliness," reiterating a proverb that apparently originated in Judaism. All religious traditions are concerned with inner purity and its external reflection in bodily cleanliness. Both connotations are captured in the Sanskrit word *shauca*, which is used in the *Yoga-Sūtra* (2.32, 40). In aphorism 2.40, Patanjali explains that by observing purity/cleanliness, the yogin acquires an inner distance from his own body as well as a desire to not be "contaminated" by others. Often this statement is misinterpreted to mean that the yogin becomes disgusted with his own body. The crucial word *jugupsā*, however, is derived from the verbal root *gup*, meaning "to protect." Mere disgust would violate the yogin's aspiration to overcome negative emotions and to neutralize the play between aversion (*dvesha*) and attraction (*rāga*). Therefore it seems more appropriate to understand this particular aphorism as conveying that the adept of Yoga develops a protective mindfulness about his body, especially in the context of interacting with others who are not similarly engaged in a program of self-purification.

This attitude, however, should not be confused with neurotic overprotectiveness. Rather we must assume that *jugupsā* has the quality of mature dispassion, or renunciation, by which the yogin becomes able to observe his body objectively, which implies that he has a certain inner aloofness from it. This dispassionate mindfulness also allows him to notice the "contaminating" effect that other, impure people have on his body-mind and to take the necessary countermeasures. This purist attitude does not spring from a haughty elitism but a genuine desire to progress on the path of self-purification. The purer, or more *sattvic*, the aspirant's body-mind becomes, the more sensitive he becomes to outside influences, and sometimes this hypersensitivity can present a real challenge. For this reason, many traditional authorities recommend that the serious practitioner should minimize his or her social contact, if not seek out complete solitude. Eventually, the yogin learns to be like the proverbial lotus, which remains unstained by the muddy water on which it floats.

The entire work of Yoga can be regarded as a progressive process of self-purification by way of mental transparency, leading to the perfect innate "purity" of the ultimate Being. In his *Yoga-Sūtra* (2.41), Patanjali refers to this mental or inner transparency as *sattva-shuddhi*, where *shuddhi* stands for "purity/purification" and *sattva* represents one's inner being, or mind, which is the most refined aspect of cosmic existence. As he makes clear in this aphorism, this systematic concern with self-purification in due course leads to a cheerful disposition, "one-pointedness" (i.e., mental concentration), mastery over the senses, and the capacity for "self-vision" (*ātma-darshana*). The last-mentioned facility, which implies a peaceful mind, opens the inner vision to the spiritual Reality hidden behind all mental activities.

Patanjali names contentment (*samtosha*) as the second of the five practices of "self-restraint" and states in aphorism 2.42 that it yields unexcelled joy. The *Manu-Smriti* (4.12), a major Sanskrit work on morality and law, confirms that "contentment is the root of joy; its opposite is the root of suffering." The operative idea in the virtue of contentment is "enough." The contented individual does not grasp for "more." Diogenes lived happily in a barrel, while Alexander the Great, who out of curiosity once visited the sage, found no satisfaction even after conquering half the civilized world. Grasping makes the mind restless and sends it on a journey away from inner light and peace. The *Yoga-Bhāshya* (2.42), a fifth-century commentary on Patanjali's compilation, quotes the following adage: "Both the pleasure of love in this world and the superlative pleasure of heaven do not compare to a sixteenth part of the pleasure of someone whose craving has dwindled."

The *Shāndilya-Upanishad* (1.2), composed between the thirteenth and fifteenth centuries, explains contentment as the condition of being satisfied with whatever comes one's way of its own accord. This definition corresponds to a more radical orientation of renunciation, which befits the ascetical yogin who has cut himself off from conventional life. He lives from day to day, trusting entirely that his good karma will provide all necessities for him. In India's warm climate and tolerant culture, many ascetics roam the countryside in the nude or scantily dressed.[2] Following the ancient custom of hospitality and charity, pious householders gladly share their meager provisions with holy men. Not a few ascetics, however, live entirely off the land. Some eat only the ripe fruit falling from trees and drink the morning dew gathered on leaves.

The situation is necessarily different for householder yogins, who have a family and must hold down a job to provide for their dependents. In Western countries, with their colder climate and cultural bias against external renunciation, the kind of radical asceticism witnessed in India, would be entirely impossible. Public nudity, whatever its reason, is found generally unacceptable, and extreme asceticism is likely to lead to psychiatric intervention. Furthermore, Western householders who are committed to a spiritual discipline are embroiled in a noisy, hurried and harried society with a high cost of living, which makes a quiet, peaceful, and simple lifestyle quite difficult. Voluntary simplicity is still possible, however, although it will never look anything like the lifestyle of India's itinerant ascetics.[3] In our Western context, it makes sense for a Yoga practitioner with a family to have a reasonably well-paying job, a savings account, health insurance, and a pension plan.

It also makes sense, however, to arrange one's life in a responsible way that minimizes the pressures of modern life as much as possible, not only for oneself but for one's entire family. This move toward voluntary simplicity calls for a fair amount of introspection and also collaboration within the household, and the eventual solution will inevitably be a compromise. For Western spiritual practitioners, the practice of contentment must start here.

The third item in Patanjali's list of self-restraints is asceticism (*tapas*). This Sanskrit term means literally "heat" and refers to any form of spiritual practice that challenges the mind's habit patterns and thereby "heats up" our inner environment. It is voluntary creative self-frustration. This archaic practice can be first encountered in the *Rig-Veda* (10.129) where the ultimate Being itself is said to undergo a process of intense self-heating in order to emanate the universe. Yoga can be interpreted as the same process in reverse at the microcosmic level: The yogin "heats" himself to melt down the cosmic structures as they manifest in the form of his own body-mind, whereby the ultimate Being is revealed.[4]

Few people nowadays have a concept of this traditional practice and virtue. Most Westerners, who are spoiled by the luxuries of our consumer society, tend to be self-indulgent rather than self-disciplined. Asceticism, in stark contrast, is drastic self-discipline. The Greek word *askesis* is frequently flatly interpreted as "extreme self-denial." Often the word "penance"—derived from Latin *paenitentia*, "penitence"—is used interchangeably, but this is equally unsatisfactory. The yogin engages in asceticism not to punish himself or repent with a contrite conscience, which would be the Christian interpretation. Instead, he simply appreciates that unless the mind is properly controlled, it is a source of never-ending suffering. Nor should tapas be equated with self-mortification that is intended to "kill" the flesh.

In a yogic context, asceticism is best understood as spiritual discipline, its essential characteristic being the transcendence of the ego. Although asceticism often involves disciplines by which a practitioner "denies" himself or herself certain customary things, notably food, sleep, and comfort. But these external "denials" are not what is important in genuine asceticism. Rather, such disciplines as fasting, staying awake for prolonged periods, or exposing oneself to discomfort, are incidental to the more important inner exertion of disallowing the mind to flow along well-worn grooves of habit. The *Bhagavad-Gītā* (17.16–19) distinguishes between three types of asceticism:

Serenity of mind, gentleness, silence, self-restraint, and purification of the [inner] states is what is called mental asceticism.

This threefold asceticism practiced with supreme faith by people who are disciplined and not longing for the fruit [of their deeds] is what is known as *sattva*-natured.

Asceticism that is performed for the sake of good treatment, honor, and reverence or out of deceitfulness is what is called here *rajas*-natured; it is fickle and unsteady.

Asceticism that is performed out of foolish notions for self-torture or in order to ruin someone else is what is named *tamas*-natured.

Verses 17.5–6 of the same text makes it abundantly clear that violent austerity merely tortures the body and bears no positive fruit. The God-man Krishna even argues that the kind of asceticism that oppresses the bodily elements also indirectly (and metaphorically) oppresses him in the form of the Spirit enshrined in the body. While India has had its share of misguided asceticism, Yoga distinctly favors balance in all things, especially spiritual practice.

Gautama the Buddha started out as a radical ascetic, who for six long years did in fact "oppress" his body, but then he realized that in order to attain authentic liberation, he had to walk the middle path between the extremes of self-denial and self-indulgence. He started to nourish his emaciated body properly and soon gained an inner balance that blossomed into the full spiritual awakening for which he became famous. His five fellow ascetics, who failed to understand his reasoning and course of action, left him in disapproval. Subsequently, however, when they saw the awakened one's luminous countenance, they became the Buddha's first disciples.

Self-study (*svādhyāya*), the fourth of Patanjali's disciplines of self-restraint, also has a long history in India, starting with the *Vedas*. As the yogic scriptures explain, *svādhyāya* means both "studying the tradition oneself" and "studying one's self." Both connotations apply to the traditional practice of scriptural learning. By studying the wisdom found in the texts, the yogin also learns about himself, mainly by seeing how his mind and life do not yet reflect the great virtues extolled by the sages. Scriptural study is an important aspect of all religio-spiritual traditions that are backed by texts (whether written or memorized). Christians study the New Testament and, more rarely, traditional hagiographies or the tracts of the great Christian mystics. The Jews study the Torah and, more rarely, the Talmud. The Muslims study the Qur'an and, more rarely, the Hadith or the writings of great Sufi masters. The Buddhists and Jainas study their particular school's canonical texts and, more rarely, the texts of other schools. The same applies to Hindus, who possess a vast sacred literature. Self-study is to be pursued as a sacred discipline. In other words, it is neither casual reading nor academic research. Its purpose is not merely to fill the mind of the aspirant with useful knowledge but to transform him or her. In other words, for study to be *svādhyāya*, it must be mind altering in the deeper sense.

Devotion to the Lord (*īshvara-pranidhāna*), the fifth and last discipline of self-restraint is the virtuous practice of devotion to a higher principle, which corresponds to love-devotion (*bhakti*) in the monotheistic schools of Yoga, and having introduced this subject in Chapter 12, I will refrain from further discussion.[5]

Post-classical Yoga texts, such as the *Tri-Shikhi-Brāhmana-Upanishad* (2.33), mention ten rather than five moral disciplines (*yama*). These include the first four virtues of Patanjali's list, which I reviewed in Chapters 6–10, plus patience, integrity/rectitude, sympathy, steadfastness, moderation in diet, and again purity, which deserve at least a brief consideration here.

In Hinduism, patience (*kshānti, kshamā*) is widely respected as a chief virtue, and it also is prominent in Jainism and even more so in Buddhism. The medieval *Yoga-Yājnavalky*a (1.64) defines it as equanimity toward all pleasant and unpleasant experiences, while the *Darshana-Upanishad* (1.16–17) explains it as one's refraining from agitation when provoked by one's enemies. The *Bhagavad-Gītā* (13.7), again, considers it to be a manifestation of wisdom. In the *Anguttara-Nikāya* (5.140), giving out the Buddha's own words, we can get a sense of the comprehensiveness of patience:

How is a practitioner patient? By being indifferent to cold, heat, hunger, and thirst; to contact with flies, mosquitoes, wind, sun, and reptiles; to ill-spoken, unwelcome words and bodily sensations that, when they arise, are painful, stinging, disagreeable, displeasing, and threatening to life.

In one of his many sermons, as recorded in the *Samyutta-Nikāya* (1.222), the Buddha told the ancient myth of the verbal battle between the gods and the anti-gods. Sakka (i.e., Indra), the leader of the former, praised forbearance (*titikshā*) as follows:

Whatever anyone may think,
when cultivating the highest goal
nothing compares to patience.
And the highest form of patience
is to tolerate the weakness and shortcomings of others.

The Buddhist *Dhamma-Pada* (184), a popular didactic Hinayana scripture, similarly extols patience as the highest form of asceticism. How fundamental this virtue is can be gauged from the fact that in the Mahayana branch of Buddhism, patience figures as one of the ten stages on the bodhisattva path. Here patience is seen as the antidote to anger. Just how extraordinary the forbearance of a bodhisattva must be can be gleaned from his or her earnest resolution to continue to work for the spiritual welfare of all beings "for as long as space endures," as Shāntideva puts it in his *Bodhicaryāvatāra* (10.55).

In contradistinction, the impatience of contemporary Westerners is proverbial. The Anglo-American poet and dramatist Wystan Hugh Auden astutely observed: "Perhaps there is only one cardinal sin: impatience. Because of impatience we were driven out of Paradise, because of impatience we cannot return." Francis Bacon expressed it more succinctly thus: "Whoever is out of patience is out of possession of their soul."

Integrity/rectitude (*ārjava*), the next moral discipline of the extended set of *yamas*, is often mentioned in yogic texts. We can see it as a function or aspect of truthfulness, which I have treated in detail in Chapter 7.

Sympathy (*dayā*) is really a subcategory of compassion, as elaborated in Chapter 11. This Sanskrit word stems from the verbal root *da*, meaning "to give," and hence it can also be translated as "compassionate giving."

Steadfastness (*dhriti*), which is frequently advocated in the Yoga texts, is a virtue without which the yogic process cannot succeed. As spiritual transformation, contrary to popular Western belief, is not an overnight or week-end achievement, the yogin must prepare for the long haul. Yoga is a lifetime undertaking and hence demands great stability in one's intention, vision, and practice. As the *Yoga-Sūtra* (1.14) emphasizes, practice becomes firmly grounded only through uninterrupted and proper cultivation over a long period of time.

Moderation in diet (*mita-āhāra*) falls under the heading of temperance. While some texts recommend fasting, most favor a balanced approach. Rather than denying the body essential nourishment, it seems better to simply practice moderation in all things, including dieting. Extreme physical practices tend to throw the mind off balance, and an equanimous mind is essential for the higher stages of the yogic work of self-transformation.

Purity (*shauca*), which I treated above as one of the meritorious practices of self-restraint (*niyama*), is also often reckoned among the moral disciplines (*yama*).

Earlier I mentioned generosity and patience in connection with the bodhisattva path, which comprises the following ten stages of "virtue perfection" (*pāramitā*): (1) generosity, (2) conduct, (3) patience, (4) vigor, (5) meditation, (6) wisdom, (7) skillful means, (8) aspiration, (9) power, and (10) knowledge.[6] I propose to sketch out the virtues not yet introduced.

The second stage of the bodhisattva path consists in the perfection of the virtue of conduct (*shīla*), meaning proper moral behavior. Specifically it means putting all the many precepts applying to a bodhisattva into practice.

By vigor or energy (*vīrya*), the theme of the fourth stage, is meant both the physical and mental stamina needed to truly serve others diligently, without the slightest hesitation and laziness.

Meditation (*dhyāna*), which is to be cultivated to perfection on the fifth stage of the bodhisattva path, is central to all forms of Yoga. This virtue is considered perfected when the yogin has flawless control over his own mind. An uncontrolled mind is scattered and of no benefit to oneself or others.

Wisdom (*prajñā*), the object of the cultivation on the sixth stage, is the great transcendental insight arising from the most profound state of meditation. This supreme wisdom relates to the weighty realization that all things are simultaneously interconnected and empty. I have addressed the interconnectedness, or interdependence, of all phenomena in various chapters. Here I would like to focus on the deep Buddhist notion of emptiness (*shūnyatā*), which originated with Gautama the Buddha and was subsequently greatly enlarged upon by the masters of Mahayana, notably the second-century adept Nāgārjuna. The concept of emptiness is simple in principle but complex in the theoretical elaborations furnished in the Mahayana and Vajrayana literature.

In essence, when the Buddhists insist that phenomena are "empty," they mean to capture the undeniable fact that whatever exists is not what it appears to be. More precisely, things lack essentiality (*sva-bhāva*). When we analyze anything into its constituent parts—whether it be our body-mind or a computer—we quickly realize that "things" are largely creations of the conceptual mind. The moment we attempt to gaze beyond the labels that we attach to phenomena, we find that they are not stable, permanent things or identities in themselves. For instance, "computer" is the name we give to an agglomeration of many components, which, upon closer inspection, themselves are made of components, and so on. Reality is fluid and rather elusive. We can say that there is "something" happening, but we can never quite pin down what that is. Philosophically, things are "empty" of an identifiable essence.

For a yogin, this recognition is important for two reasons. First, it fosters an attitude of renunciation, because if the things to which we are normally so attached do not quite exist in the way we think, there is no point in hanging on to them for dear life. Second, if phenomena are not as stable as the conceptual mind makes them out to be, we can apply the same wisdom to our own mind and successfully detach from its processes to free pristine awareness, which is transcendental. At that point all phenomena recede: the cluttered mind becomes transparent (mirror-like) mind, which stands free irrespective of arising phenomena or even whether or not phenomena are arising.

Skillful means (*upāya*), which the bodhisattva seeks to master on the seventh stage, consists in compassionate and expedient activity that is based in the dual recognition that there are suffering beings who are in need of help yet that they are, in truth, empty and already liberated.[7] Skillful means signifies knowing what to do and say in any given situation in order to uplift someone else spiritually. For example, a teacher might talk to a student about transcendental realms ("paradises"), such as Avolokiteshvara's *tushita* realm, in order to create faith and hope, while on another occasion he might teach another, more mature student that everything is empty.

Aspiration (*pranidhāna*), to be perfected on the eighth stage of the path, refers to the bodhisattva's core aspiration to liberate all beings. He becomes so sensitive to everyone's suffering that he cannot bear to rest even for an instant. This overwhelming impulse is beautifully illustrated in the myth about the transcendental bodhisattva Avalokiteshvara, the "patron saint" of Tibet. On seeing the untold suffering of all beings embroiled in cosmic existence, his head split into thousands of pieces. Amitabha Buddha reassembled that great bodhisattva, who now is usually visualized as having eleven heads and a thousand arms that compassionately extend to all beings.

Power (*bala*), the theme of the ninth stage of the altruistic path, is the incomparable spiritual puissance of a bodhisattva by which he is able to successfully effect any compassionate activity that his pure heart envisions for the benefit of others.

The knowledge (*jnāna*) that the bodhisattva is expected to perfect on the tenth and final stage is making him virtually omniscient. With the perfection in this virtue, he becomes a Buddha.

Returning to Hinduism, we may note that the vast sacred literature of this spiritual culture names many additional virtues, such as—in English alphabetical order—adherence to the path of truth (*satya-mārga-anurakti*), cheerfulness (*saumanasya*), courage (*dhrishnutva*), devotion to the teacher (*guru-bhakti*), dispassion (*virāga, vairāgya*), egality (*sama-darshana*), equanimity (*upekshā*), faith (*shraddhā*), fearlessness (*abhaya*), forgiveness (*marshana*), frugality (*amuktahasta*), gentleness (*mārdava*), gratitude (*pratyupakāra*), humility (*amānitva*), loyalty (*prativrata*), mastery over the senses (*indriya-jaya*), mastery over the mind (*mano-jaya*), mastery over sleep (*nidrā-jaya*), modesty (*hrī*), non-attachment (*nihsangatā*), nonjealousy (*anīrshya-bhāva*), piety (*āstikya*), prudence (*kāryacintā*), respect (*anunaya*), reverence for all life (*prāna-abhyarcana*), scant diet (*laghv-āhāra*), self-effacement (*anahamkāra*), self-reliance (*svādhīnatā*), softspokenness (*priyamvadā*), solitude (*ekānta-vāsa*), tolerance (*kshānti*), sobriety (*anunmatta*), and tranquility (*upashama*). Many of these virtues are variations of those that have been discussed already. I would like, however, to say a few words about faith, fearlessness, gratitude, humility, tolerance, and solitude.

Faith, which must not be confounded with mere belief, is a fundamental mental disposition by which we affirm our trust in the fundamental goodness of Reality. Yogically speaking, it is our trust and conviction that as long as we remain true to the spiritual path, everything will work out in our favor. Faith is the opposite of spiritual doubt (*samshaya*), which fragments the mind and devastates our emotional life. Elsewhere I have characterized faith as "radical openness" to something or someone who holds superlative personal significance for us, who, in Paul Tillich's terms, is our "ultimate concern."[8]

Typically, an ultimate concern is not worthy of great trust, because unless it happens to be Reality (Spirit) itself, we will inevitably be betrayed. For example, if we make another human individual the object of our faith, we are bound to experience disappointment. Or if we make wealth or nationalism our ultimate concern, we will unavoidably remain unfulfilled. Any ultimate concern other than ultimate Being is a source of disillusionment. As the *Bhagavad-Gītā* (17.3) reminds us, "A person is of the nature of his faith. Whatever his faith is, that indeed is he."

Gratitude, in yogic contexts, is not merely saying "thank you," which yogins rarely do. Rather, as the Sanskrit word *pratyupakāra* suggests, it is active reciprocation of a kindness done to us. In the West, we all too often verbalize gratitude without meaning or feeling it. "Thank you" is frequently little more than a polite formula. Genuine gratitude, however, is a positive state of mind that gives rise to positive action. As such, it is a subform of the virtue of giving. A yogin who is firmly on the path is bound to feel immense gratitude for being alive and having received a liberating teaching and a teacher (*guru*) who is dedicated to helping him realize the goal of inner freedom.

Humility, a sure sign of spiritual nobility, is the feeling of being "nothing special"—a human being full of flaws, though intent on overcoming all shortcomings. According to the Gospel of Matthew (18:4), Jesus of Nazareth said: "Whosoever humbles himself as a little child is the greatest in the kingdom of heaven." To demonstrate the virtue of humility, which consists in the attitude of being a servant to all, Jesus washed the feet of his disciples. The renowned twentieth-century Yoga master Swami Sivananda taught the same lesson to one of his young initiates when he did a full-length prostration in front of the disciple, who could not bring himself to bow to his *guru* as is customary.

Tolerance, in modern times, is a virtue that tends to be primarily applied in religious and ethnic contexts. On the spiritual path, however, it must be extended to all beings and situations. The Sanskrit language has no separate word to denote "tolerance," but generally the common word *kshānti*, meaning "patience," is used, which captures one of the ingredients of the attitude of tolerance. The other ingredient is an attitude of accepting things that are different from our expectations, which falls under the virtue of regarding everything with an even eye (*sama-darshana*).

True tolerance, on the personal level, demands a modicum of wisdom, which allows us to see common denominators rather than merely distinctions. Hinduism is one of the most tolerant cultures, periodic lapses into intolerance notwithstanding. Already the Buddhist emperor Ashoka in the third century B.C., pleaded in one of his numerous edicts as follows:

> . . . Growth in the essential teaching can be accomplished in different ways, but all have as their root verbal restraint, that is, by not extolling one's own religion or disparaging the religion of others without good reason or [if there is cause for criticism] on certain occasions, by doing so in a mild manner. . . . Therefore concord is salutary, so that everyone listens to and respects the teachings of others.[9]

This commendable attitude is foreshadowed in one of the hymns of the *Rig-Veda* (1.64.46), which states that "Truth is one, but the sages speak of it in many ways." The Jaina monks developed this laudable stance into a full-fledged philosophical teaching— the doctrine of *anekānta-vāda*.[10] According to this approach, the Jaina yogin ought to look at everything from multiple viewpoints. This orientation is epitomized in the classic parable of the blind men who are led to an elephant and asked to describe the animal. As each man grabbed hold of a different body part, their descriptions are correspondingly different and quite comical.

At this point, I would like to insert a relevant side note on U.S. politics. The official policy of "zero tolerance" in the United States' "war on drugs" is an example of the opposite attitude. As the phrase spells out very clearly, the authorities are intent on *not* exercising the virtue of tolerance in this case, and they often even err on the side of intolerance and injustice. While I do not question the appropriateness of a nation to enforce its laws, their application must be impartial and commensurate with the nature of the crime. Thus, even though three quarters of illicit drug users are white Americans, yet 56 percent of drug offenders in prison are African Americans (who make up only 13 percent of the American population).

Moreover, this zero tolerance has—seemingly irrationally— been extended even to consumer goods made from the fiber-producing, non-narcotic strain of hemp (*sativa cannabis*), only because marijuana is produced from the flower of the narcotic strain of this plant. For the United States, this represents a complete reversal of an earlier policy, when it was illegal for a farmer to *not* grow hemp, which is possibly the most versatile plant on Earth.[11] Whatever the undesirable consequences of marijuana use may be, it is an undeniable fact that the growing and utilizing of hemp was outlawed not because of any great concern for the welfare of the American public but because of political and commercial interests: Hemp, it turns out on closer examination, was in the way of corporate business, which chose to base itself on fossil fuel and its derivatives.

One of the virtues that is seldom singled out for special attention but is implicit to all yogic morality is sobriety (*anunmatta* or *anucchvāsa*). Obviously, a mind befuddled by alcohol is incapable of proper judgment or discernment (*viveka*) and concentration. Again, this is a virtue that is conspicuous by its paucity in our modern society. In fact, the abuse of alcohol is a significant problem in Northern America, Europe, and elsewhere. While apparently 90 percent of Americans regard alcoholism as a disease, the medical profession and the courts are not so sure. At any rate, alcohol abuse and dependence cost the U.S. some $170 billion every year in healthcare expenditure, not counting the medical price tag for injuries sustained from drunk driving. The human cost of alcohol abuse is inestimable.

With the exception of the ritual use of alcohol in Tantra, Yoga makes no allowance for inebriation. In the Buddhist tradition, it is considered a "root downfall," though many Western Buddhists have a conveniently lukewarm attitude toward the consumption of alcohol. Some even seek to excuse their penchant for alcoholic beverages by pointing to the Buddha's "middle way," arguing that there is no harm in occasional and moderate drinking. Abstention from intoxicating drinks and drugs is unmistakably named as one of the five precepts (*shīla*), applying equally to monastics and lay folk.

In conclusion, we may wonder how modern virtues like punctuality, orderliness, and environmental conscience fit into the picture? Punctuality seems to be a contemporary obsession. The more relaxed lifestyle of traditional cultures does not expect anyone to live by the clock (which was invented only in the last quarter of the sixteenth century). As for orderliness, this concept also belongs to the machine age where predictability and efficiency are deemed important qualities. It is a product of the rational mind, which works in binary fashion (yes/no) and demands reality to fit this model. The ancient sages, while fully valuing the conceptual mind, did not allow themselves to be hemmed in by sheer logic but also availed themselves liberally of intuition and sagacious insight. Fortunately, twentieth-century quantum mechanics, has poked holes in the Newtonian worldview created primarily by the binary logic of the rational mind, and, perhaps more importantly, has revealed the rational mind to be of limited scope. Not surprisingly, those favorable to a metaphysical and mystical interpretation of the world have pounced upon the understanding of quantum mechanics to buttress their argument that reality cannot be fit into tight conceptual boxes.

Finally, the Sanskrit language lacks an equivalent for the notion of environmental conscience. Although the ancient world has had its share of climate change and deforestation, it never had to confront the enormous ecological devastation that our own era is facing. The idea of environmental conscience, however, is an integral part of the traditional value system via the virtue of balance (*samatva*). The sages of yore were well aware of the interdependence of all things. For them, the Earth and the universe at large were sacred and brimming with life and with invisible agents, notably deities. Perhaps we are about to rediscover at least a portion of their understanding of the world.

ENDNOTES, CHAPTER 14

1   This is my own paraphrase.

2   For an excellent documentary on the Nāga Babas, or naked Hindu ascetics, see *Naked in Ashes*, directed by Paula Fouce and distributed by Paradise Film-works (Las Vegas, Nev., 2005). See also the documentary *Kumbha Mela* by Jack Hebner, published in a DVD edition by Mandala (San Rafael, Calif., 2003). See also Dolf Hartsuiker, *Sadhus: India's Mystic Holy Men* (Rochester, Vt.: Inner Traditions, 1993).

3   See Duane Elgin, *Voluntary Simplicity: Toward a Way of Life That Is Outwardly Simple, Inwardly Rich* (New York: Harper Paperbacks, rev. ed. 1998) and Janet Luhrs, *The Simple Living Guide* (New York: Broadway Books, 1997).

4   See Walter O. Kaelber, *Tapta-Marga: Asceticism and Initiation in Vedic India* (Albany, N.Y.: SUNY Press, 1989). See also the anthology by Vincent L. Wimbush and Richard Valantasis, eds., *Asceticism* (New York: Oxford University Press, 1998).

5   Patanjali's concept of *īshvara* ("lord") is quite problematic within the framework of his peculiar dualistic system of metaphysics, which makes an uncompromising distinction between the cosmos (*prakriti*) in all its aspects and the transcendental Spirit (*purusha*). The *Yoga-Sūtra* (1.24) defines *īshvara* as "a special Spirit untouched by the causes of affliction, action, fruition, and [karmic] deposits." See Georg Feuerstein, *The Philosophy of Classical Yoga* (Rochester, Vt.: Inner Traditions, repr. 1996).

6   See Robert Aitken, *The Practice of Perfection: The Paramitas from a Zen Buddhist Perspective* (Washington, D.C.: Counterpoint, 2d ed. 1997). See also Shantideva, *The Way of the Bodhisattva: A Translation of the Bodhicharyavatara*. Trans. by the Padmakara Translation Group (Boston, Mass.: Shambhala Publications, 2003).

7   See Michael Pye, *Skillful Means: A Concept in Mahayana Buddhism* (London: Duckworth, 1978).

8   See Georg Feuerstein, *The Deeper Dimension of Yoga* (Boston, Mass.: Shambhala Publications, 2003), pp. 287–288.

9   This is a partial rendering of the text of Rock Edict XII. See also Romila Tharpar, *Aśoka and the Decline of the Mauryas* (New York: Oxford University Press, 1997), p. 255.

10   See Tara Sethia, *Ahimsa, Anekanta and Jainism* (Delhi: Motilal Banarsidass, 2004).

11   For an eye-opening 1942 propaganda film on hemp produced by the U.S. government at a time when growing hemp was encouraged, see *Hemp for Victory*, which can be viewed at www.watchfilms.com/movies/.

CHAPTER 15

DEATH, FREEDOM, AND MORAL SPONTANEITY

Before we can walk and grow on the spiritual path, we must first experience an inner turning, or what the ancient Greeks appropriately called *metanoia*. The literal meaning of this word is "beyond thought," that is, "beyond the conventional mind." Usually, the term is translated as "inner turnabout" or "change of heart." The Sanskrit language has a similar word to express the same idea, namely *parāvritti*, or "reversal." The reversal intended is the kind of revolution that must occur in our thinking in order to even want to dedicate ourselves to inner growth through spiritual discipline. In Buddhist terms, we must acquire correct view (*samyag-drishti*). This means that we have to be willing to consider our life in light of existing wisdom teachings. When these teachings have made their point in us, we must then apply them to our everyday life.

All of India's spiritual traditions agree that we commonly live in the darkness of spiritual ignorance (*avidyā*). It is this fundamental nescience that is the root cause of our suffering. Spirituality consists in removing this primary ignorance. According to Jainism, there are fourteen steps to inner freedom. We begin with false vision (*mithyā-drishti*), which makes us identify with the body-mind and its diverse activities. That is to say, we construct an ego for ourselves. But, as Chögyam Trungpa put it so vividly, the ego is merely the result of "a succession of confusions."[1] As a consequence, we are under the sway of karma, that is, the far-reaching influence of all our past volitions and actions. Thus we are keeping ourselves in lock-step with our own shadow. Gradually, through the hard knocks of life and perhaps the graceful intervention of our teachers, knowledge dawns in us. We develop a taste for correct view, but we may still experience long lapses into spiritual unconsciousness, which characterizes the second step in the fourteen-step model of the path. At a certain point, correct view and false vision oscillate yielding slight relief from karmic necessity through further insight into our unconscious thought patterns and behavior. This is the third step. Next we may find that we have attained to correct view, but our emotions are still trailing behind our insights. Now the challenge before us is to cultivate self-restraint (*virati*), which is the real beginning of the spiritual work. The fifth step consists in a deepening desire to let go of worldly things and adopt the rigorous lifestyle of an ascetic. Through voluntary simplicity and a battery of ascetical practices, we can overcome the binding force of the four major vices of anger, pride, delusion, and greed.

The challenge at this stage—the six step—is to gain control over the play of attention (*pramatta-samyatā*). Our mind typically wanders from thought to thought, powered by the engine of the subconscious karmic deposits. Inattention (*pramāda*) is a significant obstacle on the yogic path and must be overcome. The next, seventh step consists in our honing the mind's capacity for concentration, which, among other things, helps us overcome sleep. This inner work continues until all our karmic self-expressions are perfectly subdued, including the sexual instinct, the emotions, and subtle mental delusions.

At long last, we penetrate the ego-delusion itself and gain total gnosis (the exact opposite of false knowledge) and what is called "active transcendence" (*sayoga-kevalī*). This thirteenth step, which superforms us into a "transcender" (*kevalin*), "victor" (*jīna*), or "worthy one" (*arhat*), corresponds to the state of transconceptual ecstasy (*asamprajnāta-samādhi*) in Patanjali's Classical Yoga. Then, upon the demise of the physical body, we automatically enter into "inactive transcendence" (*ayoga-kevalī*), which is the fourteenth and final step. This developmental stage in what amounts to a dizzying journey to the peak of spiritual development can be compared to Patanjali's "cloud of virtue" ecstasy (*dharma-megha-samādhi*), which leads directly to liberation. This is not the place to discuss what this means exactly or to compare the distinct concepts of liberation at home in the various yogic traditions. Suffice it to say that the path to liberation calls for a total reshaping of our human nature and, finally, even its complete transcendence.

We are like villagers living in an isolated valley at the foot of a huge mountain, having forgotten that there is more to the world than our immediate environment. Unless our gaze perchance falls upon the lofty peak outside the village with its endless daily concerns and worries, we will never want to experience the freedom of vision granted at the summit. We must first become aware of the possibility that we can scale the mountain and that, in fact, extraordinary individuals in our village have done so in the past. Perhaps the pain of life itself makes us look up with a vague longing. Or, if we have the good fortune, a wise fellow villager draws our attention to the mountain and its promising possibilities. Usually it takes a crisis for us to raise our habitual downward glance and look beyond the maze of samsāra, our familiar karmic world.

Whatever it may be that interrupts our routine life, we still have to *want* to look up and embrace the vista revealed by our upward gaze. Sometimes, fear prevents us from wanting to look more closely. Sometimes, the panorama revealed to our glance seems too daunting to traverse and we meekly return to our samsaric tracks through life. We do not feel up to the challenge, and thus we postpone the inevitable.

Sometimes, however, a person is awestruck by the revealed landscape and becomes excited about its possibilities. Then he or she is willing to take a risk, gear up, and scale the mountain. Upon hearing of the success of others who have reached the summit and now breathe the air of freedom, such a courageous individual will start to look for guidance. Seemingly as an inviolable rule, help is extended to those who are sincerely committed to the steep climb. Assistance comes in the form of teachings and teachers, and this is how the world's spiritual traditions have been preserved for untold ages. We can look upon this supportive response as a manifestation of the law of reciprocity that prevails in a universe governed by interdependence (*bandhu*).

Teachings and teachers provide are, as it were, external props until the teachings have become fully internalized and the authority figure of the guru has been integrated and starts to manifest in the form of the aspirant's own conscience. But this internalization of the spiritual teachings and one's teacher is not exhausted by the usual psychological process of imitation or "echoing" of external standards. The yogin is not a mindless "yes man." Rather, prompted by his own emerging wisdom, he is able to see and appreciate the wisdom inherent in the teachings and in the counsel of his teacher. Conversely, the external teachings and the presence of the charismatic figure of the guru serve as catalysts, which educe the aspirant's innate wisdom. This is the real meaning of education: to educe, or bring out, what is already present deep within.

Because, ideally, the guru is a self-transcending person in whom the wisdom function is fully activated, he reflects the same wisdom that is also at least potentially present within the disciple. The more the aspirant is able to tune into his or her deeper wisdom, the more he or she will experience the efficacy of the "inner teacher." In the final analysis, there is no distinction between the external guru and the internal teacher. At that point, the disciple's relationship to his or her guru is bound to change. On the one hand, it will deepen immensely; on the other hand, a shift in the external aspects of the relationship is likely to occur. Often the teacher will insist that a "fully baked" disciple will go his or her own way or, quite simply, circumstances will force that disciple to seriously focus on his or her own teaching work. This is the crucial moment when, as the Zen saying has it, the disciple must "kill" the Buddha when he encounters him on the road. The distinction of inner and outer guru, which previously proved essential, has become false and therefore needs to be disposed of.

Similarly, the traditional teachings, which are the repositories of the wisdom of masters, have the purpose of guiding the aspirant's behavior from outside until wisdom manifests clearly from the depths of his or her own mind. When the diverse spiritual virtues are actualized, the need for external guidelines drops away. In that case, the mature practitioner must learn to trust his or her own wisdom and moral conscience. This switch to inner guidance is liable to occur long before enlightenment, and hence the yogin must continue to be supremely mindful of his mental continuum and conduct in the world, lest he should commit renewed karmic blunders.

It is unambiguously obvious from the bodhisattva path that in order to attain full enlightenment, or Buddhahood, we must cultivate the great virtues to perfection. The Sanskrit term *pāramitā*, which is applied to the virtues to be perfected by a bodhisattva, is derived from the verbal root *pri*, meaning "to cross over." The related word *pāra* denotes "opposite shore" or "farther bank," which relates to the notion that the world of change, or samsāra, is like a vast ocean that the yogin must cross in order to reach the distant shore of liberation. Thus the feminine noun *pāramitā* suggests "extreme limit" or "perfection." In the present context, the underlying notion is that the enlightened being is infinitely generous, infinitely patient, infinitely attentive, and so forth.

I am reminded here of Lucius Annaeus Seneca's remark that virtue is "the only immortal thing that belongs to mortality." What this great Roman statesman and philosopher meant to convey by this somewhat obscure apothegm is that virtue, pertaining to the realm of perfection, touches our imperfect human life and renders it more sublime. It is like a lightning rod connecting heaven and earth. Seneca implied that we can meaningfully confront our mortality only through a virtuous life, and this is exactly what he himself aspired to. He faced death bravely when Nero, without a trial, ordered him to commit suicide as a punishment for his alleged conspiracy against the mad emperor. "I ask you," wrote Seneca to his friend Lucillius, "wouldn't you say that anyone who took the view that a lamp was worse off when it was put out than when it was lit an utter idiot? We, too, are lit and put out. We suffer in the intervening period, but at either end of it there is deep tranquility. . . . We are wrong in holding that death follows after, when in fact it precedes as well as succeeds. Death is all that was before us. What does it matter, after all, whether you cease to be or never begin, when the result of either is that you do not exist?"[2] Seneca had known the paroxysms of an asthma attack many times, which he described as "rehearsals for death," and he felt fully prepared to enter into what he believed would be peaceful oblivion.

Our own eventual demise is an absolute certainty. As biological organisms, we are preordained to fade out. Most of our life, we behave as if this were otherwise, paying little attention to death unless we are rudely reminded of it by a serious illness or the departure of loved ones and friends. But then we do our best to forget about this reminder as quickly as social etiquette permits in order to return to business as usual. Our denial of death, however, does not change the actual reality of it. In the spiritual traditions, a more salubrious attitude prevails. Here life is lived in full awareness of its inevitable finitude, without succumbing to moroseness. How, we may ask, does our inescapable mortality relate to a virtuous life?

Seneca mistakenly thought that when the flame of life becomes extinguished, there is nothing at all. He sadly lacked the great insight of Buddhism that extinction (*nirvāna*) does not equate with nothingness, or annihilation.[3] The Buddhist sages, like the teachers of India's other spiritual traditions, all affirm that the post-mortem nothingness is merely a no-thing-ness, the absence of the individuated (egocentric) consciousness and its world of objects.[4] Seneca clearly had acquired the virtue of accepting life as it comes—the great moral quality of the Stoics. Yet, the virtue of true wisdom, which gazes deep into the heart of existence, eluded him.

For the yogin, death is not a negative event that fills him with dread but yet another wonderful opportunity to both test and step up the process of inner transmutation. His entire life of yogic exertion is a meticulous preparation for the moment of death. In this final moment of physical existence, whatever mental abilities and virtues the Yoga adept has been able to develop will define the quality of his post-mortem state. The art of conscious dying is fundamental to Yoga, and the *Bhagavad-Gītā* (8.12–13), which belongs to the fifth century B.C., makes reference to the ancient practice of exiting consciously through the crown of the head with the sacred syllable *aum* on one's lips.

In Tibet, the yogic way of dying has for untold centuries been associated with the *Bardo Thödol*, which was made famous in the Western hemisphere by Carl Gustav Jung, who wrote a psychological commentary on it. This work is intended as a guide for the recently deceased person, who finds himself or herself in the phantasmagoria of after-death experiences. For the yogin, the intermediate state (*bardo*) between post-mortem existence and the next embodiment is a unique situation in which, through an all-out effort, he can burn up all karmic seeds and thereby transcend all realms and the necessity for future embodiment either on Earth or at a more subtle level of existence. Of course, only someone whose mind is fully prepared through long training in mental concentration and the cultivation of virtues will have the capacity to penetrate the veil of *bardo* experiences, overcome all fear, and unhesitatingly enter into the supreme condition of Clear Light, which he knows will dissolve his individuality forever.

Whatever or whoever remains after this event cannot be pin-pointed. When Malunkyaputta, a disciple, asked Gautama the Buddha whether a liberated being continues or ceases to exist after Buddhahood, that great sage responded as follows:

> Malunkyaputta, suppose a man wounded by a poison-tipped arrow and provided by his friends and relatives with a physician were to say, "I will not extract this arrow until I know who shot me, whether he is a warrior, priest, merchant, or farmer," he would die without ever knowing the answer. Similarly, if someone were to argue, "I will not follow the path unless the Buddha answers questions such as whether the enlightened being exists or ceases to exist after death," he would die without these questions having been answered. I have not explained them simply because they are not fundamentally connected with the path. They are not conducive to detachment, cessation, tranquility, penetrative thought, awakening, or *nirvāna*.[6]

The Buddha made the same point in his conversation with the wandering ascetic Vacchagotta.[7] Vacchagotta's busy mind, however, was not satisfied. He next sought out the adept Moggalāna, one of the Buddha's advanced disciples, to pose the same question and to his astonishment received the exact same answer.

The state of liberation, which we can talk about only in paradoxical terms and which is best left untypified, in any case represents the end of all incarnations. In other words, it interrupts once and for all the vicious cycle of repeated births and deaths in the conditional realms. Prior to final release (*parinirvāna*), however, the liberated being manifests a virtuous character, and this is so even when a master chooses to teach in the controversial style of a crazy-wise adept—*avadhūta* in Sanskrit and *nyönpa* in Tibetan—the Eastern equivalent of the Fool for Christ's Sake.

In order to facilitate the spiritual growth of others, the crazy-wise adept resorts to all kinds of unpredictable ploys that, from the perspective of the conventional mind, appear outlandish, wild, offensive, or even immoral. Many of the masters of the North Indian pantheon of eighty-four "great adepts" (*mahā-siddha*), such as Nāropa, Tilopa, Kukkuripa, and Virūpa, lived and taught in a fashion that would at least raise brows in any polite society.[8] The classic example of such a yogin is the late-fifteenth-century Bhutanese master Drukpa Kunley, whose exploits have become popular entertainment in the Himalayan region.[9] I have addressed this theme at length in my book *Holy Madness* and therefore will confine myself to a few brief comments.[10]

First of all, although the attainment of full enlightenment depends on the development of a virtuous character, enlightenment itself is thought to be beyond the mind and the realm of duality and hence also beyond the polarity of good and evil. We can find this affirmation in the soteriological texts of both Hindu and Buddhist. The Protestant theologian Paul Tillich similarly observed: "The moral conscience drives beyond the sphere in which it is valid to the sphere from which it must receive its conditional validity."[11] And yet, it is impossible for an enlightened master to be evil. If the moral behavior of a yogin were merely imitative, we would have reason to be skeptical of any notion that the moral dimension is transcended upon enlightenment. Imitative morality belongs to a preliminary stage of moral development. The yogin, however, devotes his entire life to *become* virtuous, which is to say, his ethical conduct is a function of his very state of being. He does not merely follow moral rules but *embodies* the virtues that conventional morality endeavors to mimic.

Because the advanced yogin is virtuous by nature, he does not have a self-conscious attitude about his own moral conduct. He simply knows what is morally appropriate in any given situation. If he remains silent on a particular issue, it is not because he has no answer, but only because his answer would not make sense to the conventional mind or would not be heeded.

In regard to the enlightened yogin, in whom any sense of duality has vanished and who experiences everything as "one taste," all virtues can be said to have melted into the single impulse to awaken others spiritually. Such awakening is not possible without full mastery of all the factors that normally prevent self-knowledge and active self-transcendence. Another way of putting this is to say that the enlightened being's sheer presence in the world has an enlightening effect upon his or her environment—a kind of field effect that extends even to inanimate things. While those who are spiritually immature are apt to experience that effect as an irritant, the aspirant on the spiritual path will find the enlightened master's "charismatic" presence to be peaceful, luminous, uplifting, and illuminating.

Charisma is frequently understood as a personality trait by which someone "magnetically" attracts, charms, and influences others. The original meaning of this Greek word, however, is "gift." In Christianity, the term is used to denote "divine gift"— something like grace—and this fits our present purpose better. The enlightened adept's presence is a numinous gift that evokes a corresponding state of being in those whose mind is prepared for the advent of tranquility, lucidity, or even complete transcendence (i.e., enlightenment). This gift flows spontaneously from the enlightened master to others and does not depend on an act of attention on his or her part. If such a fully accomplished adept, however, were to deliberately focus his or her attention on someone with the intention to transmit, this general field effect would become like a laser beam and predictably lead to major changes in the recipient's (usually a disciple's) mind. This is in fact at the core of what is called "mind-to-mind transmission."

For this esoteric process to blossom into enlightenment, the disciple's mind must be like fertile soil ready to receive the *guru's* gift. If the mind is not ready, however, some plowing and fertilizing needs to occur first. Most teachers are willing to assist a worthy disciple in taking these initial steps, and in the case of a crazy-wisdom master, this assistance can take a rather unusual form. Drukpa Kunley, for instance, is known to have "seduced" numerous female disciples, which provoked a great deal of indignation and criticism among his contemporaries. He also was an outspoken and fearless critic of conventional piety and the ecclesiastic hierarchy. Yet, history fondly remembers his exploits as the skillful activities of an enlightened adept. His moral transgressions have traditionally been viewed not as moral flaws but as the spontaneously compassionate work of an enlightened being, who was fully aware of the long-term consequences of his actions. Drukpa Kunley's only purpose, we are told, was to bring his disciples to the point of illumination, and the existing biographical accounts mention individual cases in which this apparently occurred in a single lifetime.

Over the last several decades, some teachers in the West have adopted the controversial crazy-wisdom style of teaching and, it would appear, have not necessarily matched either Drukpa Kunley's enlightenment or absolute compassion. At least the short-term results of their invasive methods do not inspire the outside observer with confidence that the long-term effects will be particularly benign, never mind enlightening. When the Dalai Lama was asked about crazy wisdom, he responded by saying that someone claiming to qualify as a crazy-wisdom teacher would have to be able to demonstrate Drukpa Kunley's other attainments.[12] He also referred to the Buddha's disciple Pindola Bharadvaja, who is reported to have possessed great paranormal abilities, including the art of levitation. Then the Dalai Lama observed: "As far as I know, zero lamas today can do that," quickly adding, however, the following important qualification: "Some meditators living in caves around Dharamsala are highly realized and possibly capable of such attainments." At any rate, the Dalai Lama conceded that an enlightened master like Drukpa Kunley would be qualified to deploy sexuality as a skillful means to benefit a disciple—a concession that had his Western audience puzzled.

The Dalai Lama, however, made it very clear that prior to enlightenment, crazy-wisdom behavior is fraught with karmic consequences. Only at the level of authentic enlightenment can the yogin be said to have perfected all virtues, so that no moral backsliding can ever occur. Wisdom has become infallible, and whatever the enlightened being does immediately or in the long run serves the awakening of others. For Westerners, the notion of infallibility is difficult to accept, there having been all too many abuses in religious history. But then, most people are struggling even with the idea that a person could be enlightened once and for all and that enlightenment transcends the body-mind.

To summarize, the yogic training in virtues, which starts out with emulating the virtuous conduct of exemplary sages, is concluded when the yogin attains enlightenment, which is commensurate with the perfection of all virtues. Prior to enlightenment, the yogin only approaches the perfection of virtues asymptotically and therefore errors in moral judgment are always possible, though less and less likely as he draws closer to enlightenment. It is, therefore, correct to say that on the relative level, moral perfection is impossible. Yet, because enlightenment lifts the adept's mind out of the relative level of conditioned existence, his or her virtue perfection is not merely metaphorical but actual.

The transvaluation of values, which Friedrich Nietzsche saw as a new mission for philosophy, is accomplished only in the state of enlightenment.[13] It supersedes all conceivable moral codes, just as it supersedes all traditions, because it transcends the mind itself. This, however, does not make the enlightened being an anarchist and enlightenment a condition of chaos. Rather, the enlightened one is truly whole and the repository of the deepest insights and most sublime virtues of which any sentient being is capable. Nietzsche demanded the transvalued values must be "life affirming," and what could be more life affirming than enlightenment, which neither rejects nor grasps but renders absolutely everything transparent?

ENDNOTES, CHAPTER 15

1   Chögyam Trungpa, *The Myth of Freedom and the Way of Meditation* (Berkeley, Calif.: Shambhala Publications, 1976), p. 12.
2   Seneca, *Letters From a Stoic*. Translated by Robin Campbell (London: Penguin Books, 1969), pp. 104–105 (letter LIV).
3   On *nirvāna*, see Theodore Stcherbatsky, *The Conception of Buddhist Nirvāna* (Delhi: Motilal Banarsidass, 2d rev. ed., 1977) and Peter Harvey, *The Selfless Mind: Personality, Consciousness and Nirvana in Early Buddhism* (Abingdon, England: RoutledgeCurzon, repr. 2004).
4   See Gian Giuseppe Filippi, *Mrtyu: Concept of Death in Indian Traditions— Transformation of the Body and Funeral Rites*. Transl. Antonio Rigopoulos (New Delhi: D. K. Printworld, 1996) and Elisabeth Schombucher and Claus Peter Zoller, eds., *Ways of Dying: Death and Its Meaning in South Asia* (New Delhi: Manohar, 1999).
5   See Walter Y. Evans-Wentz, ed., *The Tibetan Book of the Dead or the After-Death Experiences on the Bardo Plane, According to Lama Kazi Dawa-Samdup's English Rendering* (Delhi: Munshiram Manoharlal, repr. 2000). First publ. by Oxford University Press in 1927. Jung's commentary was written in 1938, which was published for the first time in English in the 1957 Oxford University Press edition. See also Chögyam Trungpa and Francesca Fremantle, *The Tibetan Book of the Dead: The Great Liberation Through Hearing in the Bardo* (Berkeley, Calif.: Shambhala Publications, 1975), Detlef Ingo Lauf, *Secret Doctrines of the Tibetan Books of the Dead*. Transl. from the German by Graham Parkes (Boston, Mass.: Shambhala Publications, 1977), and Sogyal Rinpoche, *The Tibetan Book of Living and Dying* (San Francisco: Harper Collins, 1992).
6   This is a paraphrase of a section of the *Cula-Malunkya-Sutta* found in the *Majjhīma-Nikāya* (7.3; i.e., sermon 63).
7   The *Vacchagotta-Sutta* can be found in the *Samyutta-Nikāya* (4.395).
8   See Keith Dowman, trans., *Masters of Mahāmudrā: Songs and Histories of the Eighty-Four Buddhist Siddhas* (Albany, N.Y.: SUNY Press, 1985).
9   See Keith Dowman, trans., *The Divine Madman: The Sublime Life and Songs of Drukpa Kunley* (Varanasi: Pilgrim Publishing, repr. 2000).
10   See Georg Feuerstein, *Holy Madness: Spirituality, Crazy-Wise Teachers, and Enlightenment* (Prescott, Ariz.: Hohm Press, 2d rev. ed. 2006).
11   Paul Tillich, *Morality and Beyond* (Louisville, Kent.: Westminster John Knox Press, 1963), p. 81.
12   The audience and dialogue with the Dalai Lama took place at his residence in Dharamsala and included Lama Surya Das and twenty-one other Western teachers. See the essay "Toward a new spiritual ethic" by Kate Wheeler at www.angelfire.com/electronic/bodhidharma/wheeler.html.
13   See Friedrich Nietzsche, *Beyond Good & Evil: Prelude to a Philosophy of the Future*. Translated by Walter Kaufmann (New York: Vintage Books, 1989).

EPILOGUE

I started this book by asserting that today's unprecedented global crisis calls for a deeply spiritual and moral response. I further explained how in the absence of such a mature response, we are bound to fail this particular historical lesson and thereby imperil the future not only of our own human species but conceivably of Earth's biotic environment as a whole.

As I have repeatedly affirmed throughout this book and my other writings on the subject, I believe that the spiritual and virtue-based morality of Yoga is as valid now as it was thousands of years ago. Although our lives have become far more complex, our human nature is basically the same as it was in antiquity. We are still subject to spiritual ignorance and its far-reaching consequences. We are still suffering from wrong views and negative emotions. We also are still yearning for happiness and inner freedom.

The wisdom teachings of Yoga, which over the millennia have been taught by word of mouth, have demonstrated their relevance and efficacy over and over again. The various branches of the yogic tradition have produced hundreds of great masters even in recent history—masters who have excelled in wisdom, compassion, generosity, patience, and the other sublime virtues. Their teachings on mental discipline and ethics are abundantly and freely available to anyone wishing to benefit from them. What is more, these teachings include the kind of life-enhancing values that make sense within an environmental morality, which is the greatest desideratum today.

In the preceding chapters, I have surveyed the moral teachings of Yoga within Hinduism, Buddhism, and Jainism and, I hope, have made a reasonable case for their contemporary applicability and usefulness. In order to drive home the point that a thorough moral overhaul is an urgent requirement, I have provided ample examples of the specter of moral failure that haunts our modern society, including the contemporary Yoga movement. This proved a rather sobering and often disquieting exercise for me, and I am sure my readers will experience a similar shock when confronting the full extent of our society's moral dysfunction. But we must first acknowledge the problem before we can set about tackling it. In this case, the magnitude of our society's moral failure is such that we cannot hope to bring about positive change at the systemic level without simultaneously transforming ourselves.

The idea current in some circles that spirituality has nothing to do with morality is an unproductive and even dangerous will-o'-the-wisp. If spirituality is not embodied here and now, it is nothing at all. To become inwardly free, which is the promise of Yoga, we must begin with becoming virtuous—an old-fashion ideal, I know, but nonetheless true. There simply are no shortcuts to a freer, happier, and holier life. There also are no shortcuts to an environmentally whole coexistence with other life forms on this planet. Out of ignorance and selfishness, we are currently causing untold suffering to each other and to other species and are in fact responsible for what biologists are calling the Sixth Mass Extinction, equaling the extinction that occurred 65 million years ago as the result of a natural catastrophe.

Climatologists are warning us that the point of no-return has been reached. In other words, they feel it is already too late to prevent catastrophe. We are already suffering the consequences of our laissez-faire attitude to global warming, and there is much more to come in the near future. We do, however, have a moral obligation toward our children and their children, who will inherit a vastly troubled planet. That means we absolutely must make appropriate choices NOW. We can no longer afford to be fence sitters. Particularly those who profess to tread the spiritual path must now vigorously combine their efforts of self-transformation with environmentally sound conduct. In our time, the only viable approach is a holistic and hence ecologically responsive Yoga, which acknowledges that we are teetering at the edge of planetwide collapse. I believe the principles of such a Yoga are plentifully present in the traditional morality of Hindu, Buddhist, and Jaina teachings.

I cannot understand the cavalier attitude of many Yoga practitioners, especially those professing to be Yoga teachers, toward environmental concerns. It is nice but no longer enough to merely divvy up one's garbage into paper, plastic, and cans, and ignore all the other, even more serious environmental problems. If we purport to live a spiritually sound life, we have now no choice but to implement our spiritual principles and ideals as fully as we possibly can. It has become popular, for instance, for the wealthier among Yoga practitioners to go on retreats in foreign lands or take cruises with the Yoga stars. From an ecological perspective, both these practices are incredibly wasteful. Think of the hidden cost of jet fuel alone! Would it not make more sense—ecologically and spiritually—to find alternatives closer to home and donate the saved money to a charitable cause?

Perhaps you, the reader, are already taking all the necessary steps to countermand the rampant consumerism of our own Western society by voluntarily adopting a simpler, saner lifestyle and by facilitating the efforts of environmentalists and animal rights as well as human rights activists. But if you are not, or are not yet fully committed to a transformative life, I hope that this book will impress on you the urgency of the situation. Our happiness in this world depends on the happiness of all.

To the truly ethical man, all life is sacred . . . [1]

ENDNOTE, EPILOGUE

1   Albert Schweitzer, *The Teaching of Reverence for Life* (San Diego, Calif.: Holt, Rinehart and Winston, 1965), p. 47.

Bibliography

Abbott, Elizabeth. *A History of Celibacy*. Cambridge, Mass.: Da Capo Press, 2001.

Aguilar, H. *The Sacrifice in the Rgveda*. Delhi: Bharatiya Vidya Prakasham, 1976.

Aïvanhov, Omraam Mikhaël. *Cosmic Moral Laws*. Fréjus, France: Prosveta, 1984.

_____. *Toward a Solar Civilisation*. Fréjus, France: Prosveta, 1982.

Anthony, Dick, Bruce Ecker, and Ken Wilber. *Spiritual Choices: The Problem of Recognizing Authentic Paths to Inner Transformation*. New York: Paragon House, 1987.

Aristotle, Nichomachean Ethics, in Jonathan Barnes, ed. *The Complete Works of Aristotle*. Princeton, N.J.: Princeton University Press, 1984.

Aronson, Harvey B. *Love and Sympathy in Theravada Buddhism*. Delhi: Motilal Banarsidas, 1980.

Atiśa. *A Lamp for the Path and Commentary*. Transl. Richard Sherburne. London: George Allen & Unwin, 1983.

Aurobindo, Sri. *Essays on the Gita*. Pondicherry, India: Sri Aurobindo Ashram, 1949.

_____. *On the Veda*. Pondicherry, India: Sri Aurobindo Ashram, 1964.

_____. *Synthesis of Yoga*. Pondicherry, India: Aurobindo Ashram, 1972. 2 vols.

Balsys, Bodo. *Ahimsa : Buddhism and the Vegetarian Ideal*. New Delhi: Munshiram Manoharlal, 2004.

Bauval, Robert and Adrian Gilbert. *The Orion Mystery: Unlocking the Secrets of the Pyramids*. New York: Three Rivers Press, 1995.

Bergson, Henri. *The Two Sources of Morality and Religion*. Notre Dame, Ind.: Notre Dame University Press, rev. ed. 1977.

Bhatt, G. P., ed. *The Forceful Yoga: Being the Translation of Hathayoga-Pradīpikā, Gheranda-Samhitā and Śiva-Samhitā*. Transl. by Pancham Sinh and Rai Bahadur Srisa Chandra Vasu. *Delhi: Motilal Banarsidass*, rev. and enl. ed. 2004.

Bhattacharya, Chanchal A. *The Concept of Theft in Classical Hindu Law*. New Delhi: Munshiram Manoharlal, 1990.

Bhattacharyya, Haridas, ed. *The Cultural Heritage of India*. Calcutta: Ramakrishna Mission Institute of Culture, 1956. 4 vols.

Blair, C. J. *Heat in the Rig Veda and Atharva Veda*. New Haven: American Oriental Society, 1961.

Boccio, Frank Jude. *Mindfulness Yoga: The Awakened Union of Breath, Body, and Mind*. Somerville, Mass.: Wisdom Publications, 2004.

Bonhoeffer, Dietrich. *Ethics*. Trans. by Neville Horton Smith. New York: Touchstone Books, 1955.

Bondurant, Joan V. *The Conquest of Violence: The Gandhian Philosophy of Conflict*. Princeton, N.J.: Princeton University Press, 1958.

Bonhoeffer, Dietrich. *Ethics*. New York: MacMillan, 1955.

Brennan, Joseph Gerard. *Foundations of Moral Obligation: A Practical Guide to Ethics and Morality*. Novato, Calif.: Presidio Press, 1994.

Brinton, Crane. *A History of Western Morals*. New York: Paragon House, 1990.

Brown, Lester R. *Eco-Economy: Building an Economy for the Earth*. New York: W. W. Norton, 2001.

Brownlie, Ian, ed. *Basic Documents on Human Rights*. Oxford, England: Clarendon Press, 3d ed. 1992.

Brunton, Paul. *The Notebooks of Paul Brunton. Vol. 5: Emotions and Ethics; The Intellect*. Burdett, N.Y.: Larson, 1987.

Buber, Martin. *I and Thou*. New York: Scribners, 1937.

Buddhaghosa. *The Path of Purification (Visuddhimagga)*. Trans. by Bhikkhu Nyanamoli. Berkeley and London: Shambhala, 1976. 2 vols.

Burley, Mikel. *Hatha-Yoga*. Delhi: Motilal Banarsidass, 2000.

Chapple, Christopher K. *Karma and Creativity*. Albany, N.Y.: SUNY Press, 1986.

_____. *Nonviolence to Animals, Earth, and Self in Asian Traditions*. Albany, N.Y.: SUNY Press, 1993.

Coward, Harold. *Yoga and Psychology: Language, Memory and Mysticism*. Albany, N.Y.: SUNY Press, 2002.

Cremo, Michael A. and Richard L. Thompson. *Forbidden Archaeology*. Badger, Calif.: Torchlight Publications, 1998.

Curle, Adam. *Mystics and Militants: A Study of Awareness, Identity, and Social Action*. London: Tavistock Publications, 1972.

Dalai Lama. *The Good Heart: A Buddhist Perspective on the Teachings of Jesus*. Boston: Wisdom Publications, 1996.

_____. *Many Ways to Nirvana: Reflections and Advice on Right Living*. Ed. by Renuka Singh. Toronto: Penguin Canada, 2004.

Dange, Sadashiv A. *Vedic Sacrifices: Early Nature*. New Delhi: Aryan Books International, 2000. 2 vols.

Danto, Arthur. *Mysticism and Morality: Oriental Thought and Moral Philosophy*. New York: Columbia University Press, 1987.

Dasgupta, Surendra Nath. *A History of Indian Philosophy*. Cambridge: Cambridge University Press, 1952–55. 5 vols.

Dechanet, J. M. *Christian Yoga*. London: Search Press, 1973.

Dobson, Charles. *The Troublemaker's Teaparty: A Manual for Effective Citizen Action*. Gabriola Island, British Columbia: New Society Publishers, 2002.

Dombrowski, Daniel A. *The Philosophy of Vegetarianism*. Amherst: University of Massachusetts Press, 1984.

Dossey, Larry. *Healing Words: The Power of Prayer and the Practice of Medicine*. New York: HarperCollins, 1993.

_____. *Healing Beyond the Body: Medicine and the Infinite Reach of the Mind*. Boston, Mass.: Shambhala, 2003.

Driver, Tom. *The Magic of Ritual*. San Francisco: Harper, 1991.

Edwards. Andres R. *The Sustainability Revolution: Portrait of a Paradigm Shift*. Gabriola Island, British Columbia: New Society Publishers, 2005.

Eliade, Mircea. Yoga: *Immortality and Freedom*. Princeton, N.J.: Princeton University Press, 1958.

Eppsteiner, Fred. *The Path of Compassion: Writings on Socially Engaged Buddhism*. Berkeley, Calif.: Parallax Press, 1988.

Feuerstein, Georg. *The Yoga Tradition: Its History, Literature, Philosophy and Practice*. Prescott, Ariz.: Hohm Press, 2d ed. 2001.

_____. *The Deeper Dimension of Yoga*. Boston, Mass.: Shambhala, 2003.

_____. *Tantra: The Path of Ecstasy*. Boston, Mass.: Shambhala, 1998.

_____. *The Yoga-Sutra of Patañjali: A New Translation and Commentary*. Rochester, Vt.: Inner Traditions International, repr. 1989.

_____. *Lucid Waking: Mindfulness and the Spiritual Potential of Humanity*. Rochester, Vt.: Inner Traditions International, 1997.

_____. *Wholeness or Transcendence? Ancient Lessons for the Emerging Global Civilization*. Burdett, N.Y.: Larson Publications, rev. ed. 1992.

_____, Subhash Kak, and David Frawley. *In Search of the Cradle of Civilization: New Light on Ancient India*. Wheaton, Ill.: Quest Books, 1995.

Fingarette, Herbert. *The Self in Transformation: Psychoanalysis, Philosophy and the Life of the Spirit*. New York: HarperCollins, 1977.

Fowler, J. W. *Stages of Faith: The Psychology of Human Development and the Quest for Meaning*. San Francisco: Harper & Row, 1981.

Fox, Matthew. *A Spirituality Named Compassion*. Minneapolis: Winston Press, 1979.

Frankl, Victor E. *Man's Search for Meaning*. Boston, Mass.: Beacon Press, 1962.

Frawley, David. *Yoga and the Sacred Fire: Self-Realization and Planetary Transformation*. Twin Lakes, Wisc.: Lotus Press, 2004.

Frazer, James George. *The Golden Bough: A Study in Magic and Religion*. New York: Macmillan, abridged ed. 1922, repr. 1960.

Freud, Sigmund. *Civilization and Its Discontent*. Trans. by James Strachey. New York: W. W. Norton, 1961. (Originally published in German in 1930.)

Friedel, David et al. *Maya Cosmos: Three Thousand Years on the Shaman's Path*. New York: William Morrow, 1993

Fu, Charles Wei-hsun and Sandra A. Wawrytko, eds. *Buddhist Ethics and Modern Society: An International Symposium* (Contributions to the Study of Religion). Westport, Conn.: Greenwood Press, 1991.

Gampopa. *The Jewel Ornament of Liberation*. Trans. by Herbert V. Guenther. Berkeley: Shambhala Publications, 1959.

Gandhi, Mohandas Karamchand. *Collected Works*. Washington, D.C.: Public Affairs Press, 1948.

_____. *An Autobiography: The Story of My Experiments with Truth*. Trans. by Mahadev Desai. Boston, Mass.: Beacon Press, 1993.

Ganeri, Jonardon, ed. *Philosophy, Culture, Religion: The Collected Essays of Bimal Krishna Matilal. Vol. 2: Ethics and Epics*. Delhi: Oxford University Press, 2001.

Ganguly, Kisari Mohan. *The Mahabharata of Krishna-Dwaipayana Vyasa*. New Delhi: Munshiram Manoharlal, repr. 2003. 12 vols.

Gier, Nicholas F. *The Virtue of Nonviolence: From Gautama to Gandhi*. Albany, N.Y.: SUNY Press, 2004.

_____. "*Hindu Virtue Ethics*," www.class.uidaho.edu/ngier/hinduve.htm.

Gonda, Jan. *The Vision of the Vedic Poets*. The Hague: Mouton, 1963.

Govinda, Lama Anagarika. *The Psychological Attitude of Early Buddhist Philosophy*. New York: Weiser, 1961.

Guenther, Herbert V., trans. *The Life and Teaching of Nāropa*. London: Oxford University Press, 1963.

Gyatrul Rinpoche, *Generating the Deity*. Transl. Sangye Khandro. Ithaca, N.Y.: Snow Lion Publications, 2d ed. 1996.

Hancock, Graham and Robert Bauval. *The Message of the Sphinx: A Quest for the Hidden Legacy of Mankind*. Three Rivers Press, 1997.

Hanh, Thich Nhat. *Being Peace*. Berkeley, Calif.: Parallax Press, 1987.

Harris, Judith. *Jung and Yoga: The Psyche-Body Connection*. Foreword by Marion Woodman. Toronto: Inner City Books, 2001.

Hazlitt, Henry. *The Foundations of Morality*, Princeton, N.J.: Van Nostrand, 1964.

Heard, J. and S. L. Cranson, eds. *Reincarnation: An East-West Anthology*. New York: Crown, 1961.

Heesterman, J. C. *The Broken World of Sacrifice: An Essay in Ancient Indian Ritual*. Chicago, Ill.: University of Chicago Press, 1993.

Heinberg, Richard. *Power Down: Options and Actions For a Post-Carbon World*. Gabriola Island, British Columbia: New Society Publishers, 2004.

_____. *The Party's Over: Oil, War and the Fate of Industrial Societies*. Gabriola Island, British Columbia: New Society Publishers, 2003.

Horne, James. *The Moral Mystic*. Waterloo, Ontario: Wilfrid Laurier University Press, 1986.

Hubert, Henri and Marcel Mauss. *Sacrifice: Its Nature and Functions*. Chicago, Ill.: University of Chicago Press, 1981.

Hume, David. *An Enquiry Concerning the Principles of Morals*. LaSalle, Il.: Open Court, 1930. (First published in 1750.)

Huxley, Thomas Henry. *Evolution and Ethics and Other Essays*. New York: Appleton, 1898.

Huxley, Aldous. *The Perennial Philosophy*. New York: Perennial Books, repr. 2004. (First published in 1943.)

Ingalls, Daniel H. H. "Dharma and Moksha." In: *Philosophy East & West*. Vol. 7

(1957), pp. 41-48.

Iyengar, B. K. S. *The Tree of Yoga*. Boston, Mass.: Shambhala Publications, 1989.

_____. *Light on Yoga: The Yoga Journey to Wholeness, Inner Peace, and Ultimate Freedom*. Vancouver: Raincoast Books, 2005.

Jaini, Padmanabh S. *The Jaina Path of Purification*. Delhi: Motilal Banarsidass, 1979.

James, William. *The Varieties of Religious Experience*. New York: New American Library, 1958. (First published in 1902.)

Jamieson, Dale, ed. *A Companion to Environmental Philosophy*. Malden, Mass.: Blackwell Publishing, 2003.

Johansson, R. E. A. *The Psychology of Nirvāna*. London: Allen & Unwin, 1969.

Jones, Peter. *Rights*. New York: Macmillan, 1994.

Jones, Richard. *Mysticism Examined: Philosophical Inquiries into Mysticism*. Albany, N.Y.: SUNY Press, 1993.

_____. "Must Mystics be Moral?" *Philosophy East & West*. Vol. 34, no. 3 (July 1984), pp. 273-293.

Jung, Carl Gustav. *The Psychology of Kundalini Yoga*. Princeton, N.J.: Princeton University Press, 1996.

Kak, Subhash. *The Aśvamedha: The Rite and Its Logic*. Delhi: Motilal Banarsidass, 2002.

_____. *The Gods Within: Mind, Consciousness and the Vedic Tradition*. New Delhi: Munshiram Manoharlal, 2002.

_____. *Patanjali and Cognitive Science*. Pune, India: Vitasta, 1987.

_____. *The Architecture of Knowledge: Quantum Mechanics, Neuroscience, Computers and Consciousness*. Delhi: Motilal Banarsidass, 2004.

Kane, Pandurang Vaman. *History of Dharmaśāstra*. Poona, India: Bhandarkar Oriental Research Institute, repr. 1941. 5 vols.

Kant, Immanuel. *Grounding for the Metaphysics of Morals*. Trans. by James W. Ellington. Indianapolis, Ind.: Hackett Publishing, 1985. (First published in 1785.)

_____. *Critique of Practical Reason*. Trans. by Lewis White Beck. Indianapolis, Ind.: Bobb-Merrill, 1956. (First published in 1788.)

Kaveeshwar, G. W. *The Ethics of the Gītā*. Delhi: Motilal Banarsidass, 1971.

Kaza, Stephanie, ed. *Hooked! Buddhist Writings on Greed, Desire, and the Urge to Consume*. Boston, Mass.: Shambhala Publications, 2005.

_____ and Kenneth Kraft, ed. *Dharma Rain: Sources of Buddhist Environmentalism*. Boston, Mass.: Shambhala Publications, 2000.

Khanna, Madhu. *Rta: The Cosmic Order*. New Delhi: D. K. Printworld, 2004.

Kohlberg, Lawrence. *The Philosophy of Moral Development*. New York: Harper, 1981.

_____. *The Psychology of Moral Development: Moral Stages and the Life Cycle*. New York: Harper, 1983.

Kotler, Arnold, ed. *Engaged Buddhist Reader*. Berkeley, Calif.: Parallax Press, 1996.

Kraft, Kenneth, ed. *Inner Peace, World Peace: Essays on Buddhism and Nonvio-*

lence. Albany, N.Y.: SUNY Press, 1992.

Ladner, Lorne. *The Lost Art of Compassion: Discovering the Practice of Happiness in the Meeting of Buddhism and Psychology*. San Francisco: HarperSanFrancisco, 2004.

Lasater, Judith. *Living Your Yoga: Finding the Spiritual in Everyday Life*. Berkeley, Calif.: Rodmell Press, 2000.

Laszlo, Ervin. *The Interconnected Universe: Conceptual Foundations of Transdisciplinary Unified Theory*. River Edge, N.J.: World Scientific, 1995.

Machiavelli, Niccolò. *The Prince*. Trans. by Peter Bondanella and Mark Musa. Oxford: Oxford University Press, 1984.

Meilaender, Gilbert. *The Theory and Practice of Virtue*. Notre Dame, Ind.: University of Notre Dame Press, 1984.

Maritain, Jacques. *The Rights of Man and Natural Law*. Transl. Doris Anson. New York: Scribner's Sons, 1947.

Maslow, Abraham H. *The Farther Reaches of Human Nature*. Harmondsworth: Penguin Books, 1973.

_____. *Religion, Values, and Peak Experiences*. Athens: Ohio State University Press, 1964.

Meadows, Donella H. et al. *Beyond the Limits* (White River Junction, Vt.: Chelsea Green, 1992).

Mehta, Rohit. *Yoga: The Art of Integration*. Adyar, India: Theosophical Publishing House, 1990.

Merton, Thomas. *The New Man*. New York: Farrar, Straus & Cudahy, 1961.

Miller, Jeanine. *The Vision of Cosmic Order in the Vedas*. London: Routledge & Kegan Paul, 1985.

Misra, G. S. P. *Development of Buddhist Ethics*. New Delhi: Munshiram Manoharlal Publishers, 1984.

Monroe, Kristen Renwick. *The Heart of Altruism: Perceptions of a Common Humanity*. Princeton, N.Y.: Princeton University Press, 1996.

Moore, G. E. *Principia Ethica*. Cambridge: Cambridge University Press, 1903.

Murphy, Michael. *The Future of the Body: Explorations into the Further Evolution of Human Nature*. Los Angeles: J. P. Tarcher, 1992.

Nagar, Shanti Lal. *Sūrya and the Sun Cult*. New Delhi: Aryan Books International, 1995.

Neufeldt, Ronald W., ed. *Karma & Rebirth: Post-Classical Developments*. Albany, N.Y.: SUNY Press, 1986.

Nickel, James W. *Making Sense of Human Rights: Philosophical Reflections on the Universal Declaration of Human Rights*. Berkeley: University of California Press, 1987.

Niebuhr, H. Richard. *The Responsible Self*. New York: Harper & Row, 1963.

Nietzsche, Friedrich. *"On the Genealogy of Morality" and Other Writings*. Ed. by Keith Ansell-Pearson and Carol Diethe. Cambridge: Cambridge University Press, 1994. (First published in German in 1887.)

_____. *Beyond Good and Evil*. Edited by Rolf-Peter Horstmann and Judith Norman. Cambridge, England: Cambridge University Press, 2002. (First published in German in 1886.)

Nono, Carlos. *The Ethics of Human Rights*. Oxford, England: Clarendon Press, 1991.

O'Flaherty, Wendy Doniger. *Asceticism and Eroticism in the Mythology of Śiva*. Delhi: Oxford University Press, 1973.

_____. *The Origins of Evil in Hindu Mythology*. Berkeley and Los Angeles: University of California Press, 1976.

_____, ed. *Karma and Rebirth in Classical Indian Traditions*. Berkeley: University of California Press, 1976.

Orchard, David. *The Fight for Canada: Four Centuries of Resistance to American Expansionism*. Westmount, Quebec: Robert Davies Multimedia Publishing, rev. ed. 1998.

Otto, Rudolf. *Mysticism East and West*. Transl. Bracey and Payne. New York: Macmillan, 1970. (First published in German in 1932.)

Pabongka Rinpoche. *Liberation in the Palm of Your Hand: A Concise Discourse on the Path to Enlightenment*. Ed. by Trijang Rinpoche and trans. by Michael Richards. Boston, Mass.: Wisdom, 1991.

Padel, Felix. *The Sacrifice of Human Beings: British Rule and the Konds of Orissa*. 1995.

Pal, Jagat. *Karma, Dharma and Moksha: Conceptual Essays on Indian Ethics*. Delhi, Abhijeet Pub., 2004

Parrinder, Geoffrey. *Sexual Morality in the World's Religions*. Oxford, England: Oneworld, 1996.

Perrett, Roy, W. "The Bodhisattva Paradox," *Philosophy East & West*. Vol. 36, no. 1 (1986), pp. 55-59.

Potdar, K. R. *Sacrifice in Rgveda*. Bombay: Bharatiya Vidya Bhavan, 1953.

Pye, Michael. *Skillful Means: A Concept in Mahayana Buddhism*. London: Duckworth, 1978.

Quaegebeur, Jan, ed. *Ritual and Sacrifice in the Ancient Near East*. Leuven, Belgium: Peeters, 1993.

Radhakrishnan, Sarvepalli. *The Principal Upaniṣads*. London: Allen & Unwin, 1953.

_____. *The Bhagavadgītā*. London: Routledge & Kegan Paul, 1960.

Ray, Reginald A. Secret of the Vajra World: The Tantric Buddhism of Tibet. Boston, Mass.: Shambhala Publications, 2001.

_____. *Indestructible Truth: The Living Spirituality of Tibetan Buddhism*. Boston, Mass.: Shambhala Publications, 2002.

Raz, Joseph. *The Morality of Freedom*. Oxford, England: Oxford University Press, 1986.

Regan, Tom. *The Case for Animal Rights*. Berkeley: University of California Press, 1983.

_____ and Peter Singer, eds. *Animal Rights and Human Obligations*. Englewood Cliffs, N.J.: Prentice Hall, 1976.

Rizzetto, Diane Eshin. *Waking Up to What You Do: A Zen Practice for Meeting Every Situation with Intelligence and Compassion*. Foreword by Charlotte

Joko Beck. Boston, Mass.: Shambhala Publications, 2005.

Scheffler, Samuel. *Human Morality*. Oxford, England: Oxford University Press, 1992.

Schele, Linda and David Friedel. *A Forest of Kings: The Untold Story of Ancient Maya*. New York: William Morrow, 1990.

_____ et al. *The Code of Kings: The Language of Seven Sacred Maya Temples and Tombs*. New York: Touchstone, 1999.

_____ and Mary Ellen Miller. *The Blood of Kings: Dynasty and Ritual in Maya Art*. Fort Worth, Texas: Kimbell Art Museum, 1986.

Schopenhauer, Arthur. *On the Basis of Morality*. Trans. by E. F. J. Payne. Indianapolis, Ind.: Bobbs-Merrill, 1965. (First published in German in 1840.)

Schweitzer, Albert. *The Teaching of Reverence for Life*. Trans. by Richard and Clara Winston. New York: Holt, Rinehart and Winston, 1965.

Selvanayagam, Israel. *Vedic Sacrifice: Challenge and Response*. New Delhi: Manohar Publishers & Distributors, 1996.

Shamdasani, Sonu, ed. *The Psychology of Kundalini Yoga: Notes of the Seminar Given in 1932 by C. G. Jung*. Princeton, N.J.: Princeton University Press, 1996.

Sidgwick, Henry. *Methods of Ethics*. Indianapolis, In.: Hackett, 7th ed. 1981.

Singer, Peter. *Animal Liberation*. Random House, 1975.

_____, ed. *A Companion to Ethics*. Oxford, England: Blackwell, 1993.

Singh, Jaideva. *Śiva Sūtras: The Yoga of Supreme Identity*. Delhi: Motilal Banarsidass, 1979.

_____. Spanda-Kārikās: *The Divine Creative Pulsation*. Delhi: Motilal Banarsidass, 1980.

Sivananda, Swami. *Bliss Divine*. Shivanandanagar, India: Divine Life Society, 1965.

_____. *All About Hinduism*. Shivanandanagar, India: Divine Life Society, 1947.

Skolimowski, Henryk. *Dancing Shiva in the Ecological Age*. New Delhi: Clarion Books, 1991.

Slote, Michael. *From Morality to Virtue*. New York: Oxford University Press, 1992.

Sommers, Christina Hoff, ed. *Vice and Virtue in Everyday Life: Introductory Readings in Ethics*. San Diego, Calif.: Harcourt Brace Jovanovich, 1985.

Soonthorndhammathada, Phra. *Compassion in Buddhism and Purānas*. Delhi: Nag Publishers, 1995.

Staal, Frits. *Exploring Mysticism: A Methodological Essay*. London: Penguin, 1975.

_____, ed. *Agni : The Vedic Ritual of the Fire Altar*. Delhi: Motilal Banarsidass, 2001. 2 vols.

Stace, Walter. *Mysticism and Philosophy*. New York: St. Martin's Press, 1960.

Suzuki, David. *Inventing the Future: Reflections on Science, Technology, and Nature*. Toronto: Stoddart, 1989.

_____. *Time to Change: Essays*. Toronto: Stoddart, 1994.

Suzuki, D. T., "Ethics and Zen Buddhism" in Ruth N. Ashen, ed. *Moral Principles of Action*. New York: Harper and Row, 1952.

Tähtinen, Unto. *Ahimsā: Nonviolence in Indian Tradition*. London: Rider, 1976.

_____. *Indian Traditional Values*. New Delhi: Abhinav Publications, 1983.

Taimni, I. K. *The Science of Yoga*. Adyar, India: Theosophical Publishing House, 1961.

Talbott, Rick Franklin. *Sacred Sacrifice: Ritual Paradigms in Vedic Religion and Early Christianity*. New York: Peter Lang Publishing, 1995.

Taye, Jamgon Kongdrul Lodro. *Buddhist Ethics*. Trans. and ed. by The International Translation Committee. Ithaca, N.Y.: Snow Lion, 1998.

Taylor, Gordon Rattray. *The Doomsday Book*. London: Thames and Hudson, 1970.

Taylor, James. *Sin: A New Understanding of Virtue and Vice*. Kelowna, British Columbia: Northstone Books, 1997.

Tierney, Patrick. *The Highest Altar: The Story of Human Sacrifice*. New York: Viking Adult, ill. ed. 1989.

Tillich, Paul. *Morality and Beyond*. New York: Harper, 1964.

Tripurāri, Swami B. V. *Jīva Goswāmī's Tattva-Sandarbha: Sacred India's Philosophy of Ecstasy*. Eugene, Oreg.: Clarion Call, 1995.

_____. *Aesthetic Vedānta: The Sacred Path of Passionate Love*. Eugene, Oreg.: Mandala, 1996.

Trungpa, Chögyam. *The Myth of Freedom and the Way of Meditation*. Berkeley and London: Shambhala Publications, 1976.

_____. *Crazy Wisdom*. Ed. by Sherab Chödzin. Boston, Mass.: Shambhala Publications, 2001.

_____. *Cutting Through Spiritual Materialism*. Boston, Mass.: Shambhala Publications, repr. 2002.

_____. *The Collected Works of Chögyam Trungpa*. Ed. by Carolyn Rose Gimian. Boston, Mass.: Shambhala Publications, 2003. 8 volumes.

Tsong-kha-pa. *The Great Treatise on the Stages of the Path to Enlightenment*. Trans. by The Lamrim Chenmo Translation Committee. Ithaca, N.Y.: Snow Lion, 2000.

Tsongkhapa. *Tantra in Tibet: The Great Exposition of Secret Mantra*. London: Allen & Unwin, 1980–81. 2 vols.

_____. *Tantric Ethics: An Explanation of the Precepts for Buddhist Vajrayāna Practice*. Trans. by Gareth Sparham. Foreword by Jeffrey Hopkins. Boston, Mass.: Wisdom Publications, 2005.

Vesci, Uma Marina. *Heat and Sacrifice in the Vedas*. Delhi: Motilal Banarsidass, 1985.

Vivekananda, Swami. *The Complete Works of Swami Vivekananda*. Mayavati, India: Advaita Ashrama, 1947-1955. 8 vols.

Wallis, H. W. *Cosmology of the Rigveda*. London: Williams & Norgate, 1887.

Watts, Alan. *Psychotherapy East and West*. New York: Mentor Books, 1961.

West, John Anthony. *The Serpent in the Sky*. Wheaton, Ill.: Quest Books, 2d ed. 1993.

Wilber, Ken. *The Atman Project: A Transpersonal View of Human Development.* Wheaton, Ill.: Theosophical Publishing House, 1980.

_____. *Sex, Ecology, Spirituality: The Spirit of Evolution.* Boston, Mass./London: Shambhala Publications, 1995.

Williams, R. *Jaina Yoga: A Survey of the Mediaeval Śrāvakācāras.* Delhi: Motilal Banarsidass, 1991.

Woods, Richard. "Mysticism and social action: The mystic's calling, development and social activity," *Journal of Consciousness Studies.* Vol. 3, no. 2 (1996), pp. 158-171.

Yeshe [Thubten], Lama. *Becoming the Compassion Buddha: Tantric Mahamudra for Everyday Life.* Ed. by Robina Courtin. Somerville, Mass.: Wisdom Publications, 2005.

Yogendra, Shri. *Yoga Essays.* Santacruz, India: The Yoga Institute, 1978.

INDEX

A

abhinivesha, 157
absenteeism, 149
abuse, child, 193; elder, 120, 206;
 sexual, 118, 159ff.
action, xv, 28, 51. *See also* Karma-
 Yoga
adepts, 7, 8, 261
Aeschylus, quoted, 133
Afghanistan, 114
agapae, 221
agape, 207
aggression, 104, 108
Agni, 209
Agni-Purāna, 166
ahamkāra, 4
ahimsā, as master value, 87. *See also*
 nonharming
Ahmed, Nafeez, 107
alcoholism, 250
Alexander the Great, 189, 237
alobha, 188
altruism, 11–12, 193, 196f.
Amitabha, 246
Amnesty International, 116
amsha, 212
Anathapindika, 187
anekānta-vāda, 249
Angelou, Maya, 101
anger, as root vice, 153, 184
Anguttara-Nikāya, quoted, 209, 241
animals, 63, 66, 110ff., 192, 196f.,
 199
antar-yāga, 57
anunmatta, 250
anu-vrata, 89

aparigraha, explained, 188
arcanā, 213
arhat, 255
Aristide, Jean-Bertrand, 96
Aristotle, 86, 138
ārjava, 243
Arjuna, 26, 30, 87, 91f. *et passim*
Arsenius, 165
asamprajnāta-samādhi, 255. *See also*
 ecstasy
asceticism, 61, 85, 89, 96f., 124,
 165f., 172f., 207, 237ff., 240;
 threefold, 239
Ashoka, 70; quoted, 248
askesis, explained, 238
asmitā, 4
aspiration, perfection, 245
asteya, 152
Atharva-Veda, 164; quoted, 20, 24
atithi, explained, 228f.
ātma-darshana, 236
ātma-jnāna, 15 *note 1*
ātman, 3, 24. *See also* purusha, Self,
 Spirit
ātma-nivedana, 213
ātma-samkoca, 4, 6
attachment, 5, 29, 207
attentiveness, 99. *See also*
 mindfulness
attraction, 235
Auden, Wystan Hugh, quoted, 242
Aurobindo, Sri, 24–25, 79, 173;
 quoted, 22
avadhūta, 261
Avalokiteshvara, 245f.
avatāra, 211

avarice. *See* greed.
aversion, 235
avidyā, 253
awakening, 41, 262. *See also*
    enlightenment
ayoga-kevalī, 255
Aztecs, 56

B

Bacon, Francis, 82–83
bala, 246
balance, 250
bandhu, 21, 45, 47, 229, 256. *See also*
    interconnectedness
banking, 135, 179
bankruptcy, 148
bardo, 259f.
Bardo Thödol, 259
beauty, inner, 233
Bedouins, 145
Being-Awareness, 80. *See also*
    Reality, ultimate
belief, 8, 247
Benedict XVI (Pope), 138
benevolence, 99. *See also* generosity,
    kindness.
Bentham, Jeremy, 83
Berman, Morris, xi
Bhagavad-Gītā, xv, 26, 60, 88, 209,
    210, 241, 259; quoted, 27, 28–29,
    91f., 211, 214, 239, 247
Bhāgavata-Purāna, 213
bhakta, 215
bhakti, 210, 227, 241; explained, 207
Bhakti-Sūtra, quoted, 214
Bhaktivedanta Swami, 210
Bhakti-Yoga, xii, 29, 207, 210ff., 214
Bhave, Vinoba, 28
Bhīshma, 202
bhūta sacrifice, explained, 66
bindu, 43
bliss, 103
blood, 55, 56, 77
bodha, 41
Bodhicaryāvatāra, quoted, 242
bodhisattva, xvii, 12, 32, 46, 94,
    242ff., 257

body, 43, 78, 127, 157, 169f., 172f.,
    235, 240
Bonhoeffer, Dietrich, 87
Bosch, Hieronymus, 218
Brahma, 210
brahmacarya, explained, 164f.
brahman, 24, 43, 44, 164f.
brahma sacrifice, explained, 66, 69
brahma-vihāra, 202
brain, 14, 43, 171
Brihad-Āranyaka-Upanishad,
    quoted, 49–50
Brihaspati, 35, 36, 202
Buddha, 15 *note 2,* 47, 187, 202, 228,
    240, 244; quoted, 48, 260. *See also*
    Buddhism
buddhi, 80; explained 103
Buddhism, xiii, 3, 32, 46–47, 70, 96,
    102, 119, 167f., 184f., 202, 209, 212,
    226f., 250
Buscaglia, Leo, 206
Bush, George, Sr., 130
Bush, George W., Jr., x, 135
Bushmen, 177
Byron, Lord, 113

C

Caitanya, 211
cakra, 171
Campbell, Jeremy, 140
Canada, 116, 132, 138, 201
capitalism, 179f.
capital punishment, 116f., 194
Carey, Alex, 137
caritas, 195, 220, 221
Carlin, George, 183
Carrette, Jeremy, xiii
categorical imperative, 83
chanting. *See* kīrtana
character, and virtue, 90, 232; as
    destiny, 36, 41. *See also* personality
charisma, 262
charity, 195, 218, 220, 227, 237. *See
    also* generosity
chastity, 90, 157–174
cheerfulness, 246
Cheney, Dick, 129, 136

Chinnamastā, 72, 76–77
Christianity, 18, 57, 81, 87, 137ff.,
    165, 166, 183, 185, 206ff., 219, 240,
    262; and sexual abuse, 159ff.
Churchill, Ward LeRoy, 115
CIA, 134
CIWF, 199
civilization, and suffering, 158;
    contemporary, xv, 118, 178, 206,
    237f., 268 et passim
Clarkson, Adrienne, quoted, 201
Clear Light, 260
Clinton, William J., 130
colonialism, and suffering, 113f.
compassion, 191–203; and
    emptiness, 46; and lying, 138
competitiveness, 109
concern. See ultimate concern
Confucius, 131
conscience, 94, 152, 261;
    environmental, 250, 251
consciousness, and death, 50; and
    material reality, 126
consensus reality, 128f. et passim
consumerism, xx, 52, 113, 150, 153,
    177, 181ff., 185f.
contemplation, 10, 227. See also
    meditation
contemporary civilization. See
    civilization, contemporary
contentment, 155, 227, 236f.
cooperation, 104, 197
copyright theft, 152. See also theft
Corinthians, 153
corporations, 149 et passim
cosmic order. See order, cosmic
cosmology, 43, 75
courage, 86, 246
crazy wisdom, 261ff.
credit cards, 147f., 180
crime, 116, 151, 160f., 193
crisis, global, ix–x, 52, 267ff.
cruises, Yoga, 269

D

Dalai Lama, 119; quoted, 121, 168,
    202, 264

dāna, 223, 224, 228
Dāna-Nibandhas, 224
Darshana-Upanishad, 241
Darwin, Charles, 141, 196
Dashā-Vaikālika-Sūtra, quoted, 85,
    97f.
dāsya, 213
dayā, 243
death, 48–50, 62, 65, 68, 106, 128,
    257, 259. See also dying.
death instinct, 158
debt, financial, 147f., 179f.
desire, 29
destiny, 36. See also karma.
Deuteronomy, quoted, 208, 220
deva, 228
development, moral, 93f.
Devil, 68
devotion to the Lord, 241
devotionalism, 207, 209f., 213, 227;
    nine stages, 213f. See also love
Dhamma-Pada, 187, 242; quoted,
    227
dharma, defined, 8, 20; in Buddhism,
    32; in Jainism, 85; in *Mahābhārata,*
    31, 35; in *Rig-Veda,* 60
dharma-megha-samādhi, 38 note 13,
    255. See also ecstasy
Dharma-Shāstras, 224
dhriti, 243
DHS (Dept. of Homeland Security), x
Dickens, Charles, 217
diet, 241, 243, 246; and Gandhi, 173;
    Western, 110, 183
Diogenes, 189, 237
discernment, 103, 142, 250
discipline, spiritual. See practice,
    spiritual
dispassion, 142, 236, 246
Dobson, Charles, xi
Donatello, 218
doubt, 247
Drake, Francis, 151
drugs, 117, 249
Drukpa Kunley, 261, 263, 264
duality, and language, 41;
    vs. nonduality, 4, 40

gluttony, 183
goals, and ethics, 85; four human, 25
God, 2, 9, 13, 138, 207f. *See also* religion
gold, 178, 187, 215
Gold Rush, 178
good and evil, 17, 261
goodness, 8, 82, 215, 234
grace, 92, 212, 215
gratitude, 246, 247
Great Britain, 90, 108, 114, 149, 199, 218
greed, 152, 154, 177ff.; 184ff.; and violence, 107, 185
greedlessness, 177–189
Greeley, Andrew, quoted, 184
Greenspan, Alan, quoted, 184
growth, inner, xviii
guru, 233, 247, 256f.
guru-bhakti, 246
Gyatrul Rinpoche, quoted, 42

H

Halliburton scandal, 136
Halloween, 67
happiness, 84, 269
Haribhadra Sūrī, 32
harming, 98, 108, 121. *See also* nonharming
Harrison, George, 211
Hatha-Yoga, xviii
health, and sexuality, 172; in Hatha-Yoga, xviii; mental, xvi, xxi *note 11,* 150
heart, 55, 56
heaven, 35–36, 237
Heidegger, Martin, 139
Heinberg, Richard, xi
hell, 35–36
Hemacandra, 97
hemp, 249f.
Heraclitus, quoted, 102
himsā, 98
Hinduism, xiii, 3, 25–26, 58, 207, 209f., 223ff., 246ff. *et passim*
Hitler, Adolf, 87, 118. *See also* Third Reich

Hoffer, Eric, quoted, 192
homa sacrifice, explained, 66
homelessness, 200, 221
homicide, 115f.
honesty, 89, 125
hospitality, 71, 228f., 237
householder, in Hinduism, 25–26 *et passim*
Humane Slaughter Act, 111
humanism, 18–19
humility, 234, 246, 247
hunger, 113, 129, 200, 221, 223
hypocrisy, 125, 138f.

I

identity theft, 151. *See also* theft
I-am-ness, 4. *See also* ego
ignorance, as root vice, 153, 182, 184f., 253
I-maker, 4. *See also* ego
impatience, 242
impurity, 102f.
inattention, 254
individualism, modern, 44–45
Indra, 31, 209
Indus-Sarasvati Civilization, 37 *note 7,* 64
injustice, 179
Inner Ruler, 9
instinct, survival, 5
integralism, vs. verticalism, 172
Integral Yoga, 173. *See also* Aurobindo
integrity, 125, 241, 243
interconnectedness, 21–22, 24, 44, 47, 51, 229, 244. *See also* bandhu
invisible, the, 67
Iraq, 108, 114, 133, 136
īshvara-pranidhāna, 241
Islam, 220, 229,240

J

Jainism, xiii, 3, 31–32, 89, 96–98, 119, 226, 227, 249, 253 *et passim*
Janabāī, 214
japa, 124
Japan, and altruism, 193

Jeanne des Anges, 166
Jesus, xix, 57, 127, 208, 220; quoted, 166, 223, 248
Jews, 118, 240
jīna, 255
jnāna, 246
Jnāna-Yoga, xii
John XII (Pope), 159
joy, 236f.
jugupsā, explained, 235, 236
Julian (Emperor), 164
Jung, Carl Gustav, 259
jurisprudence, 151
justice, 82, 89, 151, 220

K

Kabīr, 214
Kālī, 62, 63, 66
kali-yuga, xvi, xxi *note 10*
kāma, 207
Kāmadeva, 77
Kanishka, 70
Kant, Immanuel, 34, 83, 141; quoted, 20
karma, 12, 21, 29, 31–32, 222, 254; explained, 49–52; of yogin, 36. *See also* destiny
Karma-Yoga, xii, xiv, 28–30, 88, 105
karunā, 202
Kaviraj, Gopinath, 79
kevalin, 255
Kevorkian, Jack, 118f.
kindness, 46, 65, 155, 191
King, Martin Luther, 28, 96
King, Richard, xiii
kinship, 21, 44, 67; and morality, 45. *See also* bandhu, interconnectedness
kīrtana, 213
knowledge, 246
Kohlberg, Lawrence, 93f., 105
Krishna, 31, 61, 62, 87, 92, 210ff.; quoted, 27, 91. *See also Bhagavad-Gītā*
Krishna Consciousness Movement, 210f.
krodha, 184
kshamā, 241

kshānti, 241, 248
Kukkuripa, 261
kula, 46
Kulārnava-Tantra, 140
Kundalinī-Yoga, xii
Kurtz, Paul, 18
Kyoto Treaty, 150

L

Lao Tzu, 35, 36, 202; quoted, 34, 233
language, 167; and duality, 41
law, inner. *See* sva-dharma
law, three strikes, 194. *See also* crime
leadership, xvi–xvii
Leviticus, 208
liberation, 23–24, 260f.; in Sanskrit epics, 26; of all beings, 79. *See also* enlightenment
libido. *See* sexuality
life, and death, 106; as gift, 229; as Yoga, 22
life energy, 158, 170
Linga-Purāna, 166
listening. *See* shravana
lobha, 153, 184
logos, 102, 103
loka-samgraha, 215
love, 191, 206–215, 241
loyalty, 246
Luke (Gospel), quoted, 208, 219
lust, 166, 207. *See also* sexuality.
lying, 125, 138; and contemporary Yoga, 140; and U.S. government, 130

M

MacIntyre, Alasdair, 85
Macranthropos, 11, 58–61, 75, 92
Mādrī, self-immolation, 65
Mahābhārata, 65, 91; and dharma, 31; and liberation, 26; quoted, 35, 229
Mahākashyapa, 41
Mahānirvāna-Tantra, quoted, 124
mahā-siddha, 261
mahā-vrata, 89
Mahayana, 70–71, 192, 242. *See also*

Buddhism.
Mahayana Sūtras, 209
Maimonides, 220
maitrī, 202
Majjhima-Nikāya, 227; quoted, 260
Malunkyaputta, 260
manana, 69
manas, 80
mantra, 230
Mantra Project, 52
manushya sacrifice, explained, 66,
   71. *See also* sacrifice, human
Manu-Smriti, 236f.
marks, three, 102
Martin, Paul, 138f.
Maslow, Abraham, 82, 126
mastery, over mind, senses, sleep,
   246
materialism, 18, 68, 126f.
Matthew (Gospel), 208, 248
Matilal, Bimal K., 33
Mayas, 55–56
McChesney, Robert W., 136
Meadows, Dennis, xi
Meadows, Donella, xi
meat, 63; industry, 197, 199
media, 129, 136f.
meditation, 32, 70, 110, 119, 243,
   244. *See also* contemplation
Mehta, Rohit, 39
menos, 86
mental health. *See* health, mental
mercy, 195
merit, 225
Merton, Thomas, 10
metanoía, explained, 253
mettā, 202
military, 184; and lying, 132f.
Mill, John Stuart, 34, 83; quoted, 84
Milošević, Slobodan, 131
Mimamsa, 62
mind, 23, 43, 142, 244; higher, 103f.;
   training, 202; two streams of, 141f.
mindfulness, 35, 99, 154, 235f., 254
miserliness, 217f.
mita-āhāra, 243
mithyā-drishti, 253

modesty, 167, 246
Moggalāna, 260
moha, 184
money, 146, 147
Montagu, Ashley, 192
moral development.
   See development, moral
moral principles. *See* principles,
   moral.
moral relativism. *See* relativism,
   moral
morality, and cultural variation,
   17–18; and kinship, 45; and
   spirituality, xiii, 268; and Yoga, xiv,
   93; environmental, 267
Mother Teresa, 206
muditā, 202
Muhammad, 229. *See also* Islam
muhpatti, 98

N

Nāgārjuna, 244
Nārada, 214
Nāropa, 261
Narayana Guru, 28
Native Americans, 145, 178
NATO, 130f., 136
Nature, 21, 101f.
Nazis, 87, 139
Neoplatonism, 103
Nero, 258
New Ageism, 82, 141, 167
New York, 201
nididhyāsana, 70
Nietzsche, Friedrich, 265
nihilism, moral, 34, 83
nirvāna, 15 *note* 2, 259. *See also*
   enlightenment, liberation
nirvikalpa-samādhi, 171. *See also*
   ecstasy
niyama, 154, 235
Nixon, Richard, 130
nonattachment, 246
nonduality, vs. duality, 4, 40
nonharming, 85, 87, 89, 96–121;
   and Gandhi, 28; *See also* ahimsā
nonjealousy, 246

nonstealing, 145–155
nyönpa, 261

O

obligations, five social, 66–67
oceans, 198
oil, 107f., 114
Olympic Games, 109
Orchard, David, 132
order, cosmic, 7–8, 75, 78. *See also* rita
orderliness, 250, 251
Orwell, George, 150
overconsumption. *See* consumerism

P

pacifism, 88
pāda-sevana, 213
pain, and animals, 197f. *See also* suffering
pāramitā, 243, 257
paranormal, 68–69
parāvritti, 253
Pareto, Vilfredo, 13
parigraha, 188
parināma, 102
parinirvāna, 261
Patanjali. *See Yoga-Sūtra*
patience, 115, 222, 227, 241f., 243, 248
peace, 6
penance, 238. *See also* asceticism
Penny, Timothy J., 129
personality, 30, 86, 103; of liberated beings, 7. *See also* character
PETA, 198
pharmaceutical industry, 134
philanthropy, 218f., 221
piety, 246
Pindola Bharadvaja, 264
piracy, 151f.
pitri sacrifice, explained, 66
Plato, 232
pleasure, 170, 237; and pain, 79; and welfare, 53, 84; of killing, 63
politicians, and lying, 130ff.; and mental health, xvii

politics, 45, 115, 129f., 138, 215; and media, 136
pollution, 112
poverty, 200, 219
power, perfection, 246
practice, spiritual, 3, 65, 97, 106, 127, 212f., 239. *See also* self-transcendence
pramāda, 254
pramatta-samyatā, 254
pranidhāna, 245. *See also* īshvara-pranidhāna
prasāda, 212
pratyupakāra, 246, 247
preman, explained, 207
pride, 153
principles, moral, 89
prisons, 118
privacy, 89f.
problems, global, ix–x
prostration, 213
Proverbs, 125
prudence, 246
pūjā, 63
punctuality, 250
punya, 225
purification. *See* self-purification
purity, inner, 235f., 243
purusha, 3, 58. *See also* ātman, Self, Spirit
purusha-medha, 56, 64

Q

Quetzalcoatl, 56

R

Radhakrishnan, Sarvepalli, quoted, 60–61
radioactive waste, 182
rāga, 235
rajas, 239; explained, 225f.
Rāmāyana, and liberation, 26
Rand, Ayn, 11–13
Randers, Jørgen, xi
Rātī, 77
Ravven, Heidi M., 14
realism, moral, 81, 82

Reality, ultimate, xii, 2, 9, 247 *et passim. See also* consensus reality.
reason, and feeling, 79–80
rebirth, 50–51
reciprocity, 256
recitation, 124
Red Cross, 194f.
relativism, moral, 18, 82, 125, 140
religion, and spirituality, 2, 9–10
renunciation, 26, 30, 166, 227, 236, 245, 254
repentance, xix
repression, 169, 171
Resnik, David, 89f.
respect, 246
responsibility, and spiritual life, 106, 115
reverence for life, 46, 51, 246
reversal, principle of, 61, 253
rights, and ethics, 85; constitutional, 150
Rig-Veda, 3, 20, 146, 209, 210, 238; quoted, 24, 58–60, 223f., 249
rita, 75; explained, 20, 229. *See also* order, cosmic
rituals, religious, 213; secular, 71; sexual, 171
Roberts, Peter, 199
Romans, 193
Romero, Oscar, 96
Roosevelt, Theodore, 134
Rose, James D., 198
Rousseau, Jean-Jacques, 139
Roy, Ram Mohan, 28
RSPCA, 199
Russell, Bertrand, quoted, 13

S

sacrifice, 55–71; animal, 63, 66; five types of, 66–67; human, 56, 64; inner, 57, 63, 76
sage, and will, 34
sākhya, 213
sallekhana, 119
sama-darshana, 214, 246, 248
samatva, 251
Samnyāsa-Yoga, 30

samsāra, 255, 257
samshaya, 247
samtosha, 236
samyag-drishti, 253
Samyutta-Nikāya, quoted, 227, 242
Sātī, 62, 63, 65
sattva, 102, 215, 232, 236, 239; explained, 53, 85f., 95 *note 12,* 225f., 227
sattva-shuddhi, 236
satya, explained, 124
Schweitzer, Albert, 51
saumanasya, 246
Savitri, 230
sayoga-kevalī, 254
Scharping, Rudolf, 131
scientific materialism. *See* materialism, scientific
scriptures, religious, 69, 71, 240f.
Scrooge, 217
Second Harvest, 200
Self, transcendental, 3–4; plurality of Selves, 4; as concept, 40
self-contraction, 4. *See also* ego
self-effacement, 246
selfishness, 85; as virtue, 11–12
self-offering, 213
self-purification, 42, 86, 234ff.
self-reliance, 246
self-restraint, 239, 254; five disciplines of, 154, 235
self-transcendence, 10, 17, 22, 23, 82, 254f.; as sacrifice, 57, 78. *See also* practice, spiritual
self-transformation, 41, 76, 233
self-vision, 236
Seneca, 259; quoted, 234, 258
serenity, 239
service, devotional, 213
sexuality, 77–78, 100, 157ff., 162f., 169f., 173 *et passim*
sexual revolution, 162
Shaivism, Kashmiri, 4, 6
shakti-pīthas, 62
shama, 88
Shāndilya-Upanishad, 237
Shāntideva, 242

Sharp, Gene, 115
shauca, 235, 243
shīla, 250
Shiva, 62, 65, 210
shraddhā, 226, 246
shravana, 69, 213
shuddhi, 236
shūnyatā, 47, 244
Shvetāshvatara-Upanishad, 210
silence, 239
simplicity, voluntary, 154, 238, 254
sin, 169, 185, 242. *See also* good and
  evil
Singer, June, 67
Sivananda, Swami, 248; quoted on
  ethics, xiv
Sixth Mass Extinction, 168
skillful means, perfection, 245
smarana, 213
smriti, 92
Sneddon, Lynne U., 112f.
sobriety, 246, 249
Socrates, 233
softspokenness, 246
Solar Yoga, 61, 230
solitude, 246
soup kitchens, 221
speech, 99, 108f., 167
Spinoza, Baruch, 13
Spirit, defined, xii; as ātman,
  purusha, or Self, 3. *See also* Reality,
  ultimate
spiritual, defined, xii
spiritual practice. *See* practice,
  spiritual
spirituality, explained, xii–xiii, 253;
  and religion, 2, 9–10; and morality,
  9, 268;
St. Ammon, 166
St. Augustine, 138, 153
St. Benedict, 166
steadfastness, 241, 243
Stewart, Martha, 135
Sthānakavāsins, 98
Stoics, 81, 259
St. Paul, 153
study, scriptural, 69, 71, 240f.

sublimation, 171
suffering, 48, 81, 102f., 223; and
  civilization, 158; of animals, 111ff.,
  268
suicide, 118ff.,
Sun, 229f.
superlimation, 171
supreme Reality. *See* Reality,
  ultimate
survival instinct, 5, 157
suttee, 65–66
sva-bhāva, 30, 90, 244
sva-dharma, 30–31, 91
svādhyāya, explained, 240
symbolism, of Chinnamastā, 78
sympathy, 241, 243

T
Taimni, I. K., 39
tamas, 239; explained, 225f.
Tantra, 76–78, 124, 140, 167, 169,
  207
Taoism, 34
Tao Te Ching, quoted, 34–35, 233
tapas, 61, 124, 238f.
Tasker, Peter, 193
Tattvārtha-Sutra, 98; quoted, 99
technology, xvi, 18
televangelism, 137
terrorism. *See* war on terrorism.
theft, 146, 150ff.
Theravada, 70. *See also* Buddhism.
Third Reich, xix, 87, 118
thoughts, 6, 99, 114
Tillich, Paul, 247; quoted, 207, 261
Tilopa, 261
Tiru-Kural, 223; quoted, 138, 142
Tiruvalluvar, 138, 223
tithing, 220f.
titikshā, 242
tobacco industry, 134
tolerance, 228, 246, 248
Transcendental Meditation, 110. *See
  also* meditation
tranquility, 246
Tri-Shikhi-Brāhmana-Upanishad, 241
Trujillo, Alfonso L., 137

Truman, Harry S., 134
Trungpa, Chögyam, quoted, 254
truth, 92, 124ff., 133, 249
truthfulness, 90, 124–142, 243
Tukārām, 214

U

Uechtritz, Max, 133
ultimate concern, 247
Umāsvāmin, 98
unconscious, 141, 142
United Nations, 116f., 160f.
United States, and oil, 107f.;
  and constitutional rights, 150;
  and human rights, 116f.; and
  religious fundamentalism, 129;
  and sexual abuse, 161; animal
  slaughter, 111; competitiveness
  of, 109; government, x; hunger
  and homelessness, 200;
  imperialism, xi, 114, 184;
  jurisprudence, 193; national debt,
  147, 179f.; philanthropy, 218f.; zero
  tolerance, 249
universal virtues. See virtues,
  universal
Upāli, 227
Upanishads, 49, 57, 70. See also
  individual Upanishads
upāya, 245
upekshā, 202
ūrdhva-retas, 171
utilitarianism, 83–84

V

Vacchagotta, 260
vairāgya, 246
Vaishnavism, 210
Vajrayana, 46, 167f. See also
  Buddhism.
values, 82, 125, 265
vandana, 213
Vatican, 137, 138f., 159f. See also
  Christianity
Vedas, 49, 64, 69, 209. See also
  individual Vedas
vegetarianism, 63, 110

verticalism, vs. integralism, 172
vice, 254; defined, 141, 153
view, correct, 253, 254
vigor, perfection, 244
violence. See harming
virati, 254
virtue, 97, 227f.; and children, 86;
  and cosmic order, 7; and
  knowledge of God, 13; as natural,
  14; as power, 6; of nonharming, 87;
  of quiescence, 88; of selfishness, 11
virtue ethics, 14, 33–34, 84–85, 93
virtues, universal, 5, 9, 19, 75–94;
  five key, 88–89; miscellaneous
  yogic, 232–251; perfections, 33,
  243, 257, 264; specialization of,
  232; thirteen, 234
virtus, explained, 235
Virūpa, 261
vīrya, 244
Vishnu, 62, 210ff.
vision, false, 253
viveka, 250
Vivekananda, Swami, 22
vivekin, 103
vivisection, 199
Voltaire, 139
vow, great, 89, 97, 105, 124, 152;
  subsidiary, 89

W

Walmart, 180, 186
war, 133f., 179, 196; and oil, 108;
  in Bhagavad-Gītā, 27; just, 84; on
  drugs, 117, 249; on terrorism, x,
  130, 150
wealth, 148, 186f., 223f.
Web of Life, 42, 47
welfare, 89, 195f., 215; and pleasure, 53
Wesley, John, 235
WHO, 137
will, and sage, 34; free, 91
Williams, Stanley Tookie, 117
wisdom, 103, 243, 256, 264; and
  compassion, 46. See also crazy
  wisdom
witnessing, 15 note 6

Y

yāga, explained, 57
yajna, 57, 58
Yama (God of Death), 31
yama, 96, 105; ten, 241
yoga, meaning of, 39, 57; as
  "integration," 39
Yoga, activist, 27; and belief, 8; as
  ego deconstruction, 5; as discipline
  of enlightenment, 1, 17, 40; as
  inner sacrifice, 76; as spirituality,
  3; branches, xii; commodification,
  xiii; competitiveness in, 110;
  contemporary, 140, 167f., 268;
  forms, xiii, 3; inner freedom,
  xiv; Integral, 173; life as, 22;
  miscellaneous virtues, 232–251;
  morality, 5, 93; stereotype, 1; Solar,
  61, 230. *See also* individual types of
  Yoga
Yoga Alliance, 168f.
Yoga-Bhāshya, quoted, 141, 237
Yoga-Shāstra, 97
Yoga-Sūtra (of Patanjali), brahma-
  vihāra, 202; chastity, 173;
  contentment, 155, 236; ecstasy,
  255; five key virtues, 88–89;
  greedlessness, 188; nonharming,
  96, 99; plurality of Selves, 4, 36;
  practice, 243; quoted on suffering,
  103; shauca, 235; truthfulness,
  124f.
Yoga-Yājnavalkya, 241
youth, 163
Yudhishthira, 31, 35
Yugoslavia, 130f., 136

Z

zakat, 220
Zen, 41, 256

AS IT IS
A Year on the Road with a Tantric Teacher
by M. Young

A first-hand account of a one-year journey around the world in the company of a *tantric* teacher. This book catalogues the trials and wonders of day-to-day interactions between a teacher and his students, and presents a broad range of his teachings given in seminars from San Francisco, California to Rishikesh, India. *As It Is* considers the core principles of *tantra*, including non-duality, compassion (the Bodhisattva ideal), service to others, and transformation within daily life. Written as a narrative, this captivating book will appeal to practitioners of *any* spiritual path. Readers interested in a life of clarity, genuine creativity, wisdom and harmony will find this an invaluable resource.

paper, 725 pages, 24 b&w photos, $29.95
ISBN: 0-934252-99-8

HALFWAY UP THE MOUNTAIN
The Error of Premature Claims to Enlightenment
by Mariana Caplan   Foreword by Fleet Maull

Dozens of first-hand interviews with students, respected spiritual teachers and masters, together with broad research are synthesized here to assist readers in avoiding the pitfalls of the spiritual path. Topics include: mistaking mystical experience for enlightenment; ego inflation, power and corruption among spiritual leaders; the question of the need for a teacher; disillusionment on the path . . . and much more.

"Caplan's illuminating book . . . urges seekers to pay the price of traveling the hard road to true enlightenment." — *Publisher's Weekly*

Paper, 600 pages, $21.95
ISBN: 0-934252-91-2

To Order: call 1-800-381-2700. Visit our website, www.hohmpress.com

KISHIDO: *The Way of the Western Warrior*
by Peter Hobart

The code of the samurai and the path of the knight-warrior—traditions from opposite sides of the globe—find a common ground in *Kishido: the Way of the Western Warrior*. In fifty short essays, Peter Hobart presents the wisdom, philosophy and teachings of the mysterious Master who first united the noble houses of East and West. Kishido prioritizes the ideals of duty, ethics, courtesy and chivalry, from whatever source they derive. This cross-cultural approach represents a return to time-honored principles from many traditions, and allows the modern reader from virtually any background to find the master within.

Paper, 130 pages, $12.95
ISBN: 1-890772-31-3

ZEN TRASH
The Irreverent and Sacred Teaching Stories of Lee Lozowick
Edited and with Commentary by Sylvan Incao

This book contains dozens of teaching stories from many world religious traditions—including Zen, Christianity, Tibetan Buddhism, Sufism and Hinduism—rendered with a twist of humor, irony or provocation by contemporary spiritual teacher Lee Lozowick. They are compiled from thirty years of Lozowick's talks and seminars in the U.S., Canada, Europe, Mexico and India.

These stories will typically confound the mind and challenge any conventional seriousness about the spiritual path. In essence, however, they hold what every traditional teaching story has always held—the possibility of glimpsing reality, beyond the multiple illusions that surround the truth. Even if they derive from a three-thousand-year-old tradition, Lozowick's unique style makes these stories contemporary and practical. He has no compunction about changing the details while retaining the context, applying them to the struggles, dreams, successes and failures that men and women typically encounter daily in their approach to spiritual life and practice.

Paper, 150 pages, $12. 95
ISBN: 1-890772-21-6

To Order: call 1-800-381-2700. Visit our website, www.hohmpress.com

THE SHADOW ON THE PATH
Clearing the Psychological Blocks to Spiritual Development
by VJ Fedorschak
Foreword by Claudio Naranjo, M.D.

Tracing the development of the human psychological shadow from Freud to the present, this readable analysis presents five contemporary approaches to spiritual psychotherapy for those who find themselves needing help on the spiritual path. Offers insight into the phenomenon of denial and projection.

Topics include: the shadow in the work of notable therapists; the principles of inner spiritual development in the major world religions; examples of the disowned shadow in contemporary religious movements; and case studies of clients in spiritual groups who have worked with their shadow issues.

Paper, 300 pages, $17.95
ISBN: 0-934252-81-5

YOU HAVE THE RIGHT TO REMAIN SILENT
Bringing Meditation to Life
by Rick Lewis

With sparkling clarity and humor, Rick Lewis explains exactly what meditation can offer to those who are ready to establish an island of sanity in the midst of an active life. This book is a comprehensive look at everything a beginner would need to start a meditation practice, including how to befriend an overactive mind and how to bring the fruits of meditation into all aspects of daily life. Experienced meditators will also find refreshing perspectives to both nourish and refine their practice.

Paper, 201 pages; $14.95
ISBN: 1-890772-23-2

To Order: call 1-800-381-2700. Visit our website, www.hohmpress.com

Home Study
with Georg Feuerstein

Traditional Yoga Studies is offering several distance-learning courses on Yoga, designed and tutored by Georg Feuerstein and leading to a diploma. Each course includes a comprehensive typeset manual, which comprises readings, questions for reflection, practical exercises, suggested reading, questionnaires (for homework), and numerous illustrations. The courses have attracted many students from around the world, some of whose testimonials can, along with more information about the courses, be found online at **www.traditionalyogastudies.com/**.

Each course has a number of homework assignments but can also be taken without this option. Homework is submitted by email for tutorial feedback.

800-Hour Course on the Philosophy, History and Literature of Yoga

Although challenging, this course offers the most comprehensive introduction to Yoga available today. It is based on Georg Feuerstein's 500-page work *The Yoga Tradition* (2nd edition, Hohm Press). It comes with a 1,000-page manual printed on recycled paper, which took well over 3,000 hours to create. The curriculum can be inspected online.

250-Hour Course on Patanjali's Classical Yoga

The *Yoga-Sūtra* offers the most coherent philosophical framework of Yoga and is studied by thousands of sincere students worldwide. This course, which comes with a 300-page typeset and illustrated manual, makes Patanjali's philosophy readily accessible and also shows how it can be applied on a day-to-day basis. See our online information

A Course on the Bhagavad-Gītā

In preparation.

TRADITIONAL YOGA STUDIES
www.traditionalyogastudies.com

ABOUT THE AUTHOR

Georg Feuerstein, Ph.D., was born in Germany shortly after World War II and conducted his postgraduate research in Indian philosophy at the University of Durham in England. He is one of the leading voices of the East/West dialogue and since the late 1960s has made many significant contributions to our understanding of India's spiritual heritage, notably Hindu Yoga.

He has authored more than 30 books, including *The Shambhala Encyclopedia of Yoga, The Yoga Tradition, The Deeper Dimension of Yoga, Lucid Waking, Wholeness or Transcendence?, Tantra: Path of Ecstasy*, and *Holy Madness*. His most recent works include *Transparent Leaves From the Tree of Life: Metaphysical Poems* and *Aha! Reflections on the Meaning of Everything*.

He offers distance-learning courses on Yoga philosophy and history through Traditional Yoga Studies at www.traditionalyogastudies.com, and his socio-political thoughts are featured at www.alternativecenter.ca.

For many years, he has been a practitioner of Tibetan Buddhist Yoga and since 2004 has resided in Canada.